A
RARE
AND
PRECIOUS
THING

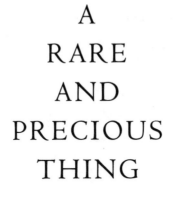

ALSO BY JOHN KAIN

Cheater's Paradise (poetry)

A
RARE
AND
PRECIOUS
THING

*The Possibilities and
Pitfalls of Working with
a Spiritual Teacher*

JOHN KAIN

BELL TOWER

New York

Some of the material in "Master of the Ordinary" and
"Undiscovered Genetics" first appeared in different
form in the *Shambhala Sun.*

See page 273 for a complete list of permissions acknowledgments.

Library of Congress Cataloging-in-Publication Data
Kain, John
A rare and precious thing : the possibilities and pitfalls of working with
a spiritual teacher / John Kain.—1st ed.
p.   cm.
Includes bibliographical references.
1. Interpersonal relations—Religious aspects.   2. Teacher-student
relationships—Religious aspects.
3. Spiritual life.   I. Title.
BL626.33.K35 2006
206'.1—dc22   2006005994

ISBN-13: 978-0-307-33592-0
ISBN-10: 0-307-33592-5

Printed in the United States of America

Design by JoAnne Metsch

10 9 8 7 6 5 4 3 2 1

First Edition

For the Zen Mountain Monastery Sangha

and all the treasured gifts

I can never repay

CONTENTS

In our tradition a teacher is called "a dangerous friend."

They can love you and tell you about yourself, too.

They can give you everything they possibly can to make your life better

and also tell you that you need to straighten up.

—CHOYIN RANGDROL

A
RARE
AND
PRECIOUS
THING

I

RETURNING TO THE CIRCLE

*You have noticed that everything an Indian does
is in a circle, and that is because the Power of the
World always works in circles, and everything tries
to be round.*[1]

—BLACK ELK

There are an infinite number of reasons for wanting a spiritual teacher, some as clear as an alpine stream, others as blurred and haunting as an inscription on an ancient tombstone. We might come to our desire through suffering—the piercing loss of a loved one, or the all-too-pervasive sense of numbing isolation in the modern world, for instance. Perhaps, though, we've experienced ecstatic and fleeting moments of insight, where in a quick flash we see *it*, the extraordinary beauty of the world, the absolute miracle in the most daily occurrence—*Haze breaking over fir and bamboo, / Clears and concentrates / The mind and spirit*, said the Chinese poet Chien Chang.[2] In the first circumstance we want a teacher to show us the way out, in the second the way back in. Underlying both is a yearning for the clarification of who we really are and the palpable ache for connection, for contact, for merging. We, in our secular consumer society (having divorced ourselves from wildness), have lost touch with the ancient but living tissue that connects us to the mystery of creation.

In *The Varieties of Religious Experience,* William James surmised, by way of his examination of a multiplex of experiences (the first study of its kind, published in 1902, and still a classic), "that the visible world is part of a more spiritual universe from which it draws its chief significance; that union or harmonious relation with that higher universe is our true end; that prayer or inner communion with the spirit thereof—be that spirit 'God' or 'law'—is a process wherein work is really done, and spiritual energy flows in and produces effects, psychological or material, within the phenomenal world."[3] James's statements, though a tad starched for modern ears, are still valid, not so much for what they say—you can find the same themes in any number of popular magazines—but for the emphasis of his study. The true radicalism of James (at least to the Western world of the day) was his recognition of personal spiritual awakening as the nadir of religiosity—beyond ritual, beyond tradition, beyond race or standing or "expertise." We didn't need an intermediary, James proclaimed.

His assertion was nothing new: the mystics had been saying such things for thousands of years, be they from East or West or from the luminous circles of indigenous tribes. Yet James was offering a broader invitation to the Western public. It was the beginning of the paradigm shift that melded the external with the internal, science with religion. Solitude, and by this I do not mean being alone but that primary place in each of us where we meet spirit, was for James the truest state. The spiritual teacher-student relationship is of this realm, a primary connection nourished in intimacy, which is at once most private and most universal.

This relationship, however, presents its own set of problems. If the visible world is indeed a part of a more spiritual universe, then we are all, in every second of existence, swimming in spirit. Unfortunately (and this is the devil's bargain), we've entered a truncated dreamscape of division and separation, believing, more often than not, that God, spirit, presence, or whatever you want to call it, is over *there* and we are over *here*. Spiritual teachers and many nonteachers alike have simply seen through, or at least glimpsed, this dream loop and do not take it at collective face value. How, then, do you teach a person to swim when that person is already swimming? Animals know what to do; a loon sings its loon song. How do you teach a human how to be human?

No one can teach us these things. It's impossible, and all of the "teachers" in this book add a disclaimer to that title. But "keepers," "guides," "whistleblowers," "friends," as they call themselves, can model for us a saner and more connected way to be. Each teacher in these pages believes in the direct connection with spirit: they feel it; they carry forward (and back) the mystical path. "Authority" and "obedience" are not simply external abstractions, but palpable connections and a balance between inside and out. The Hasidic master Rabbi Zusya told his disciples who had gathered around his deathbed, "When I get to the world to come, they will not ask me 'Why were you not Moses?,' they will ask me, 'Why were you not Zusya?' "[4] Yet Zusya's cry is not for more isolation or self-centeredness—the elevation of the "I."

The cry—through all of the teachers and students herein—is for communion, intimacy, service, and faithfulness. The individual *is* necessary to spiritual growth, but individualism is not. Each of these teachers helps us, through their call and presence to reinhabit a realm that has its anchor in nature, in wildness with all its complexity, not in the enervating sham of materialism and ego-centered motives. Nothing exists in a vacuum and neither does spirituality—it is always relational. In this sense, spiritual practice is revolutionary. But this path is not tidy. We continually wish life to be controllable and sanitary, but it's not. The world, even in its present debilitated state, is essentially wild, and much of what lies beneath our skin responds to that essence. We are sensitive to the weight and pull of other forces—the energy behind wind, the magnetism of the moon, or someone's warm breath upon our neck.

Accordingly, life is painful, and it's hard to find a stable purchase or peace of mind in our perennial yearnings—spiritual or otherwise. Celestial orphans, all. Quite naturally we look for someone, something, or some system to help us navigate through our tangled interior (at present such inner disarray is catastrophically reflected in the "external" world), a territory where our busy minds no longer speak the local language. "We've become marvelous at self-delusion,"[5] said Thomas Merton, that most eloquent and literary Cistercian monk.

As we moved from the mysterious and sacred to the scientific scaffolding of secular humanism, psychology (and by extension social science) rushed in to pick up the "slack." It gave us a new map to our interior, and for many made religion obsolete. Yet psychology (and likewise Western science) lives, for the most part, in the realm of the knowable and can never subsume the mystery of spirit, which incidentally includes the nonhuman world.

This does not by any means suggest that psychology and science (i.e., ecology, systems theory, neurobiology, and so on) cannot complement religion or vice versa. Happily, much has been done in the last few decades to bring the jilted lovers closer together, and each has been enriched by the other's embrace. If we are to evolve, both spiritually and materially (or for that matter if we are to survive), we must come to recognize the interdependence of all sentient and nonsentient beings—the two-leggeds, the four-leggeds, rocks and trees. *Mitakuye Oyasin,* say the members of the Lakota, Dakota, Nakota Nation, "all our relations."

The unfortunate return to fundamentalism (and here I refer to its most recent incarnation of ethnic and/or ideological extremism) is ironically a violent reaction against this untamable complexity, this infinite spirit. Fundamentalism, it would seem, reduces God to definable and ego-centered concepts, based in fear and the desire to control. "Conceptual idolatry" is what Robert Thurman

(Tibetan Buddhist scholar, author, and cofounder of Tibet House in New York) calls these fundamentalist tendencies—a rabid attachment to ideas that become "etched in stone," immovable, unquestionable. "Holy" wars are fought, global consumerism is unleashed, fascist doctrine is pounded down citizens' throats, patriarchy held as the standard of Godhood—all based on malformed concepts of human nature and our proper place in the landscape. Each of us has some portion of fundamentalism within us—stale ideas, ingrained patterns—and spiritual teachers can help us discover their contours.

Still there always exists the resurgent spirit pulsing in the ligaments of our lives. As Gary Synder, the poet, Buddhist, and eco-activist points out, "The world is our consciousness, and it surrounds us. There are more things in mind, in the imagination, than 'you' can keep track of—thoughts, memories, images, angers, delights, rise unbidden. The depths of mind, the unconscious, are our inner wilderness areas."[6] When we turn to a spiritual teacher we look for a guide, not one who is familiar with well-worn paths, but one who knows, as Snyder puts it, the "etiquette of freedom."

Yet in wanting a teacher to illuminate the lush and tangled undergrowth of our interior, we inevitably step into a paradox. As the late Chögyam Trungpa Rinpoche (gifted Tibetan teacher, author, and founder of the Shambhala organization, who introduced thousands of Westerners to Tibetan practice) said, "When you hear of someone that possesses remarkable qualities, you regard them as significant beings and yourself as insignificant."[7] In other words, our perceived inadequacy—that feeling which often got us looking for a teacher in the first place—is reinforced when we look upon someone or something as "more advanced," "wiser," "more enlightened," and so forth. We want what we think they "have." I've been studying Zen for more than twenty years and have been a student of Zen master John Daido Loori for seven years and continue to struggle with the teacher-student paradigm—thus the impetus for writing this book.

"Is the existence of so many religious types and sects and creeds regrettable? . . . I answer 'No' emphatically. . . . No two of us have identical difficulties, nor should we be expected to work out identical solutions,"[8] wrote James. We are genuinely lucky in the West to have so many choices, but then an endless supply of options can lead to inaction, to a dysfunctional stupor or an attitude of "shopping" frenzy in which desire trumps truth. We have to find the heart of our own sincerity—not the prepackaged kind found in greeting cards—to give the spiritual journey meaning. Intimacy is essential and inherently risky.

The feeling of inadequacy is not all bad: it is good that we want to change our often shrunken and self-absorbed view of the world and become more compassionate. Yet we must stop wanting to fix ourselves. In the spiritual world, continually wanting to "get somewhere" gets us nowhere. Because it's the ego that's never satisfied, that's always thinking there is something right around the corner and therefore keeps us from just "being," keeps us feeling separate.

It is the spiritual teacher's job to offer new ways of seeing. But this process entails a delicate surgery that places both the student and the teacher in a vulnerable position. The exchanges of power in these situations can do considerable damage if not held in balance. Recent history—from Jonestown to the Branch Davidians to 9/11 and untold religious scandals—is filled with this traumatic and bloody power play. If teachers think that they have personal power, that the "I" is teaching, then they are just transmitting more self-centered and diseased ways of being. "I cured with the power that came through me. Of course, it was not I who cured. It was the power from the outer world, and the visions and ceremonies had only made me like a hole through which the power could come to the two-leggeds. If I thought that I was doing it myself, the hole would close up and no power could come through. Then everything I could do would be foolish," said Black Elk.[9] Much foolishness has been wrought in the name of spirituality, both here in the West and around the world. I touch on some of these missteps in chapter 10, which deals with teacher abuses.

There is not just one type of teacher-student relationship. As we find in this book, the permutations are endless. Students can (and do) view their teacher as a parent, as a lover (both figuratively and literally), as a friend, as an enemy, as a god, and as a demon—perhaps all within an hour's time. The psychological pitfalls of the relationship are complex and varied. Transference and projection run rampant, and there's plenty more where that came from, as they say. Alexander Berzin, in his book about Tibetan Buddhist practice, *Relating to a Spiritual Teacher: Building a Healthy Relationship,* describes six different attributes of the teacher-student relationship:

(1) Almost all spiritual seekers progress through stages along the spiritual path. (2) Most practitioners study with several teachers during their lifetimes and build up different relationships with each. (3) Not every spiritual teacher has reached the same level of accomplishment. (4) The type of relationship appropriate between a specific seeker and a specific teacher depends upon the spiritual level of each. (5) People usually relate to their teachers in progressively deeper manners as they advance along the spiritual path. (6) Because the same teacher may play different roles in the spiritual life of each seeker, the most appropriate relationship each seeker has with that teacher may be different.[10]

This list is filled with sober insights and common sense. Yet for some mysterious reason students often check their practicality at the door, like an overcoat at a fancy restaurant, when entering spiritual practice. The best thing teachers can do for their students is to convince them that common sense is a valuable attribute. If a teacher is sleeping with a student, nine times out of ten it's a bad idea. If a teacher is an alcoholic, that teacher is an alcoholic. Some things are *exactly* as they appear. In the book *How to Meditate: A Guide to Self-Discovery*, an early work on spiritual practice (published in 1974), the author, Lawrence LeShan, gave some practical and sage advice about choosing a spiritual teacher: "Watch how they treat their spouse." At the same time, teachers do make mistakes, all of them, and if we think otherwise we're on the wrong track.

There's a razor-fine line between taming the ego—and thus unearthing compassion—and taming the person. I mentioned the difference between the individual and individualism above, but it bears repeating. A sense of self as an entity intricately connected to the web of the universe—a selfless self—is a healthy thing. A sense of self as the center of the universe around which everything revolves—me, me, me, me—is, other than being ridiculous, unhealthy for everyone concerned. It's a touchy process, then, negotiating the building up of one and the softening of the other. Every teacher and student I interviewed for this book has struggled with the tension between the two.

Thomas Merton writes:

"Religion," in the sense of something emanating from man's nature and tending to God, does not really change man or save him, but brings him into a false relationship with God: for a religion that starts in man is nothing but man's wish for himself. Man "wishes himself" (magically) to become godly, holy, gentle, pure, etc. His wish terminates not in God but in himself. This is no more than the religion of those who wish themselves to be in a certain state in which they can live with themselves, approve of themselves, God is at peace with them. How many Christians seriously believe that Christianity itself consists of nothing more than this? Yet it is anathema to true Christianity.[11]

Many students want their spiritual teachers to "magically" bestow upon them a "godly, holy, gentle, pure" nature. Believing themselves separate from the teachings (whatever they are) keeps their desire for union within the closed walls of their ego—they move farther away from what they seek. Most of us, however, start on the spiritual journey with these ideas in our heads. It's quite natural, actually. The intentions we begin with often change as we move along.

"I woke up one day and I wanted a teacher," a friend told me. She's been a student of a Tibetan lama for seven years. "I'd just seen the movie *Seven Years in Tibet* with Brad Pitt, and I wanted a spiritual 'thing' in my life. It was like I wanted a new necklace, something shiny I could wear out on the town. I liked the thought of being able to say, 'I have a teacher.' It's silly, but that's how it started. Still, here I am seven years later—something stuck. The necklace is long gone."

Having a profound experience is not a prerequisite for entering the spiritual path—a flat tire, a love affair, throwing your back out while working on a tractor, an invitation to a concert, and food poisoning are a few examples of serendipity that led students to their teachers. The universe, it seems, has a sense of humor. Often we haven't a clue as to what ignites the flame. Sometimes we show up at a church, a temple, or a mosque simply looking for community. There needn't be a central spiritual figure in our lives for us to practice in the spiritual realm. In fact, some people think no teacher is the best teacher of all, or that teachers are everywhere. Once again the key is the seeker's sincerity. We must continually ask ourselves what's at stake. What are we really after?

The spiritual teacher-student relationship is an alchemical process. It is predicated on change and not a little risk. But we are living in dangerous times, wobbling, as it were, into a theater of the absurd. Our choices, though it might seem otherwise, are narrowing. Spiritual practice is not an escape, and there are no hard and fast rules—how can we navigate something that is essentially a mystery without embracing mystery? We are, all of us, a community that can help each other. *And there will never be any more perfection than there is now, / Nor any more heaven and hell than there is now,*[12] said Walt Whitman. No sense in waiting.

2

THE WHISTLEBLOWER

Murat Yagan

A true saint has to fall in the trouble of love;
His task won't be done just dreaming:
he needs to fall in the trouble of love.[1]
— SUN'ULLAH GAÏBI

I think it's safe to assume that Murat Yagan is the only spiritual teacher to receive flowers from both Hitler and Mussolini. The story is extraordinary, yet it's only a minor aside when put in the larger mix of Murat's high-wire life, which reads like a Rider Haggard adventure novel. It includes princes, sultans, and thieves, treasure hunts and Olympic horsemanship, swords and ritual dancing. There is sex and romance, existential anguish, travel to foreign lands, and, most important to this story, a mystical embodiment of a 26,000-year-old spiritual teaching from the Caucasus Mountains called Kebzeh—the knowledge of which Murat and his wife, Maisie, have saved from the brink of extinction and brought to the West, where his students give it new life.

Though ninety years of age, Murat could pass for sixty-five. Circassians (the tribes from the Caucasus) are famous for their longevity, many living well beyond the century mark. "One of the tribal elders who instructed me in Ahmsta Kebzeh was 179 years old," Murat informs me nonchalantly. Murat is from the Abkhazian tribe, slight of build and wiry; he has a close-cropped white beard and mustache under a slightly hooked nose. He speaks with a whispered and throaty Turkish accent, using the word "darling" in a most heartwarming way, and moves with natural ease and a hint of regal charm—he was born a prince, after all. Yet his luminous life, royal blood (his father comes from a long line of Abkhazian tribal elders, and his mother, Hikmet Othman, is from the Ottoman family of Sultan Muhammad VI), and exotic past are pleasantly subsumed by his open, warm, and disarming manner. His charisma, if one can call it that, resides below the surface, like the building blocks of DNA.

"A Sufi teacher cannot be an earthshaking personality who attracts millions of adherents and whose fame reverberates into every corner of the earth," wrote Idries Shah in his classic book *The Sufis*. Shah was an illustrious Sufi sheikh, scholar, writer, and illuminating religious thinker. "His [the teacher's] stage of illumination is visible for the most part only to the enlightened. . . . The man (or woman) who is bemused and impressed by the personality of a teacher will be the person whose awareness is insufficient to handle the impact and make use of it."[2] Sufism, in other words, is a practice of essentials. "Love the pitcher less and the water more," say the Sufis. Murat tells me, "People are not attracted to me; they are attracted to the way they are treated." First and foremost, Murat treats all people with kindness, compassion, and humility. But occasionally when he's guiding his students and an ego needs softening, his love can be fierce.

"Sometimes the community thinks that I'm a hard person to get along with. I cannot say they are completely wrong because I am not perfect. I will ask a participant if they think they can bear me because it is a difficult task," Murat told me. The burden his students must bear is the way Murat continually exposes their sticking points, their delusions (be they grand or their opposite). "I don't trust a teaching that makes me feel good inside. I want to be broken down and built up again," Sharron Allen told me plainly. She came to the Kebzeh community a little over six years ago, is the assistant to Murat and Maisie, and is an older practitioner with a sober grasp of what studying with a spiritual teacher can bring, much of which is based on trust.

"I had simply reached a measure of trust in my own inner guidance by the time I came here to meet Murat," Sharron continued. "And the experiences leading up to meeting him predisposed me to trust on a certain level. When I first met him I had one of those flash experiences; it happens and it registers and it's over. But I felt recognized and I didn't need to be something else; maybe *need* isn't the right word. I simply felt an exposure of myself in his eyes, a kind of recognition, and certainly with any teacher that trust is essential, but also if you aren't challenged then you're not alive."

There's a paradox here, of course. We suffer, so we seek a spiritual teacher to help us relieve that suffering. We *do* want to feel better. We want to be filled up with good feelings or at least not overflowing with bad. We must not, however, confuse the pain of freedom with the pain of bondage, and trade one type of suffering for another. Attaching to spiritual ideals or the teacher is as troublesome as attaching to sloth.

It could be said, and often is, that a teacher is like a mirror; teachers simply reflect back what we, as students, show them—the clearer the teacher, the clearer the reflection. When a teacher exposes our weaknesses, our ignorance, our pettiness, our greed, it's painful. Often students have told me that when they first started studying with a teacher, they felt as though their suffering got worse. In some ways that's true: they're getting a taste of their own poison, beginning to see things clearly. But it's a homeopathic remedy, where a little of the poison slowly turns to the medicine of healing. Feeling "good" under this scenario gains a deeper meaning—"good" means connection with reality and not some preconceived idea of "happy." The spiritual journey is unpredictable, not a stroll across a suburban lawn. When we can let go into reality, the reflection gets clearer and the mirror starts exposing the truer parts of our nature. But this takes time and much emptying of our bundle of sorrows and hang-ups, and the teacher is there to create a consistent atmosphere of healing.

Murat calls himself a "whistleblower" because, like a mirror, he exposes reality and makes noise when a student's vision gets blurry. "In Kebzeh tradition they say you cannot teach anyone," Murat tells me, meaning, in a general sense (and I'll explain the more particular Kebzeh definition later), that he does not actively direct students. Rather he creates a tinderbox where a tiny spark can begin the burning away of one's false self. A teacher, by not teaching, simply "holds" clarity and plays with the tension between appearance and reality (which is sometimes the same, sometimes not), essence and form. Murat, in fact, embodies that very tension and continually emanates an energy that pushes his students into a wobble and then back to center again, each time strengthening the essential pivot.

Kebzeh and Sufism, for example, are not the same thing, but they're not different. Murat was trained in both forms and also has a deep connection with Christ (in Sufism, all the prophets are embraced as authentic light holders). Over the years Murat has moved seamlessly among different traditions, particularly Sufism and Christianity, but he has remained true to the essential teachings of Kebzeh and his Circassian roots. If you had met Murat twenty-eight years ago—as many of the current community members did—you would have considered him a Sufi sheikh. If you met him today, you might think him a Christian. Murat sees no conflict in this. But being a Sufi sheikh one day and deciding to open a Christian church the next was more than a minor shock for many of Murat's students and gives a good example of his teaching (or non-teaching) methods.

Mary Anne Kingsmill, a longtime Kebzeh student, was shocked by the shift. She had trained in Mevlevi Sufism (the lineage of Mevlana Jelaluddin Rumi) and began studying with Murat when he and Maisie were living in Vancouver in the 1970s. "I was raised by a man who thought there were two things that were a curse to humanity. One was the Catholic Church, the other was cats," she told me. "I had a fantastically hard time, in fact we all did, when Murat said we were going to start a church. I found it embarrassing. I wasn't going to tell anyone that I was going to church or involved with a church. It was denial. It's taken quite a long time. Now I have no problem saying, 'I'm going to church. Would you like to join me?'" You can imagine how difficult it must have been for Murat's students, one day you're seeing the world watch as you study with a Sufi sheikh—which you must admit is pretty hip and counterculture—and the next day you're seeing the world view you as part of a Christian community, so mainstream!

When Joan McIntyre, who has been with Murat for nearly thirty years and is the co-leader of the Kebzeh community, heard that Murat wanted to start the church, she balked (Joan is Jewish). "I had a couple of days where I thought 'I'm not doing this,' and then I woke up one morning and started laughing. 'What kind of a big deal is it that you belong to a Christian church?' I thought. 'The truth is the truth, get on with it,'" she exclaimed as we sat in her apartment drinking tea—Murat introducing a wobble and things returning to center. Thus the Essentialist Church of Christ was born. It offers regular Sunday sermons (usually given by one of the two acting ministers, Wayne Wilson and Bob Wilson—not related), a Sunday school, and numerous outreach programs.

Starting the church is a reflection of Murat's style. Certainly it was, as I mentioned, an example of a tinderbox and underscored the importance of flexibility. But it also tells much about the function of the teacher within the Kebzeh community and the world at large. "Why did I decide to start a church? Because I believe if I was in a Muslim country I would start a new path of Sufism with a mosque and if I was in a Buddhist country I would behave the same way or in a Jewish country the same. I believe there is no difference between recognized light holders in the history of mankind," Murat told me softly.

"I am not a knowledgeable person. I have no knowledge at all. If I talk about some elementary things, like the definitions according to the teachings of Sufism and so on, I can talk about them because I memorized them. But if people ask me about certain subjects which are very meaningful to them, what happens is that the vibrations, the receptivity of the people asking, makes me talk and sometimes I hear the answer for the first time myself. I am nothing but a channel and this channel is opened by the people around me according to their inclination. If they don't ask, I cannot say anything."[3] In Kebzeh the guest is always considered the teacher. As Murat told me, "The community becomes the teacher of the teacher." The idea of group synergy is fundamental to Kebzeh's existence.

Murat and I are sitting in the wood-paneled office of his and Maisie's tract home in Vernon, British Columbia, a midsized town with a gold-mining past, surrounded by fruit orchards and vineyards nestled in the picturesque Okanagan Lake country of the Northern Rockies. Murat is a retired carpenter—though he was

actively working on various building projects the week I visited—
and has never taken money for passing on the Kebzeh teachings.
Kebzeh is a householder practice, and all the members of the community in Vernon and elsewhere earn their own living but often
come together to practice, attend church, study, socialize, and once
a year participate in Circassian dance. Some of the community
members chipped in together in common tenancy to buy two historic buildings in which a few have apartments; the buildings,
called the Green House and the Sage House, also contain a meeting hall, an office, and guest rooms.

"Sufism is the process of awakening and developing latent
human powers under divine grace and guidance. . . . A Sufi is an essentialist: someone who meets all things in life on the basis of their
essential meaning."[4] This definition echoes that given for Ahmsta
Kebzeh, yet it would be misleading to say that the ancient Circassian tradition is simply a form of Sufism because the practice's historical arc stretches back well before the time of Muhammad,
though there are some Sufis and non-Sufis—Murat included—
who believe Sufism existed before Islam. "The association of the
Sufi process of transformation with the word Sufism is a relatively
recent phenomenon."[5]

Kebzeh consists of three distinct yet overlapping categories:
Aleishwah, which consists of the conventional rules of social behavior—etiquette and civility; Kebzeh, the moral, spiritual, and social
concepts of the tradition; and Ahmsta Kebzeh, the mystical practices of the tradition, which were originally taught (in the Circassian tribes) only to certain male members of the ruling class.
Murat has opened up Ahmsta Kebzeh (the main emphasis of his
teaching) to anyone, male or female, who is willing, available, and
open. "Ahmsta Kebzeh is not a religion and does not interfere with
any existing religion. It is an applied science; it is the art of living as

a human being fully exercising human faculties holistically as applied to life. But religions may be made out of it."[6]

In Sufism, when you are accepted into teaching by your sheikh, you are put under *chille,* which means "ordeal." In Kebzeh this process—which is essentially the slow (or in some cases rapid) transformation of ego and the rebuilding of a healthier functioning—is labeled *deconditioning* and *reconditioning,* the juicy part of practice. Spiritual progress is not easy, and in the Kebzeh tradition, when you align yourself with a teacher you are agreeing to a certain amount of psychic upheaval. "The big thing is letting go of strong opinions about anything," said Lisa Talesnick, a Kebzeh student for ten years. She is Jewish, lives in Jerusalem, and comes to Vernon as often as she can, staying for weeks and sometimes months at a time. "Even what you think is most dear, letting go of those strong opinions and creating a place for receptivity is so important," she adds. Jean Robillard put it this way: "You don't practice Kebzeh; you become Kebzeh. All those years of doing Kebzeh and you just become it." He has had Murat for a spiritual guide for twenty-six years now and lives in Vancouver with frequent visits to Vernon.

Though Kebzeh readily pours itself into different cultural forms, it is not some namby-pamby soup of borrowed traditions. Its meticulousness is apparent upon first contact with the community. During my visit (and even weeks before, through correspondence) I was treated regally, with every detail planned and covered. I was met graciously at the airport, car doors were opened for me, rest periods considered, every comfort made available, and the community didn't let me spend a dime. I was welcomed into Murat and Maisie's home and essentially had the run of the place. "No need to knock on any doors," Murat told me. "Just walk on in." Maisie, even though she was seriously ill with the flu, made breakfast every morning, brewing wonderful Turkish coffee.

These actions are more than just manners. They are an intricate part of the Kebzeh teachings and reminded me of my days at Zen Mountain Monastery, where every detail—from cleaning the toilets to lighting incense on the altars—was an opportunity for increased awareness and service. In Kebzeh this is the practice known as *aleishwah*, the code of etiquette and civility (there are hundreds of rules, including never crossing your legs when sitting), and it is taken seriously, but with good cheer. Ahmsta Kebzeh is no less disciplined and includes yogic bodywork and cleansing (rubbing the skin briskly with a rough cloth or brush every morning), breathing exercises, meditation, contemplation, visualizations, practice of contentment, and *sohbet* (dialogue with the teacher or a seminar). When the community switched from an outwardly Sufi form to an outwardly Christian form, these individual and group practices, for the most part, stayed the same.

Though Kebzeh is universal in nature, it does carry—particularly as it emanates from Murat and Maisie—a definite Circassian flavor, which still exists in ceremonies and dance. When Ralph Maddess, who has been with Murat for over twenty-five years, was initiated into a leadership position (he now shares the role with Joan), he participated in what is known as the Ahmsta Dubbing Ceremony, in which he stood in front of the community and repeated the words that had been handed down for thousands of years: "In case of thirst, I believe the horses have to be watered first. After horses, the guests have to be watered first. After the guests, the feminine folks of the Society have to be watered first. After that, all the children who don't carry any weapons have to be watered first," and on down until he, as the leader, is the last to drink.

Circassian dance, whose origins stretch back thousands of years, continues to be a central component of Ahmsta Kebzeh practice, though because of space limitations it is only performed formally in the group once a year. "No society can be truly healthy without a traditional folk-style dance," Murat offered. Circassian dance is unlike Mevlevi turning (the Dervish dance) in that it is more communal, relational, and flirtatious. It is said that Circassians flirt with everything—life, death, and each other. When Lisa first visited the group in Vernon from Jerusalem, she was hesitant and didn't feel as though she quite fit in, until she saw the dance. "It was everything, the dance really got me. I saw it all in the dance, it just clinched it for me," Lisa said.

To Murat's knowledge, he is the last native-born Circassian to carry on the teachings of Ahmsta Kebzeh. Abkhazia is now an autonomous region of Georgia, and on his visits there Murat found no remaining elders or practitioners, just the echoes of the wisdom teachings etched on the local faces. It is an oral tradition, so the only books written about the ancient practice are written by Murat. All the participants and leaders of Ahmsta Kebzeh have been guided—in one way or another—by him.

In this way, perhaps more intensely than with many other teachers, Murat's life *is* the tradition—he (and Maisie, too) is our only frame of reference. His life mimics the arc of Kebzeh, the practice moving us from above-it-all self-absorption to common and pervasively shared humanity. In this sense, by tracing Murat's past we get a palpable feel of Kebzeh's unfolding contours. "A person can only teach, in the metaphysical area, what he actually believes to be true. If he teaches you that through standing on your head you will reach some sort of mystic goal, he must first arouse in you some degree of belief that it has already been attained by this method," wrote Idries Shah.[7]

Kebzeh comes from the Caucasus Mountains, that grand range that rises in permanent cloud between the Black and Caspian seas. It was from there that Murat was taken, with fifteen thousand others, down to the dry plains of Turkey by his grandfather Sat, an Abkhazian tribal leader, in 1918 when Murat was three years old. The move was a part of the ongoing Circassian diaspora, which was forced by the Russians in 1864 after the surrender of Shamyl, the last imam of the North Caucasus. Because of the Yagan royal lineage, Murat soon found himself living in a 120-room mansion in Istanbul.

Though Murat's mother was connected to the Sultan's family, his father, Mehmet, was a prominent figure in Turkey's War of Independence, which ended the reign of the Ottoman court. After the establishment of the Turkish Republic in 1923, Mehmet was appointed to the parliament but retired from politics in 1926. Unfortunately, old political grudges persisted and Mehmet was shot in one lung while he fended off an assassination attempt, killing two of the gunmen. Eight months later he died of complications from this wound. Murat was ten years old, and suddenly his life changed in unexpected ways. A few weeks after his father's death, Murat was chosen by the tribal elders (they were still a very close-knit community) to be trained in Ahmsta Kebzeh.

Originally, Ahmsta Kebzeh grew from the beliefs and practices of the Circassians, who thought that they shared the high mountains with beings called Narts, who possessed all the wisdom on earth, and were the "Source." The Narts made contact with the people through heads of families who had reached a high level of attainment by means of dedicated and intense training. These leaders became chieftains, and Murat was born into this lineage. "When I was taken under the instruction of the elders, I wasn't taught anything contradictory. What I was given was above religion. Instead of the orthodox teaching of Islam, which was founded on the idea of punishment and reward and our indebtedness to the Creator, I was told about love. 'The Cause of All Being,' as it was explained, is a certain love affair which took place in the Cosmos. We belong to this love affair. We exist with our understanding as companions to this creative power."[8]

Murat wasn't happy about being chosen. He was getting a Western education and studying Islam. He accepted the training begrudgingly. "I was given special exercises to improve my body faculties and was instructed on how to handle, control, and activate the inner centers of the body which were called cosmic 'nests.' "[9] There was one martial arts practice Murat learned that would later bring trouble. It was known as the "clay exercise." For months on end Murat thrust his hands, fingers straightened, into a large mound of clay nearly up to his elbow, first one hand and then the other, in and out, over and over again, until he was exhausted. After a time the practitioner's fingernails fall off and grow back thicker and glossier, then fall off again and grow back glossier still. "The time comes when you can recognize a well-trained clay-exercise person by looking at the beauty of his fingers. Unfortunately, the more dangerous they become, the more beautiful they become, like a snake."[10]

The harder Murat trained, the more his resistance and skepticism grew. "My opinion of my tribal teachers was that they were a backward people, a graveyard people, and that they were trying to find meaning in dead things."[11] So Murat up and quit. "As you wish," the elders told him, and their courtesy impressed him. Soon after that, at age sixteen, for reasons he doesn't remember, he thrust his hand—in the manner he had been taught—into the ribcage of a live bull. When he withdrew his hand, the bull's intestines splattered the front of his body. He feared the elders were trying to make a killer out of him and distanced himself even further from his heritage.

"I didn't understand the spiritual benefit and merits of martial arts. When I killed this bull, I was just afraid of what I had done. And after that I started to become, little by little, the most docile, the most soft person," Murat told me. "I was afraid of getting into any kind of confrontation with anybody. Decade after decade, the softer and softer I became; before that I was a troublemaker wher-

ever I went," he said. Murat was finished with Ahmsta Kebzeh, or
so he thought. He had little inkling of the tectonic shifts that had
been put in motion. We often have no idea how spiritual practice is
unfolding below our rational radar. "There are three things you
need to be successful in Ahmsta Kebzeh," Murat told me when we
first met, "patience, patience, and patience."

After Murat quit his formal training, he turned to his love of
horses, which had grown steadily from childhood, and his dedicated practice of Islam. When he wasn't absorbed in study or
prayer, he spent every waking hour with his beloved creatures. "I
came to such an understanding of horses that I could talk with
them. A horse would tell me, 'Don't spend your time with me. I
cannot do this work. I am sorry, but look for another one.' I happened to be a good rider, and two years after I started I became a
name in national riding."[12] Murat would soon win the non-medal
steeplechase in the 1936 Berlin Olympics, and set a world record in
high-jumping in Vienna in 1937.

During the 1938 equestrian championships in Rome, Murat
took a fall in the steeplechase that ended his riding career. During
one of the jumps his horse tumbled and fell on top of him. "I
looked down and my boot was filling with blood, but I couldn't
understand why," Murat told me. "My belly had split open and
only my pants were holding my intestines together. I got back on
my horse and finished the course with blood overflowing from my
boots. At the finish I dismounted, saluted to the crowd, and then
passed out," he said. That he had completed the course with such
an injury became instant legend. During his recovery in a hospital
in Rome, he received flowers from Hitler and Mussolini, who con-
gratulated him on his heroism. He was twenty-five years old.

As with many Sufi teachers, Murat is a grand storyteller, but his
stories are often told in circular fashion. "I must warn you," he
proclaimed before I began the interview, "I might start my reply

quite a bit before or quite a bit after the answer to your question."
He quickly added that he wouldn't be offended if I cut him off
and steered him to a more direct response, but I soon found that if
I constricted his reply to what I thought the answer or even the
subject should be, I missed most of what was being given. The stories had not a hint of nostalgia and were told, quite naturally, in a
teaching fashion.

Though Murat doesn't instruct students in martial arts, as he
was taught when young (it is now presented as a different kind of
warriorship), the practice contains that essence—there's nothing
to push against, the force of a student's inquiry is used as the main
energy of transformation for the teacher and the participant. The
stories of his life have this quality; they glow with invitation—
there's a sense that you could fall into them and be transformed,
like Alice down the rabbit hole.

After Murat's riding career ended, he dropped out of orthodox
Islam. "God seemed like a bank manager."[13] He soon turned his
vast energies to medicine (he would drop out before finishing his
studies) and women. Murat became quite a rascal and writes un-
abashedly about those days in his autobiography. "I didn't want to
give people a false impression of me," he said. "I wasn't an angel. I
liked disturbing people and I liked teasing them. I liked playing
dangerous games with people. I was a real troublemaker." One
morning at 2:00 a.m. he left his school with his gun and walked to
Taksim Square in the middle of Istanbul and shot the clock six
times "because it said two a.m. instead of twelve!"[14] Though the
incident of killing the bull had begun to temper his anger, he still
smoldered. Fate (or perhaps the spiritual energy that his elders had
awakened in him), however, brought difficulties that dulled Murat's
jagged personality.

One day Murat came upon a house fire. A young woman was on
the balcony of the burning building, holding a newborn infant and

screaming for help. There was no way to reach her without a tall ladder. Suddenly a large, muscular man with a shaved head and a big mustache appeared as if from nowhere, carrying an ax and a rope. He climbed a nearby tree, tied the rope to one of the branches, dropped to the roof, smashed a hole with his ax, jumped down, and came back out holding the woman and baby under one arm. It was a remarkable rescue and the crowd cheered. Murat, however, felt as though he'd been robbed.

"Instead of being joyful and applauding and cheering like the rest of the crowd, I felt like a child from whose hands a new and desirable toy had been taken. Apparently, I was going to enjoy seeing this poor woman and her child burn. It was a very ugly experience for me. I came from a noble family. I believed that I had a generous heart, that I was different from others, that I was distinguished. . . . I believed that I was so special all the ordinary people were like insects, like worms. This was the way I had been raised in the traditional aristocratic teaching and training. In that moment I was faced with myself and saw how wicked I really was."[15] Murat, filled with anguish, ran home in shame. "The first people who met me said, 'What happened to you? Your face is dark green! Something has happened to your face.'"[16] Murat passed out on the bed and had a fever for two weeks. "I suffered a nervous breakdown for nearly three years and when I recovered I was not the same person I had been."[17]

A year after the fire, Murat had a dream in which he visited a building where the man who had rescued the woman answered the door. Inside he met another man with a red beard. When he described the dream in detail to his mother, who was a practicing Sufi in the Mevlevi order, she told him that he had visited the Bektashi *tekke* (monastery or teaching house) in the village of Merdivenkoy (a suburb of Istanbul). The Bektashis are a Sufi sect. She suggested he visit them. When he did, everything was exactly as he'd seen it in his dream: the hero from the fire answered the door, and the red-bearded man, Hasan Tashin Baba (a Sufi sheikh), seemed to be waiting for him. It was the beginning of his Sufi training.

"My connection with Hasan Tashin Baba was very strong. Anytime I remembered him, he was with me. I received full protection from him. Wherever I went, whether in Istanbul or outside of town, he was with me in a very tangible way."[18] He studied for three and a half years with his sheikh, attending evening classes, *sohbet*s, and retreats—participating at one point in an intense nineteen-day solo fast in a cell. After a year of study he was still assaulted by the shame from the fire. He talked to his sheikh about the incident, and Hasan Tashin Baba did everything in his power to help Murat heal from his existential wound.

One evening Murat was reading the Bible and decided to pray to Jesus to be healed. While he was praying he fell into a dream. In it he saw a large pile of manure with millions of worms wriggling in it. Each worm had a white face and a black nose, and Murat recognized one of them as himself. He suddenly felt great compassion for himself down in the manure. Then something picked him up by the scruff of his neck, as a cat would pick up a kitten, and when he twisted his head around, he saw Jesus carrying him down to the worm. "I grabbed the worm that had my own face and I lifted it up. As I lifted it up I hugged it with compassion and while I was doing so the worm disappeared." When Murat awoke, all traces of anguish had vanished. "From that moment I started accepting everyone the way they were, even myself. . . . I stayed with Jesus for a long time at that level."[19]

When Murat told his sheikh of the incident, Hasan Tashin Baba was very pleased and said, "You should stick with Him and maybe through you we will have benefit also." During Murat's time at the *tekke*, his sheikh began to recognize his student's previous immersion in Kebzeh. When Murat completed his training, Hasan

Tashin Baba steered him back to his roots. "My sheikh said to me, 'My wish, my recommendation to you is go back to your tradition. You made a big mistake by stopping with the elders who were trying to give you the most precious thing that exists on the surface of this planet. Go back to your ancient tradition. You deserve it,' " Murat told me, and tears welled up in his eyes. He has deep gratitude to his sheikh for helping him reconnect with Ahmsta Kebzeh. "That opened my eyes. After that I started opening myself. I meditated all the time. And I started meditating the way the Kebzeh elders had taught me."

Soon after his time in the Bektashi *tekke,* he married Maisie, a fellow Abkhazian, and eventually moved to Chorlu, west of Istanbul, to work his family's six-thousand-acre farm, which he had inherited from his father. A family squabble ensued and he sold his share, moving his family to the remote eastern region of Turkey. During this time he reconnected more and more with his Kebzeh training. But Turkey had become an increasingly difficult place to live, and at the age of forty-eight, Murat decided to emigrate to Canada. He had spent the previous year learning English and teaching it to his family. In November 1963, Murat, Maisie, and their four children flew to Montreal, and the next day boarded a train to Vancouver.

Murat's preferred method of teaching is *sohbet,* working with the energy of the group in a seminar setting. He is extremely good at it, and his facility arises quite naturally. Though he has always been a reluctant teacher and was not looking to move into that position in his adopted homeland, his exceptional quality could not be hidden. Shortly after his arrival in Canada he was offered a job as a draftsman in Vernon—the Turkish government had confiscated all of his family's money, so he was in need of work (no different from most immigrants). In Vernon he and his family attended the local Christian church, and soon Murat was invited to a study group.

"In the group they were discussing Nietzsche's assertion, 'God is dead,' " Murat told me. "Someone said, 'We no longer have God in our daily lives, so at least part of that statement is true,' and then another one said, 'No, it is not.' So they asked me, 'Mr. Yagan, what is your view? Is God dead or alive?' I said, 'I cannot answer this question, if God is dead or not. I would like to make a statement totally separate and independent and I would like to ask what this respectful group of people thinks about it. You tell me whether it is true or not.' 'Okay. Whatever you say,' they said. '*Demir* is dead,' I said. All of them asked, 'What is *demir?*'

" '*Demir* is just a word that came to my mind, and in Turkish it means the metal which is iron. I picked it purposefully. But now you see that in the statement that I make there is one word that you don't know what it means and all of a sudden you changed from 'death' to *demir,* and so when you talk about 'God is dead' you are so sure that you know what God is that you forget about it, you take it for granted that you know and you concentrate on the word *dead.* First of all, I would say humbly and gently let us explore what is God.' And then a revolutionary spirit arose in the room. 'Yes, we want to know what God is,' they said. And I said, 'It is in the very first sentence of the Gospel of John, "In the beginning is the Word and the Word is with God." What is 'the Word'? 'The Word is the Bible,' they said. 'No, the Word is consciousness at the level of *Homo sapiens.*

" 'So therefore I can change this Word into consciousness and I can say any consciousness that is aware of its environment is God. So, just imagine yourself, if you lose your consciousness, would you exist? Do you exist when you are put to sleep in surgery? When you open your eyes you find out you are alive. If you say "God is dead," then there is no awareness, and if there is no God, then everything, particularly humans, doesn't exist. That's what my understanding of God is,' I said. You know what happened? All of the people from the churches in the valley were there at the next meeting. That's how I got involved."

In Ahmsta Kebzeh, as in Sufism, the intellect is neither rejected nor exalted. Instead it is used as a vehicle to carry the aspirant farther along the path, with the understanding that the carriage of inquiry will eventually be abandoned in favor of intuition, spontaneity—spirit. "There can be no soft answers in our tradition; there must be rational and real answers to soften the intellect," Murat told me. "One should never belittle the question or the asker. We are taught that very early on as Circassians. My wife Maisie is nine years younger than I am. I knew her as a child. One day she asked her father, maybe she was ten or eleven, 'Daddy, you have two sons and two daughters. Which one do you love the most?' He answered, 'My dear child, you have two eyes. Which one do you love the most?' "

Within the practice of Ahmsta Kebzeh there are three methodological approaches: "careful observation" (listening well, watching well, and thinking twice before you speak or act), "correct interpretation" (this develops during *sohbet*s), and "practical application" (putting into action everything developed through observation and interpretation). When these are applied in the teacher-student framework they break down into four consecutive steps. First, the teacher discovers the student's "conditioning" (being raised in a religious tradition, coming from a broken home, and so on); second, the teacher works on "deconditioning" the student (freeing the person from negative conditioning); third, the teacher "reconditions" the student (educating them in the teaching, which forms the main body of learning); the fourth step is "unconditioning." This is understood as a spontaneous arising of the student's "real self" or true nature: there are no prescribed conditions, no set way of doing or understanding. The student acts in a correct manner spontaneously, without any influence from the teacher.

Much like Tibetan Buddhism's graded approach to spiritual practice, Ahmsta Kebzeh has intricately defined steps. It presents a ten-step ladder that maps the student's movement (known as the "chart of transformation") from coarse levels of energy to subtle levels. The chart begins at the "physical body energy of consciousness," and works its way through the "instinctive body," "intellectual," "emotional," "spiritual," "psychic," "ecological," "global," "universal," and finally to the "Christ body energy of consciousness." This chart is only a template and is not set in stone. "There's always movement forward and back on the chart, sometimes within a day, within a minute," says Joan. "Nothing is static and the chart is simply a guide; the steps are not coursework to be completed for graduation."

Students use a variety of practices (breathing, visualization, meditation, contemplation, and so on). Most of these methods are in some way working to soften the ego and one's narrow definition of self. "Dealing with the ego is the most difficult thing. You are continually tricked by its disguising ability," Murat told me. "Ego doesn't show itself in its real identity. It shows itself as dignity, as self-respect, and as keeping your word, making a stand. Nobody would submit to ego if they knew. It's a very strong energy. But does it work for you? Ego is like somebody smiling to bite you. The oldest thing is ego," he said. In Ahmsta Kebzeh, a teacher can create situations that help transform a person's ego but is not allowed to tamper with a person's will. "When you consider all these things, only a human by the virtue of his will can teach himself," Murat told me.

This is a very important component of the teaching and Murat's role as a whistleblower. He is not there to tell participants what to do, and this is readily apparent in the strong men and women who form the community—there is a healthy dose of individual responsibility among the long-term practitioners, which underscores Murat's nondirect approach. This does not mean that Murat is completely aloof; on the contrary, when a rogue ego and resentment is running amok, he is sharp. "I struggled with Judaism, and Murat consciously played that up. He said all kinds of stuff about the Holocaust. He was really messing with me," Lisa said. "I'd walk into the house and he'd raise his arm and say, 'Heil Hitler!' I thought, 'This is crazy, I'm out of here.' But I worked through a lot. My generation grew up with so much grief and anger and blame about the Holocaust, and Murat brought me back to the moment through that experience. I suddenly felt this huge letting go of it." Each student I spoke with had their own version of Murat "messing" with them in varying degrees.

For Mary Anne, a simple word or tone of voice from Murat cut her to the quick. "I was burnt to a point of nearly losing all my skin. I don't know how to describe it any better to you. One of the things that he will do—you might notice some of them over a period of time (talk about cumulative effect)—is cut you off or completely ignore you in a group of people when you are talking from your ego. You might not figure it out until a couple of weeks after you've recovered." For students who have developed a particularly close relationship with a teacher over time, the lessons get more subtle and often more painful as they work on cutting the deeper patterns of ego. I've often heard students talk about their teachers, saying, "She just looked at me in a certain way and my heart dropped," or "He didn't look at me at all during lunch and I was crushed." This sounds strange, but anyone who has ever been in love knows that seemingly insignificant acts can have overwhelming repercussions and the spiritual teacher-student relationship has much the same timbre as romantic love.

These "lashings" are not simple punishments, nor are they instigated for the purpose of doing away with ego altogether. We need our egos for survival. The message is that of transformation: stop allowing ego to rule the roost. By lessening ego's power, we create space for something fresher to arise. "It always comes back to my own mistrust of myself. This gets me into traps of trusting someone else more than I trust in myself. Like my trust in Murat: when I have a deep trust in my true essence, he meets me there. That's how I think it works," Lisa explained. The teacher, in a general sense, takes on the role of the healer by helping to siphon off the poisons of self-absorption and creating more spacious living. But a spiritual teacher can also be a healer in a specific sense.

Jean Robillard told me, "When I found out I had cancer, I was panicking and I phoned Murat and he said, 'Darling, you have to work with time. Time can be your ally or your enemy.' And I said, 'What do you mean, Murat?' and he said, 'You have to figure that out for yourself.' I really worked on trying to understand what he meant, and then I understood and I was going to make time my ally and not my enemy. That gave me the input to heal myself, just that word from Murat. Over the years Murat would tell me something and I would always do it. I would never argue with what he said."

Trust is vital in the teacher-student relationship. But it should never be blind. Even if a student feels a deep connection with a teacher from the start, and this is not uncommon, trust usually needs to sink its taproots slowly and be watered in the cycle of seasons. It is good to let this process unfold naturally and not rush it. There is no better way to develop trust in a teacher than by observing how they are in the world, how they react to different situations, and how they treat people.

Diane Wilson, who, with her husband Wayne, has been a student of Murat's for over twenty-five years and runs the church's children's program, said, "I have personally witnessed many times Murat staying up nights to answer students' questions and listen to life problems and concerns. He has offered his life to pass on all that he can without any personal financial benefit. All his years in Canada he worked and earned wages as a carpenter and even in this effort often took students to work with him, paying them regular wages even as he taught them, and giving the rest of his time to everyone else. He is the consummate example of the Kebzeh teaching, which says that a true leader is a servant. Also Maisie has been his loving companion and support in this, embodying the Kebzeh teachings on hospitality of spirit."

In essence, spiritual teachers are there to serve the community. It is a difficult role for many reasons, but none is more trying than keeping the community itself together as a whole and healthy unit. When I asked each group member which Kebzeh practice they found most difficult, nearly all of them said, "Community." The group has managed to avoid any major scandals. It has had the normal flare-ups of jealousies and cliquish behavior, to be sure, but any group that survives more than twenty-five years is doing something right.

When addressing the common problems that communities encounter, Joan described it this way, "I don't know if I can say we've worked them out. We are in the process of working them out. The teaching that we have been offered is so all-embracing and so clear. We have someone that has lived it, and when we wobbled he presented the truth. If you could recognize that, then hallelujah. If you couldn't recognize it as the truth, you did one of two things: you waited or you left. There aren't very many people who have left, and you know how spiritual communities are, there are conflagrations, they flare up and burn very quickly, and then they ebb, and have coals left. Well, we have sustained ourselves because of Murat."

I asked Joan how she has changed as a student over the years. "I've separated the container from the contained. I have much more empathy for Murat as a teacher than when I started. Some of the questions that I asked in the beginning and the ways of operating in the world, when I look back on them, I scratch my head and wonder where was I, what was I thinking. And now I can see with empathy when he is faced with beginning students asking the same things that I did, how tough it is for a teacher to offer the student what he needs but not necessarily what he wants."

But in Kebzeh it is the community that creates the teacher. There is always that reciprocal energy. "Homogeneity is the best whistle-blower," Murat tells me. Community is the fuel for Kebzeh practice, the fuel for the teacher. When I asked what advice Murat would give to spiritual seekers, he said, "They need a teacher. But you cannot find a teacher because a teacher doesn't exist—never existed. There's one teacher and it is community. You can form a community, find a community. Go hunting with like people. When you find it, organize yourselves. And that is the teacher. And the teacher is in you. If you find the right milieu, like a citrus fruit, it will prosper in the right way." Of course, it helps tremendously to have a master gardener in the house.

Soundings

"A spiritual junkie isn't any nobler than a heroin addict. You see them in spiritual circles, some addicted to the group buzz, others who had some transcendent experience in 1974 that was so unimaginably pleasurable, so euphoric—just like a drug—that they run around the rest of their lives trying to get that feeling back. Unfortunately, people often think that high was reality; that it was enlightenment. We feel that most pleasurable experiences—because of the way we're hooked up biologically—are extraordinarily real. I like feeling good as much as the next guy, but ultimately that has little to do with the actual task of finding reality."

—ADYASHANTI

"Ask yourself what your questions are and pursue them. Find the people who will work with you. We don't need more spiritual marshmallows in the world. You must honor the answers of the past, but you must test them in the present and you must always ask what they'll do to the future. The Chinese say if we stay on the road we are on we will surely get to where we are going—keep seeking, keep testing, keep questioning. Most of the learning that we do is not about acquiring new insights, it's about putting the old ones down. There's a lot of unlearning to do about profoundly simple things, like do you have to get behind the president in a time of war. No you don't, and no you shouldn't. You should ask if this situation is right enough to get behind. You have to get beyond that knee-jerk reaction to authority figures so you can become a valuable part of the answer, not a part of the problem."

—JOAN CHITTISTER, OSB

"When someone advertises 'this guru is great and did this and that' or some organization says 'this is our fantastic teacher, blah, blah, blah'—personally I think that is not so good. The teacher-student bond is really a deep, deep, deep spiritual relationship that is very rare. But whenever I say something is exceptional there is a danger that a person will want to be the exceptional one; I am simply saying that such a relationship will develop very, very slowly. It will usually take ten years to establish. Don't look for some *mahasiddhi* [a person with the power of absolute awareness] to hit you over the head with enlightenment because that mostly doesn't happen. If it happens it happens and then you don't have to worry about it."

—GEHLEK RIMPOCHE

"Howard Thurman [the renowned theologian] once came to visit me in Winnipeg. I asked him if he wanted to visit the Trappists and he did. I said, 'Do you want to see the abbot?' He said, 'No, the abbot is just a manager. I'd like to talk with the master of novices.' So we see the master of novices and Howard asks him, 'What's the biggest complaint you have among novices?' The master says, 'Well, they have to be up at two-thirty in the morning to attend Matins and Lauds. They aren't too happy about it. They tell me that it's so much better when they're out in the fields and they feel ecstasy and love for God and hallelujah and so on. So I say to them, "I forbid you to come to any services now except for the masses, which are an obligation." ' 'What happened then?' Howard asked. And the master replied, 'Well, after a while they came back to me and said, "We didn't come here to be farm hands." 'What happened to your ecstasies?' the master asked. 'They dried up,' said the novices. So the master told them, 'Of course, now you realize, what you are doing at two-thirty in the morning is what gives you the ecstasy in the fields.' "

—Rabbi Zalman Schachter-Shalomi

"In our way, a leader has to be humble and think about the Seventh Generation. . . . As we turn to the four cardinal directions, we hear our Ancestors in the winds, encouraging us to make decisions based on generations to come. Remember, seven generations ago our Grandfathers and Grandmothers prayed for our welfare, even though we weren't yet born. If they had forgotten those who were not yet born, if they had forgotten us, we wouldn't be here today."[1]

—Chief Arvol Looking Horse

"Authority means influence and power. So where does spiritual authority come from? Can a teacher give spiritual authority to their successors? Not on your life. You can spiritually empower a successor, but you can't give them spiritual authority. There is only one person who can grant spiritual authority to the teacher, new or old, and that is the student. Most students, when they begin to study with a teacher, don't realize they're granting spiritual authority. But it is critically important to know when you are extending such authority. Otherwise you can unknowingly get seduced into giving away your power. Real teachers won't accept your power. This Dharma is about your empowerment, not about giving your power away. In Zen, we have teachers who can point the way. They don't tell you how to live your life. That choice only you can make."[2]

—John Daido Loori Roshi

"Mataji [Srimata Gayatri Devi, Sudha Puri's teacher] was very skillful at stirring things up in the student community. We would have group meals and in her quiet way she would start some trouble and then sit back and, as she said, 'watch the monkeys dance.' When I was growing up, my mother would play Strauss waltzes while we ate; we were never allowed to say anything unpleasant at dinnertime. It was not so when I came here to the ashrama. Mataji would sit serenely at the head of the table and lob something out into the conversational banter—that she received a letter and somebody was having an affair, for instance. And kaboom! you'd see all down the table people would pounce on the bait and then the group tension would rise. She knew that if she corrected you verbally the only thing that would happen would be resistance—your ego would say, 'Well, that can't be me.' So somehow or other she would organize and create circumstances where you were confronted with that particular quality in yourself."

—Reverend Mother Sudha Puri

"As a teenager, I embraced orthodox Islam. Then one day I told my mother, who was a Dervish, that I no longer believed in God. Knowing my mother the way I did, I expected her to beat me, but her reaction took me by surprise:

'If you can deny God and stay there, for sure, without being disturbed by anything,' she said, 'this is fine. It is a great attainment. But do you think you are free from being disturbed? If you see that somebody for whom you have a great admiration believes in God and follows a godly way, wouldn't it disturb you? Don't misunderstand me. I don't say that because this man you admire believes, you should also believe. But wouldn't it at least awaken a doubt about your atheism?'

"I thought about it and decided that I knew people like that. And it truly was amazing to me at that time that they believed in God. 'How can a person of such strength, attainment, and success, believe in such an insubstantial thing?' I wondered. My mother . . . encouraged me to search: 'Search everywhere. Search in the mosques, in the churches, in the marketplace, in the whorehouses . . . but search.'

"So this is why I say that you will find yourself at first [at the beginning of the search] in a sterile, arid desert. It takes time. And always, you should be satisfied—or if not satisfied, at least you should be pleased with what you are doing. Don't see yourself as grazing all day in the same pasture, going nowhere. Don't compare yourself with others. Just say, 'I am doing well, *and* I can do better.'"[3]

—MURAT YAGAN

3

THE KEEPER

Chief Arvol Looking Horse

*Someone came to me and asked about the sacred ways and
I told them they should go take groceries to their grandmother.
That's what I mean when I say it is in everyday acts.*[1]

—DAVE CHIEF

We're riding in Arvol's pickup along a dusty dirt road to gather some ponies to be used in a traditional funeral procession. Chief Arvol Looking Horse, as he is known, is the nineteenth-generation keeper of the sacred White Buffalo Calf Pipe of the Lakota, Dakota, Nakota Nation (previously known as the Great Sioux Nation). This pipe, *C'anupa* in the Lakota language, was brought to the Nation many years ago by *Pte-san-win-yan* (White Buffalo Calf Woman). "She taught the People the Seven Sacred Rites and how to walk on Mother Earth in a sacred manner. She said, 'Only the good shall see the Pipe . . . the bad shall not see it or touch it.' "[2] Arvol is the keeper of this sacred *C'anupa*

bundle[3] and has held that responsibility since he was twelve years old, when his grandmother, Lucy Bad Warrior Looking Horse, was directed through the Spirit World to pass the bundle on to him, the youngest person ever to become its keeper.

Arvol drives along the rolling bluffs above the Moreau River, which now runs in a trickle among the ghostly cottonwoods. The South Dakota prairie stretches to the horizon in endless folds of pale ocher and brown. It's unseasonably warm for March, the tail end of another winter that never really came—more news of persistent drought and global warming. Arvol was born and raised here on the Cheyenne River Reservation, fished the Moreau when you could eat what you caught. A crow flies above us in the distance and disappears over a ridge topped by an old graveyard.

"I was really pampered by my grandparents," Arvol raises his voice above the din of the truck engine. "We went to bed early and we got up early, at sunrise, because there was no electricity. At night they would heat stones on the woodstove and then just before I went to bed they would wrap them in a white towel and they would put that on my feet. And then they would tell me stories and they would cover me with my very own blanket." Arvol smiles at the memory. "It was really a beautiful feeling when we stayed with our grandparents because they treated us with such respect. Being raised by elderly people you learn a lot of patience. That was my first teaching."

Arvol is tall, on the lanky side. He sports a mustache and wears his hair long in the traditional way—though a few months after my visit he would cut it short upon his mother Mary's death, as is the custom. When you meet Arvol you are immediately struck by his quiet presence, which you quickly understand is not about stoicism or withdrawal, but in fact their opposite. His presence seems to flow outward over his surroundings. It's calming. The more you are around him, the more you realize that his steady dignity arises from patience. And the more you watch how he interacts with the world, the more you realize that patience is the heart of peace. There is his tenderness, too, for there is no better word to describe what emanates from Arvol when he speaks of his people and their sacred ways, when he speaks of all humanity and the sacred Earth and its creatures. And that tenderness also gains its strength from patience.

"I was told that a leader is humble and respectful and never hollers down to his people," Arvol explained to me. "Long ago traditional leaders, even though they probably had a lot of anger toward whatever was disrupting them, had to maintain and act in a spiritual way. You always have to walk that line within peace and harmony. You have to choose your words before you speak because whatever you say can hurt a person long-term. If you asked one of the old leaders long ago a question it might take them a day, a week, or as long as they needed to come up with the answer. You have to respect that and give them time."

"Today in the United States non-Indians demand that Indians become militant in order to achieve political goals," writes Vine Deloria Jr., the late renowned author, philosopher, and clear-eyed Indian spokesman. "But the very quiescence of the traditional Indians and their seemingly infinite patience with the government is damning indeed when understood in the traditional Indian context. For they are bestowing dignity upon a government and a system of life with the expectation that this government and this way of life will come to a sense of understanding and will begin to act with maturity and dignity towards them. It is a great embarrassment that such expectations are unfulfilled."[4]

To describe Arvol as a teacher in the way that non-Indians understand the term is misleading. "We really don't have teachers in the sense of someone you come and study with; the society is egalitarian. Everybody is your teacher," Paula, Arvol's "other half," told me. "Arvol is centered in the knowledge of the bundle. It's the person's responsibility whether they want to be Lakota and take what he keeps as part of the bundle. He's not the one that mandates in any way whether people do that or not. He keeps what is sacred sacred; he keeps things in sync. It bothers me when people come here and say, 'Arvol is my teacher,' like it is a ticket to ride," she said. Paula, who is from the Sisseton-Wahpeton Oyate tribe and a longtime Indian rights activist, is making a point of distinguishing between authority and leadership. Arvol is not in a position to dictate how people live their lives, but he is a leader in the way he maintains the sacred pipe and its ceremonies.

"Our teachings are quite different from most Western formats," Lorain Fox Davis told me. She is Cree and Blackfeet, the founder of Rediscovery Four Corners—a youth program that teaches traditional ways—and has worked with Arvol for many years (she also studied with Lakota elder Erma Bearstops). "One can't just sign up for a workshop; it doesn't function that way. It takes years of being supportive of an entire community. That's where the teaching happens. There's a constant exchange, a flow both ways. With Erma, I was there whenever she needed help for community—it was never for herself, it was always for others, so I was expected to help support that also. With Arvol it is the same. I've known him for years and have traveled around the world with him. He has always been so respectful. He honors the ancestors and the teachings that came down through them. He would never aggrandize himself—it was always the teachings and the power of the pipe," she explained.

When Arvol was young he was bitten in the face by a black widow spider. His grandmother prayed hard for him and he believes it was her prayers that pulled him through. But the venom had spread across his face and eaten away some of his skin, leaving a bad scar, which made him very shy. He stayed away from people because he was ashamed of his disfigurement. He rode his horse and spent a lot of time on the prairie and always felt at peace there, safe and secure. Arvol received the bundle in 1966, upon the death of his grandmother, during his Coming of Age Ceremony, which all Lakota children went through the year before becoming a teenager. It was a tremendous responsibility for someone so young and set his life on a course that further separated him from an "ordinary" way of living.

"I was told that the spirit chose me. When I was taken through the ceremony, the many elders that used to come and pray with the bundle were there to witness. I was very sad that my grandmother left me; it was kind of confusing for me to carry all those lonely feelings while we were going through the ceremony. Suddenly I felt like my life was not my own. I did not understand what this all meant, or the challenges that I would face in the future, but somehow inside, I knew, I could never turn back."[5]

"Arvol isn't some superhero," Elaine Martinez exclaimed, "he's a guy, just a regular guy." Elaine has known Arvol for ten years, has traveled with him extensively, and has helped him, Paula, and others with World Peace and Prayer Day (I will explain more about this later). She is part Siboney and part Spanish. "But still I honestly believe that I've never met anyone with as much compassion," Elaine continues. "Arvol has certain responsibilities that make his life pass differently. There should be more sympathy for him and greater generosity because of the burden he was given. It wasn't a choice. In Indian Country we have a lot of choices. We don't have to follow any specific leader; we don't have to have a specific sexuality. Historically you could be whatever you wanted, but then there are rare occasions—when a medicine man comes up in your family, well, my condolences. Your freedoms are thwarted in a sense, it is your calling."

The egalitarian nature of the Lakota tribes springs from how they view themselves within the universe. "The Plains Indians arranged their knowledge in a circular format—which is to say, there were no ultimate terms or constituents of their universe, only sets of relationships that sought to describe phenomena,"[6] writes Deloria. Meaning and substance, for the Lakota people, has always been relational, communal (including the two-leggeds, the four-leggeds, the green beings, and all else), and cannot be extracted in portions, particularly from place. "American Indians hold their lands—places—as having the highest possible meaning, and all their statements are made with this reference point in mind,"[7] Deloria adds. Arvol's leadership role is a direct outgrowth of the way the Lakotas' spirituality functions. In fact, there is not a single aspect of American Indian social structure that lacks spirit or sacred meaning. Hierarchy doesn't exist; the system unfolds as varying points of contact in the circle of the Sacred Hoop, and Arvol helps hold that hoop together.

"Being regional, being in place, has its own sort of bias, but it cannot be too inflated because it is rooted in the inviolable processes of the natural world,"[8] wrote Gary Snyder, the poet and eco-activist, and he was talking particularly about indigenous and "village" values as opposed to "special interests of corporations . . . or centralized religious bureaucracies and other such institutions."[9] Indian spirituality, indeed all indigenous spirituality, is, as a matter of scale, inherently ecological; it cannot be otherwise. That is what sets it apart. With traditional Indian religion there's no separation between its healthy practice and a healthy ecosystem.

The White Buffalo Calf Pipe bowl is made of red stone, which symbolizes the blood of the People and the female. The wooden stem represents the Tree of Life and the male. When you connect the bowl and the stem, you connect the world above and the world below. But it is more than just a physical artifact. It is a living thing; it is energy. Stella Pretty Sounding Flute, who is Lakota, first saw the sacred bundle when she was five (she is now in her eighties), and it made such an impression on her that she couldn't erase the memory of it from her mind; even though she was sent to a Catholic school and told that her family's traditional ways were evil, she never forgot what she had seen and the power that she had felt. When she saw it again during a ceremony with Arvol, she had the same deep connection. "I felt that sacred bundle, oh my goodness, it was like it was building up energy inside of me," she said.

From the time Arvol received the bundle, there were protocols he had to follow—he could not swear, carry a weapon of any kind, speak badly of other people, perform any ceremony for money, or enter tribal politics, and he has always been committed to staying alcohol- and drug-free. The tribe was to take care of him. "She [Arvol's grandmother] said the sacred *C'anupa* is a spirit and that the bag it's kept in is just as sacred. The bag is called *C'an-te o-j'u-ha* (heart bag), meaning we should carry this in our heart with love and compassion. She said that when we offer tobacco to our relatives and to every spirit, such as our medicines, these energies would help us. I was told that the prayers should be for health, protection, guidance, and wisdom, nothing more."[10]

The White Buffalo Calf Woman brought the sacred bundle at a time, long ago, when the Lakota Nation had fallen on hard times. They had tried to control one another and had forgotten the sacred ways and the teachings. The buffalo had disappeared, and the people were starving. Every morning the tribe sent out scouts, but they returned empty-handed. Then one day two scouts were sent out and they came upon a beautiful woman in a white buckskin dress. One of the scouts lusted after her. He told the other that he was going to take her. As he approached the woman and reached out his hand, a black cloud descended and engulfed him. When it lifted, all that was left was a skeleton with snakes writhing about its bones. The woman then turned to the other scout, who was trembling, and told him to tell his people what he had seen, to prepare an altar of sage and cherry branches, and to put up a great tipi, because she was going to visit them the next day and bring a great gift that she kept in her sacred bundle.

The people did as they were told, and the woman visited them as promised. She told them of the sacred pipe—the very pipe that Arvol keeps—and instructed them on its use. She said, "This is the *C'anupa.* The person who smokes it achieves union with all beings and with all things of the world. By smoking this *C'anupa* you will make direct personal contact with *Wakan Tankan* (the Great Mystery). Following the way of the sacred *C'anupa,* you will walk in a sacred manner upon the earth, for the earth is your grandmother and your mother and she is sacred."[11] She told them that when they pray with the *C'anupa* they should humble themselves. She warned them that they must have a good heart and mind to go to the ceremonies. She told them to honor the sacred sites and gave them the teachings on the correct way to live.

The White Buffalo Calf Woman instructed them on the Seven Sacred Rites that came with the bundle: the *Wi-wanyang-wa-c'i-pi* (Sundance Ceremony), the *Han-ble-c'i-ya* (Vision Quest), the *I-ni-pi* (Purification Ceremony), the *Hun-ka ka-g'a* (Making of a Relative), the *Ta-pa kah'-g'o-ya* (Throwing of the Sacred Ball), the *Wi-yan is'-na ti* (Womanhood Ceremony), and the *Na-g'i glu-ha* (Keeping of the Spirit Ceremony). When the White Buffalo Calf Woman left the people, she stopped on the top of a hill and turned to look at them. She then rolled over and became a young black buffalo. She rolled again and became a red buffalo. Again a yellow buffalo, and then finally she rolled and became a white buffalo—these are the four colors used in the ceremonies.

To speak of Lakota spirituality is to speak of place and the people's connection to the landscape. It is to speak of the inextricable communal bonds that make spirituality tangible and vital. But it is also to speak of survival and the historical context in which the Lakota traditions have struggled to maintain their essential nature. The list of abuses against Indians (and all indigenous people, for that matter) is long and shameful and need not be repeated here, though I am tempted to do so in response to America's perennial amnesia in the face of the darkest, most shameful parts of our history. But only two items, directly related to the Lakota People, need be underscored to get the point across.

One of those is the slaughter of the buffalo—a nightmarish travesty of unparalleled sadness—which reduced in a short forty-five years (1840 to 1885) the largest herd of animals on the face of the planet (estimated at 30 million) to a total of two hundred (in the wild)—yes, two hundred. This carnage was carried out, in large measure, to feed industrialization and to starve and demoralize the Plains Indians—the buffalo is a sacred animal for the Lakota Nation—and drive them onto reservations. The other atrocity was the Wounded Knee massacre, where three hundred Lakota men, women, and children were murdered by the U.S. Seventh Cavalry on December 29, 1890. This act effectively ended the Indian Wars and the free expression of the traditional Lakota way of life. As Black Elk wrote:

I did not know then how much was ended. When I look back now from this high hill of my old age, I can still see the butchered women and children lying heaped and scattered all along the crooked gulch as plain as when I saw them with eyes still young. And I can see that something else died there in the bloody mud, and was buried in the blizzard. A people's dream died there. It was a beautiful dream. And I, to whom so great a vision was given in my youth,—you see me now a pitiful old man who has done nothing, for the nation's hoop is broken and scattered. There is no center any longer, and the sacred tree is dead.[12]

From the close of the nineteenth century on, the Lakota Nation was "attacked" from every angle—children were forced to attend Christian boarding schools and not allowed to speak their native language and were beaten and told their culture was evil, tribal members were forced to cut their hair (the part of the body where it is believed spirit resides) and keep it short, spiritual practices were outlawed, and Indians were forced into degrading poverty (something they had never known) and reliance on government rations. Not to mention the slew of broken treaties and the outright theft of the sacred Black Hills, which the Lakota call the "heart of everything that is."

For the Plains Indians the arrival of the Europeans, except for the introduction of the horse by the Spanish (for which they have a ceremony of gratitude), has been, in a word, catastrophic. As Gary Snyder put it, "If we actually tried to teach the values of western civilization, we'd just be peddling the ideology of individualism, of human uniqueness, special human dignity, the boundless potential of Man, and the glory of success."[13] Spirituality of any flavor, and certainly every teacher in this book would agree, is not about the primacy of human beings at the expense of the natural world. Nor does it contain any ideology; contrary to popular belief, the truth has no agenda. This does not mean that Indians were perfect: they had their wars, their jealousies and greed, and all those human foibles. But once again it's a matter of scale and priority— how much damage can be done when you hold the earth and its local places sacred?

Alex White Plume, who is the Pine Ridge Reservation vice-chairman and a staunch supporter of Arvol, says that the main problem among his people is what he calls the "colonization of the mind." And truly that is what threatens us all—the assumption that individualism trumps community and connectedness, that one race is superior to another, that material success trumps harmony and spiritual equanimity. "We've done a lot of work in recent years," Alex White Plume tells me, "to get young people interested once again in traditional ways, and it is very pleasing to see their enthusiasm returning for the ceremonies, for the language."

It was only relatively recently, through the American Indian Religious Freedom Act of 1973, that Indian spiritual leaders could legally perform any of their ceremonies in public, and they have made great strides in renewing and invigorating their traditional culture. The problem now is not the disuse of the ceremonies or a sense of shame from practicing them (long a debilitating reality for the tribe); it is the opposite. The Sundance, the Purification Ceremony, and the Vision Quest have become so popular that they are threatened by the hungry embrace of pop spirituality whose central themes, it would seem, are commercialism, self-aggrandizement, and triviality.

We are sitting around Arvol and Paula's dining-room table in their mobile home, eating cheese danish and drinking coffee. We had returned the ponies to their owner after they'd been used as part of the funeral ceremony in town. But when we dropped them off, one of the family's dogs, a recent addition, had been left behind and now the children were out looking for it on horseback. Arvol will go and pick them up with the horse trailer in a couple of hours—he seems in perpetual motion, running from one place to another, his face nearly always relaxed, his humor dry and acutely perceptive, frequently animating the conversation. As we sip our coffee he jokes about the popularity of the movie *Dances with Wolves.* "After the movie everybody wanted to be an Indian and they were showing up by the carload. But what they were really after was to be a star like Kevin Costner and act like an Indian, to be famous," he told me, laughing at the sheer and nearly painful absurdity of it.

"Laughter is probably the Indian's most treasured commodity, if I can call it that," Elaine said. "It's much more appreciated than government cheese. Individuals are valued for having a sense of humor, but the seriousness is there too, often right beneath the humor." Indians are great teasers, and it's a test of character to see how well you handle being teased and how easily you can laugh at yourself. "The Indian people are exactly the opposite of the popular stereotype. I sometimes wonder how anything is accomplished by Indians because of the apparent overemphasis on humor within the Indian world," writes Deloria. "Indians have found a humorous side of nearly every problem."[14]

Arvol's humor is hard to describe because of its subtlety and tone. Sometimes it's not what he says; it's what he doesn't say. Or it arises in the rhythm, the pauses, and inflection of his speech. Because Arvol cannot accept money for ceremonies and because, as a chief, he cannot live off the reservation, he has little means of making money. He can accept money for speaking engagements, but these are few and far between. In other words, Arvol and Paula are poor. Some months they can't afford to pay their minimal mortgage or buy enough hay for the dozen or so horses in the corral, which he uses for his youth rides. It's more than a little ironic that Arvol, who speaks at the UN—performs the opening ceremony there for Indigenous Day every year—who has traveled around the globe and met with world leaders and in turn is recognized as a powerful spiritual dignitary, can barely afford to buy groceries.

When I ask why the tribe isn't taking care of him, which is their traditional role, he says, "I was supposed to be taken care of by the Nation, but I got to say that I am not." And when he tells me this he is laughing, because as he spoke there was surprise in his voice, as if he still couldn't believe that the tribe could be so irresponsible, as if he should, after all these years, know better, as if the universe has a grand sense of humor and he continues to be the butt of its jokes. His humor is healing and hopeful and tragic all at once. When he stops chuckling he says, "I'm just barely getting by. I mean, in ceremony it is good because people bring food and such, but I need to pay my bills and my gas and to haul horses and to pay electricity."

The popularity of Lakota spirituality has brought some serious consequences. The abuses of the ceremonies have reached such a level that traditional spiritual leaders and bundle keepers gathered together and issued a controversial proclamation calling for the protection of the Seven Sacred Rites. Arvol is at the center of the controversy because, as the keeper of the original bundle, he has the final word in decisions that could not be settled by consensus among the elders, which was the situation in this case. The proclamation, dated March 9, 2003, calls for an immediate end to the desecration and exploitation of the Seven Sacred Rites, particularly the Sundance, Vision Quest, and Purification Ceremonies. The proclamation reasserts the original protocols handed down from *Pte-san-win-yan.* Charging money for ceremonies, sexual molestation and drug use during ceremony, mockery, and the mixing of New Age beliefs—all common in recent years—must be stopped.

Furthermore, and this is a large part of the controversy, non-Indians cannot lead any of these rites. This doesn't exclude non-Indians from participating in the ceremonies, but they cannot function as elders. Actually, federal law backs the proclamation on this point, as eagle feathers, a necessary talisman for ceremonial leaders, are illegal for non-Indians to possess. Unfortunately, Arvol has gotten much of the heat from both Indians (within his tribe and outside it) and non-Indians alike. He has been called a racist, a charlatan, and power-hungry—all of which, if you knew Arvol, are completely absurd.

To say that the proclamation is racially motivated misses the point. More accurately, it is an affirmation of indigenous culture, of a people and their language, and of the continuation of a way of life rooted in nature, a call to all people to reexamine the destructive mindset of materialism. Keeping, protecting, and performing cere-monies are the responsibility of the bundle keepers, and every bun-dle relates back to the original, to the one Arvol maintains. He is a living example of the original energy that is tied directly to the sa-cred bundle and all that was brought with it, which both define and nourish the Lakota: the White Buffalo Calf Pipe Bundle is the core of the Nation.

I bring up this controversy because it opens a window onto the way Arvol functions as a leader and the way the Lakota Nation and non-Indians perceive him—sometimes clearly, sometimes through the haze of great dysfunction. "If . . . non-Natives have concern for this decision, they must understand that we have been guided through prayer to reach this resolution," Arvol explains in the proclamation. "Our purpose . . . is for the survival of the future generations to come, first and foremost. If the non-Natives truly understand this purpose, they will also understand this decision and know that their departure from this *Ho-c'o-ka* (our sacred altar) is their sincere contribution to the survival of our future genera-tions."[15] Arvol is not overstating the facts when he mentions sur-vival. As Paula put it, "We need protection because one day we are going to become Ishi if we don't watch it." (Ishi was the last of the Yahi Indians. He was found nearly starved in the California foothills in 1911.)

Surprisingly (or not, depending on where you stand), much of the fire directed toward Arvol and the proclamation has come from his own people. The reservations that make up the Lakota Nation have been largely ghettoized—poverty, alcoholism, drug use, sex-ual abuse, gang violence, lack of identity, and crime in general are all real and troubling problems. The reasons behind this are both complex and obvious. Scores of studies have been done on the sub-ject, and I will not even attempt to untangle the mess, though it is safe to say that the values and practices of traditional spiritual elders are a hope and a salve to the Nation. Unfortunately, owing largely to economic pressures, there have been a number of bundle holders who have taken advantage of the popularity of the ceremonies and have been charging for their services. They are upset because the proclamation threatens their income. And the abuses don't stop there.

One Indian medicine man had been sodomizing young boys for over twenty years, traveling around Indian country and on up into Canada. "It wasn't until the proclamation that someone stood up and told the story," Paula said. "You've got to understand that these medicine bundles will heal; that's their purpose, and if the caretakers of that bundle drink or do drugs or abuse people, they can start corrupting the medicine. Finally one of those boys said, 'That's enough.'" The proclamation, once again, is only restating the original guidelines. Spiritual elders would never interfere with anyone's choice to follow or not follow them. There is no panel or inquisition. The elders are simply calling for an understanding of the sacredness of the ceremonies and hoping that decisions will be made based upon those connections.

Still, when the White Buffalo Calf Pipe holder asks certain things of the Nation, it carries some weight. Wrapped tightly within the guidelines of the proclamation is the need for all the leaders who perform the ceremonies to speak the Lakota language. This is the way it has been done from the beginning and is perhaps the hardest aspect of the proclamation to explain and abide by. More than a few of Arvol's closest supporters and friends, within the tribe and without, who were leading ceremonies do not speak Lakota and were asked to stop their leadership roles. Lorain Fox Davis and her husband, both pipe carriers, fell into this category.

"We were Sun Dancers with the Lakota. I had danced for seven years and my husband for four, so it was a shock to us because, while we fit most of the requirements, we do not speak Lakota. At sixty-seven years of age, I figure it would be very difficult for me to learn a new language. Arvol called shortly after the proclamation meeting and I asked him if I had to put my pipe away, too. He said we all have to follow the guidelines that the elders have stated. So we stopped running ceremonies out of respect for Arvol, and it was a great pain for us, it was a tremendous loss. But what it did was to encourage us to go back to my people and to seek them out, and two of my children are now dancing with the Blackfeet, so we are returning to our roots that way," Lorain told me.

To lose good friends in the process of carrying out his role as the bundle holder has been extremely difficult for Arvol. "I told Arvol he is like one of those carnival ducks in the shooting gallery. Someone says, 'Arvol, over here,' and he goes, and then someone says, 'No, come back over here,' and he goes. That little duck keeps going back and forth while being shot at from both directions, from the white society and the Indian society. We always wonder in all of our endeavors if we are favoring one side more than the other. It's just extremely difficult," Elaine said.

Arvol grew up on the spot where he lives now, with his parents and grandparents. The family calls this place Green Grass. The Looking Horse family was always a traditional clan, practicing and teaching the original Lakota ways. The White Buffalo Calf Pipe Bundle has stayed in this bloodline since the beginning—in the Looking Horse, Bad Medicine, and Elk family names.

For Arvol and his family, life was always a struggle, but the early 1970s were a particularly dark period for the clan. Before Arvol's grandmother died, she donated half of the land she owned at Green Grass, a considerable amount, to the local Christian church because at the time it was the only way to pray freely. Yet when Arvol's father, Stanley, brought the family to the church, they were called devil worshippers. Many members of the tribe had been converted to Christianity, so in various ways the Looking Horse family and other traditional clans became outcasts in their own community. Apart from religious differences, divisions also arose in tribal politics, the conflicts usually centering around economic and power struggles. At one time Stanley had eighty head of cattle, fifty horses, a number of tractors, and all the necessary equipment to run the ranch. One day members of the tribe showed up and asked to see the receipts for everything the family owned to run their business, but Stanley never kept receipts. They had bought all they had years before. The tribe confiscated everything. "It was very sad," Arvol said, "because it was the first time I saw my father cry.

"One day after a time of feeling sorry for myself, I remember crying on top of my grandmother's grave and thinking I had nothing to live for. All I had was the shirt on my back and the sacred bundle. I remembered that the four Black Angus cows and some horses that my grandfather gave to me were stolen by the tribe. My grandfather said, 'You take care of these and they will take care of you,' but now they were gone. I remember my father talked with me and told me that I should go to Rosebud, South Dakota, and get away from here for a while, so I went. My father said, 'When you feel better, come back.' At that time I was not spiritually strong, and I needed strength to be around the bundle."[16]

The turning point in Arvol's life came through tragedy. His brother Steven died, and Arvol wanted to honor him in some way. "The day he was buried, I thought about how natural he was with horses and that he would have been the best rodeo rider. So I made a commitment to ride rodeo for him, in saddle bronco riding, which he loved." Arvol went to the rodeo in Deadwood, South Dakota. "I saddled my horse, and was feeling good. I looked up at the grandstand and I got on the horse, he bucked and went straight up in the air. Then he spun around and fell backwards right on top

of me. I heard a crack in my backbone and I couldn't feel my body."
He was rushed to the hospital, and the doctors told him that he
was paralyzed from the neck down and would never walk again.

"I had broken three vertebrae, cracked one, and had a concus-
sion. I remembered my grandmother once saying to me that when
a person is getting ready to go into the Spirit World, their relatives
come to them. At different times I would open my eyes and see
them standing there. Then the phone rang, and the voice on the
line said, 'I'm your grandmother and the people need you.' This
grandmother chewed me out about the rodeo and said I had done
this to myself. I felt my mother and father entering the room, but I
kept my eyes closed because I didn't know if they were real or not.
My dad started talking to me about the Sun Dance they were having. In my mind I kept thinking about my grandmother saying that
it didn't matter how many people prayed for you—if you didn't
pray for yourself, the prayers wouldn't be effective. So I was trying
to relax my mind. I kept picturing the Sun Dance and all the people circling around the Tree of Life in the center. I prayed so much,
humbly, from my heart. When the Sun Dance was over, my bones
healed back together. The doctors couldn't believe it. A week later I
walked out of the hospital. I knew deep down in my heart that my
prayers had been answered."[17]

Anyone can come to Arvol and ask him to lead ceremonies, and
many people do. He always makes himself available. But it is necessary to offer tobacco when visiting a spiritual elder or meeting any
Nation (which can be rocks, birds, insects, or humans). "Tobacco
is very important when you meet another Nation; you've got to
give them tobacco. That's part of our tradition because it goes back
to the energy, respect that energy," Arvol said. It is also good to
bring a gift of food or other items to show your appreciation for
the spiritual leader's work. If you are a part of the Nation and want
to learn more about the ceremonies and perhaps to become a bundle

holder, you must, as stated earlier, know the Lakota language. "The tribal mindset is completely reflected in the Lakota language," Elaine told me. "If you look at the sentence structure, the 'I' factor, the 'me,' is always put last. Trees and rocks and everybody else come first. In English the 'I' usually goes at the beginning. The Indian mindset is that when we go out to work, we are working on behalf of our community, that when gifts come to us we are obligated to share them with our community."

In ceremony and prayer, one is realigned with community in a foundational and holistic way—the person reintegrates with or reaffirms natural processes. "In prayer we are speaking to the grandfathers and we are speaking from our hearts and we are singing from our hearts, so it's about feeling. Even if you pray for another person, you know you just don't pray for the one place where it is painful, you are praying for the whole body. So in that way it is holistic. It's more about energy, respecting that energy and healing, that's where it begins," Arvol stated. "In the *inipi* [purification] ceremony I have a sense of my place in life," Lorain said. "I'm very aware of the powers of the Four Directions [that supply everything we need] and my personal relationship with the powers. Before I learned the ceremonies I never felt the sacredness of fire and those Directions and the Thunder Beings. It's finding my place with the elements, with the elemental beings and natural law." At the core of all the sacred ceremonies is a deep sense of gratitude for all the things that sustain us.

"In our ceremonies you can't have any doubts. A lot of people come to our ceremonies and they hear things and see things. That's why it's so natural, because we already know it's going to be that way. No surprise," Arvol said. "People come and they can't walk and then they walk away, so we believe that can happen. It's natural we have no doubts. I've seen that all my life. We are just a common people, but it's the ceremonies and the pipe, that's where miracles happen, but it has to be done with proper protocol. That's why everything has to be in tune before miracles can happen."

The Lakota teachings are handed down through oral tradition, but if you ask an elder a question you will never get the answer outright; that's too easy. Chris Leith, Medicine Bundle Keeper of the Prairie Island Dakota Community and a good friend of Arvol's, worked for many years in the federal prisons with the Indian population. He was visiting some inmates, and they had heard that a well-known medicine man from South Dakota had died. "They said to me, 'We lost a lot of understanding, knowledge, and wisdom.' And I told them, 'No, you didn't; it's up to you to find out,' " Chris said. This doesn't mean that the wisdom of the spiritual elders is not respected or thought to be valuable. It simply means that the connection with spirit is available to everyone at any given time.

Arvol and the elders are acting from the energy of the original bundle, which taught peace and harmony and gratitude, not division and resentment. "The phrase [that accompanies all ceremonies] *Mitakuye Oyasin*—'all our relations'—has a bigger meaning than just our blood relatives. *Mitakuye Oyasin* means more than our family, more than our Nation, more even than all of humankind. Our Mother Earth herself, *Ma-ka-Un-c'i,* is our relation, and so is Grandfather Sky, and so are each of the two-leggeds, the four-leggeds, those that swim, those that fly, the root nation, and the crawling beings who share the world with us. *Mitakuye Oyasin* refers to the interconnectedness of all beings and all things."[18] Forgiveness is a powerful medicine, Arvol says, and he knows that we need forgiveness to create peace. But such a compassionate stance has not been an easy one to maintain, by any stretch of the imagination.

After hitting bottom in the early 1970s, Arvol regrouped and grew stronger spiritually. It was a time when Indians were gaining some long-deserved respect. AIM (the American Indian Movement), through many of its protests and civil rights actions, gave

voice to a generation and helped raise self-esteem. Interest in traditional spiritual practices was renewed. Arvol found his way back to
Green Grass and quickly realized that if the Nation's hoop was
going to be mended, he had to reach out beyond tribal boundaries
to the world at large. Global warming, pollution, wars, and violence were threatening the planet as a whole.

In 1989, before the Gulf War began, Arvol was directed through
ceremony to journey to Baghdad and pray with the sacred *C'anupa*.
The fear was that a black cloud foretold in prophecy could cover
the Earth and bring sickness. He went with six elders, a white reporter, and a white negotiator. When they arrived, the situation
quickly collapsed. They were put in a ramshackle trailer that was
infested with mice. They were given very little to eat, and the authorities ripped up their return tickets and confiscated their pass-
ports. The reporter went to make a phone call and came back badly
shaken after being roughed up and interrogated. They all feared for
their lives.

On the fourth day of bad food and isolation, Arvol felt helpless
and went to his room, turned off the lights, and began to look for
guidance. "My heart felt like it was scratching inside with pain. I
cried inside, praying for deliverance. And then, suddenly, a Grandfather's presence came into the room. I heard a ceremonial rattle
pound all over the wall and I felt a sense of being home once again
inside myself. I immediately jumped to my feet and told everyone
we needed to pray 'right now!' . . . We felt the presence of the
Grandfathers and knew immediately that we would be OK."[19] Ten
minutes later, four cars came and picked them up and took them to
a government building, where everyone was very polite. They completed the *C'anupa* ceremony that Arvol had been directed to do,
and then they were released. As it turned out, Muhammad Ali had
helped secure their departure, and he met them, smiling, at the
hotel in Baghdad before they left for the airport. "This journey

taught me two things—that complete faith is needed in carrying out the directives from our Sacred Ceremonies, and that the Sacred Grandfathers can journey anywhere upon Mother Earth to hear our prayers."[20]

In 1990, Arvol participated in the Big Foot Ride, which retraced the journey of Chief Big Foot's band, who were massacred at Wounded Knee, from Standing Rock, North Dakota, to the massacre site in South Dakota. The ride took place at the same time of year as the original ride, in the dead of winter from December 15 through December 28. It was the fourth year the ride had taken place—all ceremonies are done in cycles of four—so during this year the group performed the Wiping of the Tears Ceremony, which was known for its healing power. The ride was brutal, the temperature often dipping below minus 40 degrees, with a cutting wind. It was during this ride that Arvol went through his second Chief ceremony (he had the first when he was twelve), when Severt Young Bear, a respected elder, requested that Arvol wear a chief's headdress and told him that he should lead the people and continue mending the Sacred Hoop.

Four years after the completion of that ride, a white buffalo calf was born (named Miracle) in Wisconsin on the Heider family farm. White buffalo (not albino) are very rare. Biologists estimate the odds of such a birth are one in every ten million. Since Arvol was a young child he had heard the ancient prophecy that when the Earth was at a moment of great change—faced with healing or destruction—the White Buffalo Calf Woman's spirit would make her presence known. Arvol took the birth of Miracle as a fulfillment of that prophecy and renewed his efforts to promote global healing. Since 1994 there have been eight other white buffalo born. Arvol, sensing the urgency in taking action to steer us away from our present course of destruction, began holding a healing ceremony on June 21, the summer solstice. This event was the beginning of World Peace and Prayer Day, the first one taking place in 1996 at Grey Horn Butte (Devil's Tower), Wyoming. The ceremony honors the Earth's sacred sites through prayer and the gathering of people in a circle and the offering of tobacco.

Arvol has traveled around the globe planting the seed for World Peace and Prayer Day—to Canada, Costa Rica, Ireland, South Africa, Australia, and Japan. He has received tremendous support from people in those countries to carry on the work. Lorain traveled with Arvol on every one of those trips. "I've seen him in so many different situations and I have never seen him falter from integrity, humility, and truth," she said. "He stands by that. I have never seen him raise his voice, curse, or really even confront anyone, even in very extreme conditions." Lorain told me the story about their trip to South Africa. When they arrived, it was during a time of great racial tension. Arvol and the entourage were met at the airport by leaders of both the Zulu and Hindu communities; there were dancers and music and a very festive atmosphere. But the government officials told the group that there were serious security problems and that by leaving the airport their lives would be in danger. They suggested that the group get back on the plane and return home. Lorain says:

"The government officials warned us of the danger with very grave looks on all of their faces, which was a bit of a shock, and we all looked at Arvol and he stood there with his eyes closed and he said, 'I came here to pray.' So they said, 'All right. We will give you security. You will have armed guards to escort you as you travel.' And Arvol said, 'Oh no, I can't have guns around me. I come peacefully.' They said that they were responsible for our safety and insisted that we agree to the armed guards. And Arvol once again said no. They insisted. Finally, Arvol said, 'All right, let them have their guns but take the bullets out.'

"Year after year to be around that kind of person has made a huge impact on my life and that of my two daughters, who worked in the youth camp with Arvol, and on my husband, who has worked closely with him also," Lorain told me.

When jealousies and division erupted in the tribe over Arvol's role as a leader, a number of people tried to take the bundle away from him or spread rumors that it was fake. Arvol never defended himself, nor did he speak out against any of his accusers. But he has always asserted the authenticity of the bundle through his actions. Alex defended Arvol at every turn when his integrity was questioned. "I would do anything for Arvol," Alex told me. "He is the hope of the Lakota People." The last time I visited Dave Chief, here in Oregon, a month before he died, he told me, "I protect Arvol even from here. I pray for him and make flags and I tell people Arvol is going to be there. You better get there and help him."

Arvol writes:

> We must understand two ways we are free to follow—the positive way or the negative way, the spiritual way or the material way. It's our own choice—each of ours and all of ours. You yourself are the one who must decide. Whatever you decide is what you'll be, to walk in honor or to dishonor your relatives. On your decision—yes, on *your own personal decision*—depends the fate of the entire world. We are the only species destroying Mother Earth! Did you think the Creator would create unnecessary people in a time of such terrible danger? My Grandmother once told me to understand that every person can have a good heart, a heart big enough to change the world! Know that *you* yourself are essential to this world. Believe that! Understand both the blessing and the burden of that. You yourself are *desperately* needed to save the soul of this world. Did you think you were put here for something less?"[21]

Ego: Good, Bad, and Indifferent

In the West we have grown up with Freud's definition of ego as part of his structural theory of psychoanalysis—the id, the ego, and the superego. *Ego* means "I" in Latin. Freud defined ego as a set of functions: intellect, memory, organization, discernment, defense, and so on. The idea of ego quickly moved from the psychological to the spiritual, and before we knew it, ego became a convenient whipping post for everything that prevented us from being "spiritual." When Eastern religions arrived in the West, the definition of ego got filtered through various cultural structures and was interpreted to mean any number of things. We're still wrestling with its "spiritual" definition and its role in spiritual development. Does the ego need to be killed, as we assumed it did when we heard Zen masters proclaiming that we must "die on the meditation cushion"? Does it need to be transformed? Subdued? Ignored? Completely redefined?

I certainly don't have an answer, though I believe there is a contemporary consensus that trying to "kill" the ego is a wrongheaded idea. What I do know is that a teacher's particular understanding of ego—if indeed he does have an opinion—directly affects the way he teaches a student. In Judaism, ego has never been seen as something to extinguish or transcend. "Often the language they use about doing away with ego is wrong," Reb Zalman told me. "I need a good ego, a strong ego. But the ego cannot be the boss; it can only be the manager. It's a very good manager, but a lousy boss. So the boss has to be something that's behind the ego." Rabbi Tirzah Firestone, one of Reb Zalman's students, says, "Judaism is really about using the ego as a vessel. You need it. That's where Judaism and Eastern religions part. You need to keep ego transparent and porous, but it needs to be there."

Certain Eastern religious teachers do not advocate the death of the ego. In fact, much of the confusion around the notion of "killing the ego" results from a misinterpretation of its definition. It was a cultural misunderstanding that many teachers and students are still trying to sort out. Srimata Gayatri Devi, the late Hindu teacher in the Ramakrishna Order who taught in America for fifty-five years, used to say that what is necessary is "a ripe ego," that is, a healthy ego. Chögyam Trungpa Rinpoche, the renowned Tibetan Buddhist teacher, said, "It is important to see that the main point of spiritual practice is to step out of the bureaucracy of ego."[1] He said nothing about extinguishing it. Often we have interpreted a call for the renunciation of ego as a call for its annihilation. Certainly there are teachers who argue for the need for the transcendence of ego and claim that their tradition backs them on this point. The main thing here is for students to have some sense of where their teacher and their tradition stand on this question.

Twenty years ago, Jack Engler, a psychotherapist and Buddhist (a founding member of the Insight Meditation Society), wrote, "You have to be somebody before you can be nobody." He was referring to what he perceived as the tension between the Buddhist idea of "no-self" and the Western concept of psychological self-development, which is to say it's a question of ego. His line has given rise to much debate over the years, and in a recent anthology, *Psychoanalysis and Buddhism: An Unfolding Dialogue,* he revisited the statement:

"Transcending ego," which is often proposed to students as a goal of spiritual practice, has no meaning to a psychodynamically oriented therapist for whom "ego" is a collective term designating the regulatory and integrative functions. To "transcend the ego" in this frame of reference would mean to surrender the very faculties that make us human—the capacity to think, plan, remember, anticipate, organize, self-reflect, distinguish reality from fantasy, exercise voluntary control over impulses and behavior, and love.[2]

Engler's view of ego as a necessary "regulatory and integrative function" for healthy spiritual development is the emerging (if it has not already arrived) paradigm in many spiritual practices. Engler is not inferring that one must work up the hierarchical ladder from the psychological to the spiritual; he acknowledges that much spiritual practice can and rightly does nurture a healthy sense of self and self-esteem. But he also warns the student against bypassing his or her psychological neuroses for pure spiritual transcendence—we can't leap over the messy parts of ourselves in a mad rush to enlightenment.

Mariana Caplan, in her book *Halfway Up the Mountain: The Error of Premature Claims to Enlightenment*, wrote, "It seems ironic that if one enters the spiritual path with an underdeveloped ego (i.e., low self-esteem, a lack of groundedness, clarity, and internal structure), a strong ego must actually be built before it can be diminished, but that is how it works." But is that really so? Does a strong ego actually promote self-esteem, groundedness, clarity? It depends on the definition of ego.

When I asked Arvol Looking Horse about ego, he said that historically the Lakota Nation had no concept of the word. Spiritual "improvement" within his culture has always been a communal process. They've always had a very strong "we-sense" but little notion of the "I." "It seems that ego was brought over on the *Mayflower*," he joked. Once again, I do not want to romanticize the Indians—they had their wars, they have their murders, lying, adultery, and other human darkness—but if you speak with any of the traditional elders, the idea of building up the ego in order to progress along the spiritual path doesn't make any sense. And on the other hand, when Vine Deloria Jr. writes, "Indians of almost any tribe . . . can take you into communities and point out which persons or which families have had particular relationships with particular medicine animals. From those animals and their relationships some tribes have developed tremendous systems of psychoanalysis, better and more accurate, I think, than astrology or Jungian psychology or anything else the West has developed,"[3] we non-Indians can make little sense of what he's talking about. Is ego simply a cultural construct?

Adyashanti writes:

All we ever find is this proof or evidence that ego exists, but we can never find the thing itself. Everything is just arising spontaneously, and if there is any ego at all, it is just this particular movement of mind that says, "It's mine." Ego is a movement. It's a verb. It is not something static. . . . In other words, egos are always on the path. They are on the psychology path, the spiritual path, the path to get more money or a better car. . . . So in order for this verb to keep going, there has to be movement. . . . We have got to be getting somewhere because otherwise we are not becoming. So the verb—let's call it "egoing"—is not operating if we are not becoming. As soon as a verb

stops, it's not a verb anymore. As soon as you stop running, there is no such thing as running—it's gone; nothing is happening. . . . This stopping has to be done very
gently and very naturally because, if we are trying to stop,
then that is movement again. As soon as we try to do
what we think is the right spiritual thing by getting rid of
the ego, we perpetuate it.[4]

Does ego really exist? Is it, as Engler proposes, "a collective
term designating the regulatory and integrative functions," or
is it more fluid, like a verb? "You see a little baby two seconds
out of its mama's womb and it hasn't learned anything about
ego, but you can see that it has a personality," Adyashanti
said. "So the stopping of this verb called ego has nothing to
do with personality stopping."[5] This is really the crux of the
matter. In Zen they say, "I am not you, you are not me, but
we are not different." Where does ego stop and personality
begin or is there any difference? Jack Kornfield, the psychotherapist, author, and co-founder of the Insight Meditation Center, writes, "There are two parallel tasks in spiritual
life. One is to discover selflessness, the other is to develop a
healthy sense of self. Both sides of that apparent paradox
must be fulfilled for us to awaken."[6]

When I asked Joan Chittister why she rarely mentions the
word *ego* in her more than thirty books, she says, "I guess I
don't use that language because I'm steeped in this Benedictine concept of humility. It is so strong for us that you probably don't hear much about ego at any Benedictine monastery.
Instead, you'll hear a lot about humility and your relation to
God and to other people."

Ultimately these "spiritual ego" questions cannot be answered in psychological terms. But this doesn't mean that

psychotherapy or other forms of psychological treatment are not valid partners in the spiritual process. Certainly, many traumas are cured through therapy, and conversely it has been shown that meditation and prayer and simply helping other people can be powerful curatives for depression, low self-esteem, and other psychological ailments.

"Of course the realization is that there isn't a separate self," Adyashanti told me. "But it doesn't mean what our mind thinks it means. It doesn't mean that you have no sense of self. It doesn't mean that you have no ego in its rudimentary sense. It just means that the seeker and the seeking disappear. In fact, anybody who is really awake has a very definite sense of themselves. Look at Jesus. He would go around and say, 'I'm the Son of God.' "

4

UNTYING THE CAT

Joan Chittister, OSB

*I gave away my pen / Now I sit /
In my wooden chair / And listen /
Soon one of the Teachings / Will leave the page /
And enter my heart.*[1]

—MARY LOU KOWNACKI

Sister Joan Chittister is a spiritual raconteur, both in person and on the page. She speaks through Sufi parables, Zen stories, Hasidic tales, heart songs of Christian mystics, and, predominantly, through the dissonance of her own soulful struggles—all of which she blends into freshly relevant tales invoking a communal spirituality of renewal and personal responsibility. "I'm not a teacher. I don't require either a given body of information or even a regimen. I don't impart regimens, but I probably provoke and I certainly imagine, and to me those are the two most essential elements of life at any time, but definitely at the present time in U.S.-global history. We must question everything. It isn't that we have the answers, but we have to cling to our questions, because if you honor your questions you will always find God. If you are not asking questions you are probably farther from God than you imagine. If you have all the answers you have no sense of mystery as far as I'm concerned, and you have no sense of your own responsibility to envision the next layer of God-ness in the universe or your part in it. So I do provoke responses."

There's an old Hindu story Sister Joan likes to tell, about the master who tied up his cat during prayer time. Every time the community prayed together the cat disturbed the group, so the master tethered it in his room. Eventually the master died and they got a new cat that wasn't nearly as rambunctious, but they kept tying it up. After a time you couldn't have group prayer unless there was a cat tied up in the room. In the end no one knew why the cat needed to be tied up, they just knew it "had" to be done. "It's very easy for spiritual types to get trapped in the past and really believe what we did yesterday is the ultimate norm of the spiritual presence today," Sister Joan explained. "I don't think that you have to institutionalize the past in the name of holiness in the present and development of the future. In fact, if you do, that's when you become a cult or a subculture—it's people with strange behaviors for strange reasons doing even stranger things. And it has absolutely no real relationship to what's going on around them now."

When Sister Joan entered the Catholic monastery of the Benedictine Sisters of Erie (BSE)—just down the road from where she grew up—on September 8, 1952, at age sixteen, she joined an institution built on conformity, regularity, and continuity. The style of dress was modeled on the tastes of the French in the sixteenth century. The Customs Book, which prescribed every behavior in detail, hadn't changed in hundreds of years, and the daily schedule was so finely tuned that not a minute of the day went untouched by programming. The spiritual formation process was, in a word, unchanging. During her first interview in the pre-entrance process, Sister Joan was told that she would take French as part of her curriculum to finish high school. But she didn't like French and let Mother Sylvester Groner—the prioress at the time—know as much. "My dear child," the prioress responded, "we don't say we don't like anything." Sister Joan thought about it for a minute and then said, "Do we lie?"[2]

The writer Annie Dillard wrote, "Establishing that things are here is, so far as I know, a new goal for art."[3] Isn't it similar for our present spirituality? We have become so removed from our surroundings, so institutionalized in our thinking and actions—in both the secular and religious worlds—that our first step toward health should be to dismantle the rote and faulty assumptions we inflict on the world. Sister Joan, a Benedictine for over fifty-three years now, is an expert at provoking—from within the sharp angles of institution—the spiritual community (within the Church and beyond its boundaries) to uncover what really exists, or at least what certainly doesn't. She does so not to cancel spiritual tradition but to renew it, to uncap its perennial fizz. She is refreshingly anti-spin, be it the hucksterism of current fads and politics or the unquestioning (and unquestioned) drone of ancient but long-irrelevant religious practices. "As a Roman Catholic I'm informed a great deal by rite and ritual and what we call 'smells and bells,' and it's wonderful, it's absolutely glorious," she says, "but when I sell only that, when I live only that, then I'm selling snake oil."

Sister Joan is considered, by some within the Church, to be a radical, a 1960s leftist, and a consistently articulate agitator. She is, by her own admission, a feminist and a questioner of institutional thinking. The Vatican, not surprisingly, at one time called her a "source of scandal to the faithful."[4] But the list of labels and the melodramatic accusations of an increasingly isolationist Church do little to clarify Sister Joan's deep spiritual impulses: she is working tirelessly not only to renew tradition but to renew faith. "To question is not to deny. It may, in fact, be the truest type of faith a person can muster,"[5] wrote Sister Joan. Don't stop asking, she says.

"What is the struggle that's going on right now in institutional religions? If there is no struggle, what is that saying? How do you explain or relate to what the newspapers are calling radical fundamentalism? How much of your own posture is fundamentalist? How much of it is really visionary? How much of it is more contemplative than dogmatic, how much of it is more experiential than circumstantial? I've always said—for years and years I was a classroom teacher—how is it that you can erect an entire school system based on a religious tradition and at the other end of it you get students who learned how to obey but never learned how to be good?"

Why, then, the reader may ask, does Sister Joan continue to stay within the confines of an organization that rarely questions and that finds many of her views distasteful? The answer or answers are not simple. "I said once about twenty-five years ago that I began committed to the Church, then I became committed to Jesus. The way of the spirit is to negotiate always between the two," she told me. Her statement points to the long-admired and continually misunderstood Christian notion of obedience. "I seek not mine own will but the will of the Father which has sent me," said Jesus (John 5:30). Is it necessary to pledge our obedience first to an institution, or for that matter a teacher, and second to God? What is the meaning of obedience in this context? To whom, to what really do we owe such fidelity? "It is God that religion must be about, not itself,"[6] writes Sister Joan.

The Vatican's rebuke of Joan as a "source of scandal" was made in a letter to Sister Christine Vladimiroff, the present prioress of the BSE, where Sister Joan has lived, worked, and prayed for all of these years. The Church was trying to prevent Sister Joan from attending—and giving a presentation there as the keynote speaker—the Women's Ordination Worldwide Conference in Dublin, Ireland, in the summer of 2001. They were asking Sister Christine to use her "authority" to censor one of her own community members. It was a serious matter, and Sister Christine traveled to Rome to meet with Vatican officials, discussed the matter with various bishops, prioresses, and other religious leaders, and, most important, invited her community to confer on the matter. Sister Christine decided against any action. Her decision was supported by 127 of the 128 sisters in residence. Sister Christine wrote:

> After much deliberation and prayer, I concluded that I would decline the request of the Vatican. It is out of the Benedictine, or monastic, tradition of obedience that I formed my decision. There is a fundamental difference in the understanding of obedience in the monastic tradition and that which is being used by the Vatican to exert power and control and prompt a false sense of unity inspired by fear. Benedictine authority and obedience are achieved through dialogue between a community member and her prioress in a spirit of co-responsibility. The role of the prioress in a Benedictine community is to be a center of unity and a guide in the seeking of God. While lived in community, it is the individual member who does the seeking [i.e., while an individual lives in community, it is the individual who does the seeking; the leader cannot do the seeking for her].[7]

Sister Joan's allegiance to the teachings of Jesus is primary; her obedience to God through deep questioning defines her spirituality, and her immersion in a community of women religious is the underpinning of her spiritual practice—it's what authenticates religious life. "Cenobites [monastics] are the seekers of the spiritual life who live in a monastery—live with others—and are not a law unto themselves," Sister Joan tells us in her commentary on the Rule of Saint Benedict. "Holiness, he [Benedict] argues, is not something that happens in a vacuum. It has something to do with the way we live our community lives and our family lives and our public lives as well as the way we say our prayers."[8]

Though Sister Joan is an internationally recognized writer, speaker, activist, and spiritual leader, she has never misunderstood her place in the neighborhood. "I can tell you that it is the monastic rhythm that enables me to be public at all. It's the quiet, the centeredness, the immersion in the scriptures, the community form, the community flow, you can always just step right back into it and the waters wash back over you. That's the essence." Negotiating the two commitments between the Church and Jesus, then, is not, for Sister Joan, a theological abstraction. "Joan's not afraid of her own journey, wherever that takes her. And I think the strength of her conviction and the passion for which she lives is contagious. She teaches through her own living. She does a lot just by being herself and there's a real sense of humility in her," Sister Rosanne Loneck told me—she entered the BSE community in 1966.

Benedict of Nursia (near Spoleto, Italy) was born in the year 480. As a young man he traveled to Rome and found the corruption and decadence of a crumbling empire completely untenable— the connection to our times is duly noted. He retreated to the countryside, became a hermit, and lived in a cave for three years. Others of like mind gathered, and in time a monastic community formed. Early in the sixth century he wrote the Rule of Benedict, an impeccably simple document of spiritual guidance and universal insight for the monastic community and the world at large. The Rule's longevity—the Benedictine religious family is the oldest monastic order in the Roman Catholic Church—and profound substance spring from Benedict's refusal of extremes (lacking austerities, it tracks a decidedly middle course) and its refreshing common sense. It is simultaneously spiritual, philosophical, and psychological, attending to both our human weaknesses and our no less common godliness with compassion and insight.

The Benedictines have radical roots, and Sister Joan quite naturally has a similar affinity. "We trace our tradition to the early Desert Fathers and Mothers of the fourth century who lived on the margin of society in order to be a prayerful and questioning presence to both Church and society," Sister Christine continued in her letter to the Vatican. "Benedictine communities of men and women were never intended to be part of the hierarchical or clerical status of the Church, but to stand apart from this structure and offer a different voice. . . . Only in this way can we be faithful to the gift that women have within the Church."

"A Sufi is traveling to Mecca," Sister Joan tells me. "He has been on the highway for days and is very tired, so he lies down on the side of the road to sleep. A pilgrim comes by and is horrified at what he sees. He shakes the Sufi awake and tells him that it's sacrilege to be sleeping with his feet toward Mecca. 'It should be your head facing Mecca, not your toes,' he scolds. 'Pray tell,' the Sufi says, 'could you let me know what position it is that God won't be there?'"

The Benedictine monastic structure—its schedule, ritual, and rhythm—arises from the dictates of the Rule. For all of these years Sister Joan has been digesting the Rule, living it communally, and letting the fragrance and flavor of it permeate her being. Perhaps Sister Joan's greatest teaching gift is her permeability, how she absorbs things in full embrace, wrestling with their true weight and obscuring shadow, constantly questioning—her heart and mind like a rock polisher, tossing about the most jagged and tarnished stones until they reveal their beauty.

"It seems to me that simplicity is not a function, it's a quality of soul that grows as our own peripheral vision of life narrows down. As I need less and less, as I become more and more concentrated on the one, on the being, on the cosmic reality into which I am melting, I don't need to surround myself with all those other things," Sister Joan tells me. "In fact, they annoy me too much. They just clutter up my life. When one of the older sisters died, I remember being quite shocked to find how little she had left behind. Here's a woman with an illustrious career in the community, head of this and that, thousands of friends and colleagues, and you walk into her room after the undertaker has come, thinking that it will be absolutely rich with community history, and there is nothing there."

"I first met Joan through her writings in the late eighties. She wrote a wonderful book titled *Wisdom Distilled from the Daily* [her first of the two commentaries on the Rule of Benedict]. If I had to recommend one book, that would be it. She 'translates' the Rule and its spirituality for the twentieth century in line with Vatican II, among other things. Vatican II [more on this later], encouraged Catholics to get into the real world, find God there, bring God there, read the signs of the times. Sister Joan says we're not to take the Rule of Benedict literally; it was written in the sixth century Roman/European culture. Her commentary freshens it and applies it for today," said Sister Susan Doubet, who has been with the BSE for fourteen years after spending twenty-five years across town as a Sister of Saint Joseph. "Joan is someone who can look at the tradition and recognize the good elements and see where the 'old' language doesn't work anymore," Sister Carolyn Gorny-Kopkowski, who joined the BSE in 1962, concurs. "Joan takes the tradition and wraps it in new metaphors that speak to us now."

The Second Vatican Council (Vatican II) convened from 1962 through 1965. It was instigated by Pope John XXIII and called the

Church to deep renewal and modernization. Vatican II coincided with the emerging paradigm shift in society at large. Every institution, every "authority," was being revaluated in the context of an abundance of new information. "In society we called it the New Science, meaning evolution, quantum physics, molecular biology, and chaos theory. In the Church we called it Vatican II," wrote Sister Joan. "These two streams of being, science and religion, the two pillars of life—one ancient and, at least apparently, unchanging, the other kinetic and unpredictable—crossed paths in ways that changed both our concepts of life and our understanding of spiritual growth."[9]

The Benedictine community, that 1,500-year-old institution of stability, was suddenly asked to throw open its windows to the light of contemporary issues and demands. The shift was both freeing and tumultuous. Until Vatican II, the sisters were allowed only one visit home a month. All of their mail, coming and going, was censored by the novice director, and they could write just a single letter monthly. And then the lid was taken off. "When I first came to the monastery in 1966, it was right at the beginning of the renewal period of the Church. Little did I know that a large group of people had left before I came because of all the changes," Sister Rosanne remembers. "During my first year I was asking for toothpaste, and saying, 'I'm sorry I broke a dish.' At the end of the second year we—as a group, not the Church authority—were deciding what to wear. The clothes were the external change, but the internal change was a question—how do we become adults in this day and age instead of asking for everything?"

In other words, for the Benedictine sisters, Vatican II and its consequential shift in consciousness played out both structurally—habits and veils gave way to modern dress—and in ideology and values, in which the belief in unquestioned authority over all aspects of spiritual life was rapidly waning. The idea of personal responsibility and a self within the God-sphere was, particularly for women, something revolutionary.

"The ideal, of course, was passionless acceptance of a kind of perverse suppression of the self. 'Offering it up' and 'accepting the will of God' were the mantras of holiness. The reality was that the struggles were indicators of questions that needed desperately to be asked: Was suppression of the self really meant to be offered up? Was acceptance of an organizational will for the will of God an adequate substitute for free will and personal responsibility? Was a life without passion truly a holy life?"[10] wrote Sister Joan, commenting on that period. By implication, the role of the Benedictine leader—the abbot or prioress—was evolving from a predominantly parental function to one of facilitator and companion. On a structural level the shift was actually not as difficult as it would seem, Benedictine leaders have never been seen as figureheads. Abbots and prioresses are elected by the community to serve finite terms, returning to the group to work in another ministry after their leadership role is complete.

"I really don't think a prioress is a magnet that draws people. Like in the Buddhist community you might hear of a great teacher and that teacher might attract people to the monastery. That isn't a Benedictine concept. It's not that people wouldn't hear about the wonderful women in a given Benedictine monastery. It's just not that way of life," offered Sister Joan. But after Vatican II the definitions of leadership and discipleship lost their hard edges, new boundaries needed exploring, and a new language voiced.

Chapter two of the Rule of Benedict states: "To be worthy of the task of governing a monastery, the prioress or abbot must always remember what the title signifies and act accordingly. They are believed to hold the place of Christ in the monastery. Therefore, a prioress or abbot must never teach or decree or command anything that would deviate from God's instructions."[11] Holding the place of Christ is not, of course, to be taken lightly. But what does it mean exactly? If the old model no longer functions, how does the community reframe Benedict's meaning and rediscover value in a new context?

"The prioress and abbot provide an environment that confronts the monastic with the presence of God, that shows them the Way. After that it is up to the monastic to let the practices of the community and the rhythm of prayer life work their way until the piercing good of God rises in them like yeast in bread," writes Sister Joan. "The role of the spiritual leader, in other words, is not to make martinets out of people; it is to lead them to spiritual adulthood where they themselves make the kind of choices that give life depth and quality."[12]

Sister Joan came of age under the influences of Vatican II, Vietnam, the feminist movement, and the popular rise of psychology; each had a deep impact upon her growth as an individual and as a spiritual leader. In the time between entering the monastery and her election as prioress in 1978—she would serve a total of twelve years in that capacity—Sister Joan earned a bachelor's degree in English from Mercyhurst College (Erie, Pennsylvania), a master's degree in communication arts from the University of Notre Dame, and a doctorate in speech-communication theory from Penn State University; she taught as well. Sister Joan was a new type of prioress, worldly in an educational sense and politically energized, but—most important, perhaps—she came with a bag of leadership and communication tools and a personality that were a perfect fit for the chore at hand.

"Joan as a teacher is tremendously attractive in many ways," Sister Susan told me. "She has a gift for presentation and storytelling. She makes you feel, whether you're in a group of a hundred or alone, that she wouldn't want to be any other place in the world, or talking about any other subject. She's absolutely engaging, in part naturally and in part by training. These characteristics are certainly not the essence of what people come for, but they are a part of the package, the wrapping. But with Joan the wrapping is no different from the core. We've all had teachers who weren't initially attractive, and yet we eventually found they had a golden nugget. Joan's not that way: the gold is right out front from the first meeting."

Sister Joan's predecessor, Sister Mary Margaret Kraus, had spent the previous fourteen years as prioress instigating change, testing boundaries and modes of spiritual experience. Sister Joan carried the torch forward. "The period of religious life [for the BSE community] from 1965 to 1990 tested all the theories of leadership and change ever developed. It did not feel like 'renewal' then. It felt like disaster, like loss, like liberation, like life gone wild. And it felt like all of them at once. Most of all, it felt rudderless and out of control. Finding the way through a period for which there was no recent model, no rule book, no spiritual guide, colored the years with both a giddy joy and a fearsome shadow. How would we know that what we were doing was right? How would we know how far to go? Who would decide?"[13] wrote Sister Joan.

As prioress, Sister Joan was called to be a midwife to new ideas, group dynamics, and personal relationships. "I myself set out in the midst of the disintegration of past models of life and ministry to launch a process of revitalization. The task now was to enable the group to find its way into new directions without losing the core values of the past, to become a new kind of presence in the world without abandoning the meaning and bedrock of what had been the very essence of the life for centuries."[14] The task at hand was to start chipping away at the institutional mindset that had sunk into the marrow of the body religious. Sister Joan is gifted at facilitating inquiry, but she also has a signature talent for empowering others, particularly women, to find their own center and voice.

"Joan is a good listener and she respects what people say. And she's a marvelous enabler. That for me comes at the top of the list because I wouldn't have thought I could have done all that I did in those years working with her," said Sister Rosanne. Much of what Sister Joan did as prioress was to create an atmosphere in which women—long subjugated to the opinions and decisions of men, both inside and outside the Church—could begin to feel a sense of personal power without thinking that such liberation was ungodly. This shift in spiritual relationship—to oneself and to God— which was mirroring the growing feminist movement in secular society, called for a constant reexamination of Church language and its functional manifestations. The idea of "humility," for example, held up for centuries as a particularly feminine virtue, was often shrouding the chains, wrought under the auspices of control and dominance, binding women to an inferior position.

"For a man humility is a certain way and for a woman it will have to be lived out exactly the opposite," Sister Joan explained. "She has to develop the humility to speak out loud and be faced with the possibility that she may be wrong. But she has to learn to speak. She can't sit around whining about what her husband or someone else doesn't do for her. Humility demands she make her needs known and they might or might not be met. If there's anything I can't stand it's a whining woman; just say who you are. You have no idea what it takes for women, after centuries of being told they cannot do things, to be able to say, 'I can do it.'"

When Sister Joan was three years old, her father died. During the first Christmas after his death Joan was asked continually, as a distraction, what she wanted from Santa. "A doctor's kit," was all she said. Christmas arrived and she opened first the kit-shaped package, where she found not a doctor's kit but a nurse's. "There must be some mistake," she told her uncle Lou, who had bought the present. "Jo," her uncle said, "little boys get doctor's kits, little girls get nurse's kits." "I remember pushing myself up from the floor and solemnly, slowly taking it over to him. 'Then I don't want it,' I said as I put it on his lap. 'Take it back.' Some people would have called it pride. I know now that it was humility—the kind they never taught a woman in school."[15]

"Chapter seven of the Rule is on humility and is, in my opinion, the keystone chapter. Unfortunately it has disintegrated into the worst kind of misnomer; humility and humiliation are not synonyms, but as a matter of fact in the name of humility, humiliation was commonly practiced. 'It is good for your humility, don't get that look on your face, and take this correction.' For me the beating down of the ego is nothing that I really admire. Jesus, who gave himself up, is the model of my humility. This is not a merit theology. It isn't about saying so many rosaries and going to mass so many times in order to get God. You have God, that's the foundation of humility," Sister Joan explained.

"Benedict talks about revealing yourself to the teacher," she continued. "The rule says that 'they dash their thoughts against the rock that is Christ' and not to hide anything from the abbot. It's the whole notion of exposing yourself. And once you expose yourself, nothing can happen, no one can do anything to you, they have nothing to hold over you. You have said to another, 'This is what I have inside and it's full of worms and it's really not much at all.' And the other person says, 'Yes, and what else?' You come to understand yourself and you learn from the one that has been there before and can companion with you. Eventually you understand that you're the same as everyone else—that's what we must learn."

After Vatican II, sisters from every denomination, historically delegated to teach in grade schools and high schools, were emerging to open soup kitchens, halfway houses, and peace centers; they were lobbying for environmental causes, and winding up in jail for protesting the Vietnam War (not to mention being martyred[16]). "We had, in both Mary Margaret and Joan, prioresses who were brought forth from the spirit in a time in which they were really needed," said Sister Carolyn, and there exists a Jungian presence in Sister Joan's voice—a heart receptor and throaty transmission of our collective unconscious. She articulates with precision and poetics what many people in contemporary spirituality, particularly Catholics, are feeling but are unable to express.

One of the first things Sister Joan did as prioress was set up a non-mandatory conference every Sunday on subjects as wide-ranging as political theory, feminism, examination of the Rule, and human development. "We were trying to see what would work and what wouldn't work, trying to get the groups to allow things in long enough to be able to evaluate it spiritually, psychologically, and physically. We would wait six months and then ask ourselves what was happening. We would try something for one year and then at the end of the year we'd ask ourselves what is good for us and what is not. It was like walking through a minefield with snowshoes, but I think it really worked. When I look at the community now, I really think they have a good idea of what is bedrock and what is a movable feast," Joan told me. "The conferences weren't mandatory, but everybody came," Sister Carolyn remembers. "When Joan gave a talk she would have us holding our sides with laughter, but it was laughter at ourselves, serious things in ourselves, either about community or personal development issues."

The key to Sister Joan's teaching style is her presentation of information and ideas by way of communal dialogue. "The Benedictine community had perfected the form of rank but completely missed the value. We had to recover that value by working it out together," she said. "The community teaches you the whole notion of communal wisdom. I don't ever get up in the morning thinking I have the answer, but I'll know the questions for the day. I'm good at those questions and I am surrounded by geniuses who have a piece of the answer and if I ask enough of them and we hear, as a group, one another's answers, and we really explore one another's answers, we will almost always come out with what, fifteen centuries later, is called consensus."

The written word has been a constant backdrop to Sister Joan's teaching life. To date she has written over thirty books, and unlike many spiritual teachers her pages are not flushed from a series of weekly talks nor symposium lectures. She is a genuine writer, a very talented one. She is as prolific as Thomas Merton, and like him she uses her writings to reach beyond the monastery walls, at once fulfilling an urge for social action and an impulse for contemplation. Through the form of memoir and journal, she brings her struggles to the page, where she sifts for clarity and a pattern of how she moves through the world. Writing is a cornerstone of Sister Joan's ministry. She teaches through language, by exposing, as story, the layers of her own doubts, optimism, and unending inquiries. "Joan's influence, through her writing and her person, is so prevalent, it's between the lines of everything in this community as well as the wider Benedictine world and even in the larger world of religious women throughout the last thirty-five years," said Sister Susan.

Sister Joan's celebrity, though expansive outside the monastic cloister, necessarily loses much of its famous hue within her own Benedictine community. Her books, instead of distancing her as a mythic figure—which so often happens in our culture of fame—create a shared intimacy, for her writing always rises from and interlocks with her community. Not only do the sisters recognize the universal struggles of which she writes, but they plainly see the particulars of their world: the same daily prayers, the colors of the classrooms in which they teach, the parties they've thrown, the prioresses who have come and gone, the doughnuts and coffee they often share each morning. In this way Sister Joan has given the members of her community—and this is a good portion of her gift as a teacher—a fresh view of themselves; she has given them an intimate language, a tool that has opened more doors than it has closed. Still, even though her vulnerability and struggle are explicated on the page, they sometimes absorb, through the fixative of ink, a certain unreality.

"People occasionally put Joan on a pedestal. At one point I fell into that trap. And then one time Joan was having physical problems—she contracted polio shortly after arriving at the monastery, and her symptoms returned—and I realized her vulnerability, it was very tangible," Sister Carolyn exclaimed. "When we put someone on a pedestal we dehumanize them. It's the worst thing you can do to someone. That's what I think happened to priests and nuns: you wear the garb, you say these prayers, you never went to the bathroom, you never slept at night, and you never changed your clothes. I recognized that Joan doesn't always have to reach out to me. I needed to reach out to her. She allowed us to see her faults and weaknesses and I loved her even more because of it. In that way I could give her her humanity back."

Thomas Merton wrote, a month before he died in 1968:

> I think we have now reached a stage of (long overdue) religious maturity at which it might be possible for someone to remain perfectly faithful to a Christian and Western monastic commitment and yet *to learn* in depth from, say, a Buddhist or Hindu discipline and experience. I believe some of us need to do this in order to improve the quality of our own monastic life and even to help the task of monastic renewal which has been undertaken within the Western Church.[17]

Merton was underscoring a fundamental shift in the way Western spirituality perceived itself after Vatican II, at least among the more liberal-minded. The door to the East had opened, and the notion of ecumenical dialogue became a valid currency. Sister Joan built upon this new course and poured this new world of thought into the monastic mix. "I tried to introduce the community to spiritual insight around the globe by using folklore, the Sufi tales, the Jataka tales, the Hasidic tales, the materials of the spirit in each of the great traditions," Sister Joan said. "The whole notion of seeing what you hear all your life with fresh eyes and learning that all of the human traditions are calling us to the same thing gives rise to awareness and compassion. It provokes us to risk ourselves to demand justice and to acknowledge some of the nonsense of institutional religion."

As a teacher, Sister Joan is not in the security business. "I used to say to the sisters, 'Whatever brought you here will not keep you here. Whatever bait God put in the trap to get you here will not nourish you very long. You come and then the bottom drops out of everything. If you stay long enough you find that what you didn't have the sense to come for is here. It's what you are really seeking to begin with,'" Sister Joan told me.

During Sister Rosanne's early years at the monastery, she struggled with indecision about whether she was in the right place. Her vacillation might have gone on for years more, but for Sister Joan's provocative style. "When I told Joan that I thought I needed a more contemplative atmosphere, she just blew me away. I remember her saying to me, 'And where would you like to go? I'll make the phone call tomorrow.' Now I'm on the edge of the table and I'm thinking, 'Oh my god, this is it. This is the moment of your discernment and choice,' and I'm praying like crazy and trying not to cry, and she yanks this file drawer open and she says, 'Where would you like to go?' and she starts tossing to me from the other side of the desk pamphlets from probably every community in the world. I got out of the office and I went upstairs and I sat there and I just cried. She just pushed me over. But I needed the shove. It was good because it forced me to act and I found a Benedictine community in Missouri and I went for the summer and realized that I was in the right place to begin with, and I've been here ever since."

Sister Carolyn: "One day I was in my office and Joan came by and asked how I was doing. I said, 'Joan, if I didn't have all these interruptions I could get my work done.' And she said, 'Carolyn, those interruptions *are* your work.' I've drawn on that all my life. And it wasn't just Joan's words, she taught me through example. She had thousands more interruptions than I did, but when I interrupted her, or other people interrupted her, she was really *there*, no matter how many other things were floating around. She called you by name. She was present. It changed my whole spirituality, the way she taught me to live in the present. I had lived in the past and was afraid of the future. Now there are two ways I view God—one is this great underground river that just brings everything together. The other is the God of surprises."

Most of the BSE residents live in Mount Saint Benedict Monastery (celebrating its 150th anniversary in 2006); the remaining ones are housed in other "off-campus" living quarters. The sisters work in a range of local, national, and international ministries—soup kitchens, day care, environmental work, developing spiritual retreats and ecumenical dialogue, and a peace center, to name a few. One program, called Take Back the Site, consists of vigils held at murder sites within the city of Erie, where a number of the sisters and other locals gather to pray for the victims, their family and friends, and residents of the neighborhood, as well as the accused. In 1980, during Sister Joan's tenure (1978–1990) as prioress, the sisters of Erie created a corporate commitment to peace and justice, and they joined with other groups to form Benedictines for Peace (BFP).

Sister Joan has continued that commitment through her work within the Erie community and through the International Peace Center and her activism for justice and the promotion of ecumenical dialogue. Besides her public speaking and teaching schedule and her books, she writes columns for both the *National Catholic Reporter* and the spirituality website Beliefnet. She is also the founder and executive director of Benetvision, a research and resource organization for contemporary spirituality. For Sister Joan and the rest of the Benedictine community, this whirlwind of activity and activism is always grounded in a life of prayer—rooted in the psalms and other scriptures—and the stability of the Rule of Benedict, a source of both perpetual strength and guidance.

"Many people are drawn here because of our communal prayer, including our chanting," Sister Susan told me. "Prayer is the constant, is the daily. Ministry draws people here, too, but the ministry comes out of the community life and from the daily liturgy of the Hours, which has a creative aspect as well as the repetition of the psalmody. We have a different prayer leader every day, and they take seriously their role as leaders and bring their own creativity and spirituality to it. It makes our daily prayer very rich and fulfilling."

"Benedictine prayer has several characteristics that make more for a spirituality of awareness than of consolation," writes Sister Joan. "It is regular. It is universal. It is converting. It is reflective. And it is communal. Out of those qualities a whole new life emerges and people are changed. Not in the way tornadoes change things, perhaps, but in the way that sand in oysters does."[18]

When Sister Joan was a young novitiate, her prioress was Alice Schierberl. Twice a year Mother Alice would meet with the novitiates for consultation. During one of these sessions she asked the fifteen or so sisters sitting around the table, "Why do you go to prayer?" One sister said, "To find God." "No," Alice stated, and asked another, "Why do you go, Sister?" "To meditate on the scriptures." "No." "I go to prayer because it's Benedictine and we should be praising God out loud," said another. "No," she said. "You go because everyone else is going to prayer."

"When you first hear that bell and all those people are coming, you don't just sit there," Sister Joan said, referring to the story. "You have no desire to go to prayer, you're tired and busy, you have four phone calls to make, and you haven't written your mother in more than a month, but you go and while everyone is going down the hall they pick you up and put you in the line. The form carries you when you don't have enough spirit to carry you. One day you are finally awake when you pray. You did all those prayers and preparation so that when enlightenment did come, you'd be awake."

"The community teaches you difference," Sister Joan replied when I asked what she had learned during her stretch as prioress. "The Rule of Benedict is absolutely committed to difference. Through twelve straight chapters the Rule minutely lays out the form of communal prayer—on Monday mornings say these three psalms, in the afternoon say these four psalms, at Vespers say these seven psalms—but at the very end it says if any brother knows a better way to do it, please feel free to do it. And the clothing of the monastery, the Rule says, let it be what the abbot says according to the time and place and the custom of the day. So the first thing you learn is difference." It's surprising, frankly, to learn that a monastic document written 1,500 years ago can incorporate such flexibility. We are led to believe, in and outside of the Church, that such elasticity somehow lacks moral fiber. When did that notion get lodged in our heads?

"The second thing you learn is 'like,' as opposed to difference, that you have this inscrutable, stable institution which is in a constant state of flux, the change will absolutely drive you mad. You learn that the community's life changes your life and that none of these lives can be stabilized and that God promotes change while you are vowing stability. Make your molds if it lets you feel better, but just about nobody is going to go there. I learned that wisdom is atomized—nobody has all the answers."

Spirituality doesn't come cheap, Sister Joan told me. It's hard work, particularly in a monastic setting where community is always pushing buttons and routinely challenging practitioners to reinvent themselves daily, to see the sacred in the mundane. Many of the sisters have been living this Benedictine life for more than fifty years, working to connect with God, letting go one day and holding on the next. I sit with Sister Carolyn, Sister Rosanne, and Sister Susan in one of the conference rooms at the monastery. It's July, and the air conditioner hums as I ask them questions about their lives. I mention the word *sacrifice* and they all shake their heads. "Sacrifice is a pre–Vatican II word," Sister Carolyn tells me. "We'd use the word *faithfulness.* It means continually recommitting yourself to the journey," she says. "Another word that works for me is *conversion,*" Sister Rosanne adds, "that as we go down the day and encounter the traumas and difficulties, we don't give up on each other. We pray to keep that openness; even when things are difficult we get up the next day and start all over again knowing that everyone else is doing the same. We're in here for the long haul and we help each other with the conversion and the faithfulness." Spirituality, thank goodness, is not glamorous, but it nourishes.

"I really think that religion at its best is when it moves up beyond religion. We do make a God out of religion, but the function of religion is to move us beyond itself," Sister Joan tells me. "We stop there too often," she continued. "Once again we need to look at the deep questions and what we bring to those questions. I would bring this ancient Benedictine tradition, over 1,500 years old. It must work on something at some time, and I would bring with it any modern tool with which I thought I had some expertise. I would bring social psychology and I would bring scripture and all we know about scripture study.

"But most of all I would offer a kind of holy restlessness with holy indifference at the same time, the ability to want to bring the reign of God in this world now. If we're still in a state of ongoing creation, what are we helping to create? What would God want us to create? If we are indeed co-creators of the universe, then we are in harmony with the mind of God. What does God will for this universe? Scripture says, 'I wish you well and not woe.' So it is up to us to do that. My part is to help bring well and not woe on an individual basis, on a community level, on a national level, and on a global level. It doesn't mean not bring pain. It means not bring woe. There's a big difference. So for me it might look as if teaching is a body of knowledge or tradition, but it's actually knowledge of tradition in the service of co-creation, and certainly in the service of holy restlessness."

Turning Stories

Spirit speaks to us continually, in dreams, through the melodic sounds of a stream, through deaths and illnesses, and all the dressing and undressing of the seasons. Still, we are often oblivious of its hum, wrapped as we are in a shroud of self-preoccupations—worries, fears, angers, jealousies, and other catastrophes. Yet, like a youthful injury that haunts our old age or a fierce storm that changes the landscape in an instant, spirit illuminates the world in surprising ways. We all have those turning points in our lives—either fully recognized in the moment or traced through hindsight—that spin us in a new direction.

Lisa Talesnick (Murat Yagan's student) was working for the *Boston Globe* as a Jerusalem correspondent covering suicide bombings, and the only way she could deal with what she saw was to fill herself with hate for the terrorists. But then one day when she got to the site of one more bombing, the "normal" pattern of her life stopped functioning. "I stood by the scene and the bomber was lying there dead and my body wouldn't fill with hate. It filled with something else. I didn't know the word at the time, but I felt holy. And I was confused. It didn't make sense to me that I could feel holy looking at this person who had just blown himself up to kill other people," she said. "That question stayed with me."

Rabbi David Zaslow (Reb Zalman's student) was sitting on his deck in Ashland, Oregon, minding his own business when suddenly he had a mystical revelation—a "visitation," as he called it, by an ancient *rebbe*. "It was a ten-minute experience and it was like a kid at a carnival asking the oracle questions without words. It was a very relaxed time in my body and I knew it was real," he told me. After the experience he began studying to become a rabbi.

Laura Mackenzie (Adyashanti's student) was traveling in India when she was overwhelmed by the suffering she witnessed. The impact of the pain and the feelings of guilt and shame for being well off nearly drove her to a nervous breakdown. When she staggered from a train station in Calcutta she saw a sign that said MEDITATION AT TWO O'CLOCK, with a little arrow. "It was in an ashram and they gave me a Ramana Maharshi book and a book of Teresa of Avila and that was the first time I had heard about the mystical path and that was the beginning," she said.

Lynn Hoberg was invited to the Los Angeles premier of the film *Travelers and Musicians,* which was directed by Khyentse Norbu Rimpoche, the Tibetan lama from Bhutan, and the director happened to be there. As soon as Rimpoche walked into the room to give a talk before the screening, Lynn knew that he was her teacher. It was as though someone snapped their fingers and a teacher and a spiritual life appeared. It felt that sudden. "I was simultaneously terrified and relieved," she said.

One day, Joan North (Sudha Puri's student, now known as Janapriya) called her sister and asked if she knew of any ashrams in the area. "My sister said, 'What is an ashram?'— we are very different—but her thirteen-year-old son was passing by and overheard and said there was one right up the hill. So if he hadn't been there and if she hadn't said 'ashram' right at that moment, I would have never known about the Vedanta Centre. I would have never met Mataji [Sudha Puri's teacher] and fallen in love."

By the time Netanel Miles-Yépez (Reb Zalman's student) was six years old, he knew he wanted a deeper connection to spiritual life. And his first exposure to that life came through his father, a convert to Pentecostal Christianity. When Netanel was in his late teens he decided he wanted to enter a Christian seminary. But in order to do so he needed a recommendation from the pastor of his church, who, as part of the process, asked him a series of questions. "Who is your favorite person in the Bible?" his pastor asked. And Netanel answered without missing a beat, "King David." "He got a quizzical look on his face, as if this was an unexpected answer," Netanel told me. "At that time I didn't realize that there was a correct answer to this question—if you were a Christian, it's Jesus. So he said, 'Well, that's good. How come King David?' I said, 'Because he had a heart after God. No matter how many times he fell away he always came back; I identify with that falling away and coming back.' And then he asked, 'Well, who else?' And I immediately said, 'King Hezekiah.' The pastor looked at me as if I were joking and gave up this line of questioning. We then talked a little about theology and he gave me the recommendation, but that dialogue should have told me something." Shortly after this experience, Netanel learned from his maternal grandmother that they were crypto-Jews (his ancestors were forced to give up their outward Jewishness during the Spanish Inquisition, and so their Jewish identity was pushed far underground, only to surface years later). Needless to say, the revelation changed the course of Netanel's life.

5

TYING SHOES

Rabbi Zalman Schachter-Shalomi

*"What do you learn from your master?" To this question
R. Leib Sures replied: "I come to see how he ties his shoelaces."*[1]
—MARTIN BUBER

"I saw him once at the supermarket. The cashier seemed to
have a pain in his head, and after Reb Zalman got his
groceries checked out, he went and healed this person by
putting his hands on his head—the cashier, for heaven's
sake. How many people even look the cashier in the eye?
He's a model for how a person should behave in the world.
It is not just talk and he has this fabulous sense of humor,
doesn't take himself so seriously, and that's the best kind of
person to have as an example. It's real."

—RUTH SEAGULL

"In my first few times alone with Reb Zalman he was making lunch for his kids, or folding laundry while he spoke to me; I didn't expect that. I love his connection to the same world as everyone else."

—SETH FISHMAN

"There is a quality to how Reb Zalman inhabits his body. He is so robustly in his body that there's a deliciousness about being in his physical presence."

—RABBI TIRZAH FIRESTONE

In the old days the everyday life of a Rebbe (the spiritual leader of a Hasidic sect or community) was often unavailable for viewing by his students or the community. To see him tie his shoelaces or, God forbid, make a mistake, was a privilege reserved for a select few. Rabbi Zalman Schachter-Shalomi, the spiritual grandfather (some would say founder) of the Jewish Renewal Movement, is everything *but* inaccessible. Over the years (Reb is eighty-two years old), his students have had complete access to his life—the joys and sorrows, the triumphs and missteps. And in so doing they received an open channel to the ripeness of his wisdom, how he ignites the alchemical tension between the ascending spirit and the clay-bound body, striking a perennial bloom of creative force and sustenance for those around him.

"What's more important than ascendancy, simply going up, is how to make the soul go up and at the same time keep the body grounded,"[2] he told Rabbi Tirzah upon their first meeting. (Rabbi Tirzah Firestone, a student who was ordained by Reb Zalman, is the leader of the Jewish Renewal Community of Boulder, Colorado, and the author of numerous books.)

Reb Zalman (*Reb* is a term of respect and admiration) is an arbiter of change. "I came in with a calibration that puts me about twenty-five years ahead of the pack. I can't say I'm proud of that. It's just how it is," he told me. But he nonetheless stands on the solid foundation of his Hasidic tradition, and in that sense he has been a conduit for the mystical, meditative, and kabbalistic lineage of Hasidism and pre-Hasidic Judaism.

His Midas touch—not unlike Joan Chittister's expertise—has been the ability to reformat an older model to modern times without losing its essential juice—to renew Judaism rather than restore an outdated paradigm. Much of the change that Reb Zalman has wrought couldn't have happened without his knowledge of, and grounding in, Hasidic tradition and his continuation of a well-respected lineage, which has made it easier for his students to accept some of the radical changes he has introduced. Seth Fishman, a student of his for over fifteen years, couldn't have accepted his teacher without that traditional grounding. "I asked him in the 1989 Kallah [a biennial international gathering of Jewish Renewal artists, leaders, performers, and teachers] if the things he was suggesting we do were things he was making up or things he'd learned from his teachers. I wanted to believe that the Judaism he was creating was 'kosher.' When he told me it was what he had learned from his teachers, that was it for me," he said.

Much of Reb Zalman's updating places Judaism in a web of ecumenical connections and creates a completely transparent Rebbe model. He teaches in playgrounds, in kitchens, in the classroom, in synagogues, through his books and articles (numbering more than 150), in the small *shul* (house of worship) he has made in the basement of his home, in retirement communities, and through the brilliance of his scholarship and deeply ecumenical understanding of spiritual disciplines. The breadth and depth of Reb Zalman's knowledge is staggering—from Sufism (he is, as a matter of fact, also a Sufi sheik) to Catholicism, from Freud to transpersonal psychology, from rock and roll to psychedelics, from a variety of modalities of bodywork to prayer, from child rearing (he has ten children, ranging in age from twenty to fifty-eight) to elder care. Yet through all of this he has managed to stay heart-centered and humble.

On the one hand he is simply (and magnificently) carrying on in the footsteps of his Hasidic forebears and echoing the words of the Ba'al Shem Tov ("Master of the Good Name"), the founder of Hasidism, who said, "God made the material world from the spiritual, and the Jews turn the material into the spiritual." The Ba'al Shem Tov was, of course, himself reiterating a strong tenet of Judaism: "The Jews refused to abandon the physical aspects of existence as illusory, defective, or unimportant," wrote Huston Smith in his book *The World's Religions.*[3] On the other hand, Reb Zalman has never been content with the status quo. As with many mystics, he is not housebroken; he is not willing to stay within forms that have been drained of their lifeblood through abstraction and blind faith. If another religious tradition has a better spiritual technology, he's not afraid to borrow it and integrate it into Jewish Renewal. When I asked him about his broad interest in other traditions he told me, bringing his humor to the fore, "I do this because I'm a spiritual Peeping Tom. I like so see how people get it on with God."

Reb Zalman's explorations have brought renewal and innovation to every aspect of Jewish practice. The cornerstone of Jewish ritual living is the Sabbath, and when someone asks Reb Zalman how to reconnect with the faith, he inevitably points them in that direction. Building atop the foundation laid by the renowned scholar, activist, and mystic Abraham Joshua Heschel in his classic book *The Sabbath,* which reinvigorated the ritual for thousands of post-Holocaust Jews, Reb Zalman has further reframed the Sabbath for a new generation. "Sabbaths are like periods inserted into an otherwise endless run-on sentence. They help us know when it is time to stop and take a breath. They remind us to take a weekly break from living in commodity time to reanchor ourselves in what we might call 'organic time,' a way of living more in tune with our own deepest needs—as well as those of our family and the entire community and society of which we are a part."[4] This is Reb Zalman's classic mode of teaching—using traditional and ancient threads to weave a new pattern in the present.

"When you do certain prayers or read parts of the Torah, you know that everywhere in the world Jews are doing the same thing at the same time and have done so for thousands of years. That's pretty powerful in itself. But Jewish Renewal is really personal. It's very joyful and participatory, there's more dancing, there's more singing, there's interaction during the service, there's meditation," Ruth Seagull explained. She's been studying with Reb Zalman and Reb Tirzah for many years.

Reb Zalman has also expanded the idea of kosher to include environmental concerns, what he calls "eco-kosher" (organically grown foods, "green" packaging, and consideration of farm labor practices). He has reinvigorated *mitzvot* (any act Jews believe is required of them by God). He has given new meaning to the process of aging (in his book *From Age-ing to Sage-ing*), and has been a force in creating a new covenant with the Torah (specifically the five books of Moses, but generally any Jewish teaching). Yet most pertinent to the subject at hand, he has persistently breathed fresh life (and lots of heart) into the teacher-student (or Rebbe-Hasid) relationship.

When you first meet Reb Zalman he appears larger than the dimensions of his body. Even his beard and tousled hair seem to throw off sparks of energy, yet he has a calming countenance, a grounded weight—the deliciousness that Rabbi Tirzah spoke of. His face, with its piercing eyes and warm smile, reminds me of the photo of Walt Whitman from the cover of *Leaves of Grass*; it's earthy, sensuous, touched with humor, and full of light. Reb Zalman has taken me to the *shul* in the basement of his home, a small, closetlike temple with two facing chairs. Photos of his teachers hang on the wall, stacks of books and papers rise from the floor, and there are various artifacts scattered throughout the comfortable room. His model for the Rebbe-Hasid relationship is taken directly from the traditional system, yet he has given the old bones of the ancient body new flesh.

"There is an element in much of spiritual direction of the older type, pre-paradigm shift that demanded that you give over to your teacher or your master the power of attorney over your soul," Reb Zalman tells me as we sip tea. "So, that meant that a certain dependency was demanded. It fit an earlier situation because when we lived in a ghetto setting, then you didn't have any choice, really, about whether you were Jewish or not, because you were born into it. In the new paradigm it doesn't make sense to work with people creating dependency. You want to work with people's own initiative. So the hierarchical situation in which the Rebbe represented an archetypal model that you could never possibly aspire to had to be turned into an accessible model."

Reb Zalman's open personality has demystified his teacher role and given him, in the eyes of his students and everyone who knows him, a deeper authenticity. "I remember one of the rabbis asked his advice on how to deal with his children, and Reb Zalman said, 'I was a lousy father. Why are you asking me? You should ask someone who did a better job,' " Rabbi Tirzah told me. In traditional Hasidism the Rebbe was known as a *tzaddik* (saint), one who has gotten rid of all evil inclinations. Luckily for many generations of Hasidim, Rebbe Shneur Zalman of Liadi (the first Lubavitcher Rebbe—Lubavitch is Reb Zalman's Hasidic school) came along and basically said the *tzaddikim* are too far out of reach and that there are, in fact, other types that can be Rebbes. He wrote about the *beynonim* (the intermediate ones), who were the same as *tzaddikim* on the outside yet had a different personality.

"Whereas a *Tzaddik* is by nature totally good, a *Beynoni*, with great struggle and control, manages to control all thoughts, words, and deeds in such a way that she or he doesn't slip for one moment to become an instrument of the energy system of evil,"[5] wrote Reb Zalman. But the updated model created another problem. "In other words, if these saints see themselves as average, what does that make of us who are truly average? According to Rebbe Shneur Zalman, the remaining folks (you and me) are 'people who are not altogether wicked.' "[6] It is in this "not-altogether-wicked" soup where Reb Zalman loves to swim, and it is the sphere in which Jewish Renewal creates itself.

"So we have people who are 'not altogether wicked,' who have been called to do this Rebbe-work, who don't have all the tools that are necessary, but who, *b'chemlat HaShem*, 'through the merciful grace of Providence,' are picking up 'breathing' and 'postures' and 'spiritual direction' from all kinds of places!"[7] It is the community, however, that plays a primary role in a Rebbe's calling. "The Rebbe results from the Divine flowing into the world, working through community that, in a sense, makes for itself a Rebbe. Without the community there is no Rebbe. We must use Rebbe in this sense.

"It is not that we elevate ourselves to sainthood or raise ourselves above others. Rather, we are asked by the community to be their Rebbe because they see in us something they need."[8] But without some type of downward flow the "Rebbe-work" cannot continue. Reb Zalman gives an example of a Hasid who asks a Rebbe, whom he has known since childhood (warts and all), what he must believe in order to make the Rebbe his teacher, and the Rebbe says, "All you have to believe is that I'm like the height of a tree stump, that I'm that much higher than you."[9]

To further understand the relationship, one must realize that

Reb Zalman is not simply advocating a return to hierarchy, but neither—and this is a vital point—is he calling the teacher-student relationship democratic. "If everybody is equal, there is no flow; there is stagnation," he writes. "Now, if you understand how this goes, there has to be a certain amount of raising up so that the wisdom can flow down. Inside of me, I feel what the Gemara [Talmud—rabbinical commentaries on the Torah or Jewish teachings] says: 'More than the calf wants to suck, the cow wants to give milk.' Especially at this time in my life, I feel it's so important to upload files of my life's experience on other people, so the pressure here is great. On your side, the longing for the knowledge is great. Do you understand how we are in this wonderful relationship with each other? And it is not like that flat land of democracy."[10] Reb Zalman's name for this type of relationship is "organismic," and he believes it is the foundation for the new type of Rebbe-work that the Jewish Renewal Movement is offering. The connections between people are organic, interdependent, and flowing. As Reb Zalman says, "I'm here only because you help me with your energy. This is a very important point."

Rabbi David Zaslow (ordained by Reb Zalman, he is the leader of the Jewish Renewal Community of Ashland, Oregon, and also a poet, writer, and composer) put it this way: "The Rebbe-Hasid relationship, and I have one with Reb Zalman, is that I trust his sense of divine inspiration, but the Renewal part of it is that I don't just surrender to him, it's like my own judgment gets the final say. In the old days you had the teacher in the hierarchical system. The Rebbe at the top was hard to reach and therefore mysterious, which created an exalted figure, which, in a way, disguised reality because everyone is flawed. The question is, if you show your flaws, can you be the Rebbe? Traditionally the answer has been no. So we disguise our flaws because we want people to reach the highest level. They don't have to know what I'm going through, that I'm struggling with my own demons, and my kids are having trouble with me, and my wife and I aren't getting along. So if I'm disguising it, I'm doing it with good intentions so the student can reach up to an ideal model, and when a student reaches up to the Rebbe model or the guru model or the reverend model, they have something to reach up to and they don't have to know my problems. Reb Zalman's model is to say no, no, no. It's not so much that I'm up here, I may be on some level—he knows how smart he is, how wise he is, but he also knows how flawed he is. So in sharing with us his flaws, by seeing his humanity, there is less of a chance of it becoming a cult, but also there is less of a chance of you losing your own empowerment."

This new model, which has arisen in other religious and cultural disciplines as well, puts much more responsibility on the student, where it belongs. The idea of surrender doesn't disappear, but it is turned back on the student as a question—to whom and to what are you surrendering? Netanel Miles-Yépez, a student, author, and teacher who was ordained by Reb Zalman in a new Sufi-Renewal lineage (I will explain this in more detail later), told me a story that nicely personalizes this point. Before Netanel became Reb Zalman's student, he moved to Boulder to "check him out" and enrolled in a class Reb Zalman was teaching at Naropa (he taught and held the World Wisdom Chair at Naropa Institute from 1995 to 2000). One day he saw Reb Zalman get angry at a nineteen-year-old student because he had forgotten to return the *siddurim* (Jewish prayer books) he had borrowed.

"Reb Zalman said, 'You promised,' to the young man. He didn't raise his voice when he said it, yet I felt—you know when a heavy bass is playing—I felt it hit my chest like that, and it hollowed out my whole body and I felt spiritual energy the way I'd never felt it," Netanel told me. "Even though it wasn't loud, he had been angry and everybody knew it. The young man turned tail, got on his bike, and road across town. Ten minutes later he returned the *siddurim* and Reb Zalman offered him a hug, but the young man hesitated for a moment and then they embraced." Netanel was wrecked by the experience. As crazy as it sounds, he was troubled that Reb Zalman wasn't perfect. "I didn't know what to do with it. I was upset for a few days," he said.

"Next class arrives and Reb Zalman comes in and says, 'Before I start, I owe [the young man] an apology. I don't just owe it to him. I owe it to him in front of all of you.' He said, 'I lost my temper, I'm sorry. He didn't deserve that, you didn't deserve that. He didn't deserve to be embarrassed in front of all of you,' " Netanel recalled. "Reb Zalman is a renowned public person, he doesn't have to apologize anymore; he could get away with a hug and not apologize. He didn't do that, he felt bad about it. I happen to know that he still feels bad about it. I thought, 'That's what I want: a teacher who teaches me through his mistakes and the acknowledgment of his mistakes.' I want somebody who teaches me not how to be superior to a human being but actually teaches me how to be a human being in the fullest sense. In Judaism we call that person a *mensch*. A *mensch* is somebody exceptional, but is a human being— that means that most of the time the rest of us are hardly being even that. I don't want to be enlightened, I want to be whole and that's when I knew this was the teacher for me," Netanel said.

Reb Zalman is a public figure, but he also teaches in private settings as well as through more ritualized practices. "There are at least three settings in which I teach," he told me. The public setting is good because it allows his students to see him working without a plan, to see how he spontaneously reacts to the situation at hand, like Netanel's example above. Often when Reb Zalman is teaching, someone will say, "Yeah, but what about the Holocaust?" It's something that naturally comes up. When it first happened he turned to the person and said, "What do you expect from me? I should give you answers? You think I didn't suffer from that? Show me who has come up with any decent answers to that. In the end there is only one answer left. If we are not going to be good and kind to people, kindness will not spread. And evil will overtake us." It wasn't something he planned on saying, but people later told him that it was important to see how he handled the situation. "In other words, it wasn't me against the other person; I was saying 'whatever's troubling you is troubling me, too,'" Reb Zalman told me.

The second setting is private and is very much like *yechidut* (the Hasid's private encounter with his Rebbe). "Someone comes and says, 'I have a spiritual issue that I have to deal with and I would like you to help me,'" Reb Zalman says. "Or, it would be a situation where we had agreed we would be dealing with such and such a thing, whether it's Jewish law or some other problem." The third setting is what Reb Zalman calls "the high setting." "For instance, the *Shabbat* [Hebrew for Sabbath]—this afternoon I'll be sitting with people, chanting with them beforehand. It will be after the afternoon service. We'll be sitting at a little meal, just some bread, maybe some herring, and something to drink. We will celebrate that sacramental meal. Then some teaching comes. That teaching is most likely not going to be anything that I'll warm up. For that you don't need to create that kind of scene. I want, most probably, to sit with them, wait for inspiration, and hope for input from their spirit in the moment. The likelihood is I will be doing something to do with Passover. That's because that's the season coming. And whatever inspiration there is will be likely to center around that," he explained.

Netanel Miles-Yépez says, "There are some teachers who will give you every step along the way, get you into the right forms and tell you what they are. Buddhism is extremely organized that way, 'the graded path to enlightenment.' But that's not the experience one gets with Reb Zalman. I don't expect him to be a didactic teacher, that's just not in his character. He doesn't often present things in a highly organized fashion; his wisdom comes at you all at once. Whatever he says, I try to put in some kind of informational matrix myself. The responsibility is on me, and if you don't have that sense of responsibility it's going to be very rough with a teacher like Reb Zalman. But I think this applies to all spiritual guidance relationships."

"Reb Zalman is not so much interested in raising up disciples as he is in giving them permission to fly," says Rabbi Victor Gross. "If I don't agree with him, there's no pressure to go along. I once told him that I believed in the existence of absolute evil. He got very, very excited and seemed upset that I would be at such a place. We were at his house, and he looks to the space between the transom and says, 'Will you allow for even that much goodness?' And I said no. And he looked exasperated. A week later we were studying a Hasidic text and came across a passage that allows for absolute evil, and Nadya [Victor's wife] says, 'Look, there's Victor's position.' And Reb Zalman starts laughing—he has so much lightness in him, it's such a great way of teaching."

"I love Reb Zalman and I want to have him in my life," says Seth Fishman, "but I also recognize that there are many others with the same desire; and if all of us made demands on him, we might take away his energy to do more important things. So I don't go to Reb Zalman except when it is warranted. Like when I was sick with cancer and thought I could die, that I let him know. But if there is personal work for me to do, then I do what I can on my own. If there is someone else I can go to with the question or for help, I will go to them rather than to Reb Zalman."

There is an easy gentleness and humility to the way Reb Zalman teaches. Particularly his ability to give recompense to the people he feels he has wronged. "I know Reb Zalman and what he has gone through and how he has worked on himself and the painstaking lengths he's gone through to repair the damage. He's really gone to people and made things right. He has completely made the reparations and uses them to teach," Reb Tirzah told me. Not only has Reb Zalman grafted new spiritual and psychological technologies onto the central stem of the Hasidic model; he has also used them to improve himself as a teacher, as a husband, and as a father. Yet his road has not always been an easy one. He escaped the Holocaust but, as with all Jews, felt deeply its horrific sorrows. And as a pioneer among a traumatized population, he met with much fear and resistance and struggled mightily with his Rebbe. Eventually, because of his "radicalism" he was cast out from his own tight-knit Hasidic community.

Though Reb Zalman's clock runs ahead of the pack, he was born on schedule in Poland in 1924. When his family moved to Vienna, he attended a traditional yeshiva (Jewish institution of religious study) and a socialist-Zionist high school. The rise of the Nazis forced them to move to Antwerp, then to Belgium and on to Vichy, France, where they were detained in an internment camp. Eventually they fled to America via Algeria, Morocco, and the West Indies, settling in New York in 1941. His family was of the Belzer Hasidic sect (Belz is a small town in Eastern Poland—Hasidic schools are named after towns), yet through some early contacts he became an admirer of the Lubavitcher movement (a branch of Hasidism founded by Shneur Zalman of Liadi—Lubavitch was the Russian town that served as the movement's headquarters for many years).

Shortly after his arrival in New York, Reb Zalman sought out the renowned Lubavitcher Rebbe Yosef Yitzchak Schneersohn, an immigrant from Russia (where he had many times been imprisoned and tortured for "godly activity"). The Rebbe presided over the main Lubavitcher community in Crown Heights, Brooklyn. When Reb Zalman met the Rebbe for the first time, the connection was instantaneous. "He spoke to me in a slow, deliberate way because of the paralysis [from his torture in prison], but within five minutes he had my whole life laid out. There was nothing to be hidden from him. I was to attend the yeshiva, my brother was to attend the children's yeshiva, my sisters were to attend Shulamit, the girls' school, and my parents and I were to work in the fur business. Just like that—one, two, three—it was all arranged! He gave me a blessing and I came out crying. If someone had asked why I was crying then, being a teenager, I would have told them it was 'because of the terrible things the Bolsheviks had done to such a holy being,' but the truth was, this was my first *yechidut* (private encounter) with the Rebbe, and 'when the child comes to the *mohel* [circumciser], he cries.' In some way that I couldn't explain, my heart had been circumcised of its covering, and I cried. I had become a Hasid of the Lubavitcher Rebbe."[11]

Reb Zalman was ordained in 1947 and soon was teaching and serving as a rabbi in Connecticut and Massachusetts. He had an uncanny ability to intuit the emerging architecture of the counterculture. He experimented frequently, allowing women a larger role in worship and introducing guitars into the liturgy. In 1949 (the year Jack Kerouac and Neal Cassady made their cross-country trek that was later recounted in *On the Road*), the Lubavitcher Rebbe asked him and his good friend Reb Shlomo Carlebach (the great rabbi-mystic, composer of Jewish melodies—*niggunim*—and expert storyteller) to begin visiting college campuses. It was the beginning of the work that would be central to the rest of their lives.

It's hard to imagine viewing it through its present-day orthodoxy, but Hasidism started as a radical movement and as a reaction *against* orthodoxy and elitism. "The Ba'al Shem Tov comes on the scene to build Hasidism at a time when you had the most elite people doing Talmud and the rest of the folks were down below, not having any real access to the living God. The Ba'al Shem Tov comes and opens the gate. And at the same time they put a ban on him and excommunicate him and his disciples," Reb Zalman told me. It was this earlier sense of radicalism and the dynamism of the direct connection with the living God that first attracted Reb Zalman to Hasidism. The Holocaust, however, changed everything. "Hasidism was radical and innovative and progressive at one point— the avant garde. But then it moved to a place, especially after the Holocaust, where it had to rebuild infrastructure, where the social stuff was lost, where the great teachers who knew firsthand what spirit was had been killed. Only a few had survived, and those who did survive and came here were too busy rebuilding structure, and they've been wonderful, they have been very successful, in fact they have moved from charisma to institution," Reb Zalman said. This "institution" is what Reb Zalman entered when he joined the Lubavitch community, and though he initially threw his heart into the work of restoration, he quickly found that it was not the institution that he wanted to rebuild but something more elemental.

In 1950, Reb Zalman's beloved teacher, Rebbe Yosef Yitzhak, died, and was replaced a year later by Rebbe Menachem Mendel Schneersohn, who was a brilliant scholar, scientist, and authority on the Torah. Luckily, Reb Zalman had a deep love and respect for the new Lubavitcher Rebbe and hoped that he would be a "Rebbe of modernity." Unfortunately, that hope never materialized and a growing sense of institutional claustrophobia began to push Reb Zalman away. The outreach program that he had started with Reb Shlomo Carlebach was thriving and offered an open doorway beyond the narrower confines of the Lubavitch community. When Reb Zalman began meeting Hillel (Jewish student organization) directors at the different campuses, he realized that he could be doing his outreach under an official umbrella and get paid for it (he and his wife had a growing family); all he needed was a master's degree.

It was at Boston University—where Reb Zalman was gaining

his master's in the psychology of religion—that he met the famed African American theologian (as well as mystic and poet) Howard Thurman. In Thurman the young rabbi found a kindred spirit and gifted teacher, though initially Reb Zalman had to overcome some of the institutional baggage that still clung like a wet scarf around his neck. During his first semester, Reb Zalman came across a class titled "Spiritual Disciplines and Resources, with labs" taught by Reverend Howard Thurman (the dean of Marsh Chapel). Reb Zalman couldn't believe his luck at finding such a class, but he had concerns that Thurman, a Christian minister, would try to convert him, so he made an appointment to meet with him. Reb Zalman voiced his concerns. "I said, 'Dean Thurman, I want to take this course, but I don't know if my "anchor chains" are long enough.' He sat silently for a few minutes and finally he says, 'Don't you trust the *ruach ha'kodesh*?" I was dumbfounded, he had used the Hebrew for the 'holy spirit'! I got up and ran out.

"For two weeks I was tortured by this question—was I a Jew by birth or a Jew by choice—did I trust the *ruach ha'kodesh*? In the end, there could only be one answer, 'Yes.' Yes, I was open to the Spirit of Guidance in whatever form it took. From that point on, I became a true experimenter in spirituality, reaching out to every religious tradition I came into contact with. This led me down strange roads and untrodden territory, and eventually into a growing conflict with Lubavitch."[12] It was this experience that began to purge the notion of triumphalism, the idea that any one religion has the exclusive possession of the truth and salvation, from Reb Zalman's bones.

This was quite a break from traditional Judaism, and it was this shift that formed the foundation of the Jewish Renewal Movement and was, perhaps more than any other component, the biggest draw for Jews to return to their native faith. Jewish Buddhists, Jewish Hindus, and Jewish Sufis found that they could reinhabit Judaism through the open door of Jewish Renewal without unloading anything they had learned on their journeys through other spiritual and scientific disciplines. In fact, the "new technologies" of meditation, psychology, and yoga (to name a few) could be grafted onto the old stock to great advantage. Hyphenated spirituality was embraced. "I believe today everybody is a Jew by choice," Reb Zalman told me. "And look at all the hyphenated people—the Bu-Jews and Hin-Jews and Jew-Fis. The variety is great. I can't imagine anyone today who is outside the enclave that can do it without some kind of hyphenation."

During the period between 1959 and 1966 (the year he finished his doctoral studies), Reb Zalman began reaching out more and more to teachers and practitioners of other faiths. He corresponded frequently with Thomas Merton, and met with Native American leaders as well as Sufis and Muslims. He wrote numerous articles and became popular on the lecture circuit. Reb Zalman's radical ecumenism is fundamental to his personality and the way he functions in the world. I am giving it added emphasis here because he and the Jewish Renewal Movement have been such a strong force in breaking down religious barriers between Jews and Christians, Jews and Muslims, Jews and Buddhists, Jews and Hindus, and on and on.

The ecumenical dialogue is not just a paper tiger. When he ordained Rabbi Tirzah Firestone, who lives in Boulder, she became the first rabbi to be ordained who was in an interfaith marriage. This was a big leap. Ten years earlier the Rocky Mountain Rabbinical Council had put a ban on rabbis of any denomination performing interfaith marriages in the region. "He ordained me when I was married to a Christian. It was such a huge thing and it hit the papers and he put himself out so far for me. I remember rabbis were calling him and railing against him, they weren't even calling me, and he stood by me," Rabbi Tirzah told me. There is a poignant account of Rabbi Tirzah's ordination in her book *With Roots in Heaven,* which includes the following words spoken by Reb Zalman:

"So I have to do some mighty god-wrestling—this is the meaning of the word 'Israel'—with my teachers and the tradition of the past, as well as with the vision of the future, which calls us, saying, You cannot just run a religion by looking in the rearview mirror! You have to look ahead, too, and be guided by the prophecy that says: *'On that day, God's house will be a house for all peoples,'* and *'On that day, God will be one and God's name will be one'!"* [13]

Jewish Renewal teachers are fighting for peace in Israel, opening dialogues with Palestinians; they are working for women's rights all around the globe. Rabbi David Zaslow has created a strong ecumenical outreach program among different spiritual teachers in Ashland, Oregon. Netanel Miles-Yépez and Reb Zalman have created together a new Sufi-Hasidic lineage called the Chishti-Maimuniyya Sufi-Hasidic Order, which arose out of Reb Zalman being appointed a sheikh by Pir Zia, the famous Sufi teacher, and bestowing that lineage upon one of his students. And last but not least are rabbis Victor and Nadia Gross, who have started an interfaith congregation of Jews and Lutherans (the first of its kind) in Boulder, Colorado, which is simply amazing to see. "The big sticking point for the Jewish world is Christianity. It's not a big stretch for Jews to have a dialogue with Buddhists and Hindus and even Sufis. But Christianity, phew!" Nadia told me. Nadia and her husband, Victor, met two forward-thinking Lutheran pastors, Linda and Larry Daniels-Block, who were willing to share their church with a Jewish congregation. "In order to pray together, we had to examine which language we could use that would be authentic with all of us praying and not pushing anybody's buttons. So on their turf we all came together and our musician and their musician played together and they were careful to leave out the 'Jesus language.' " The "experiment" has been going on for nearly two years, and, as Nadia says, "The healing that is going on here is tremendous."

Victor and Nadia had been the heads of a non-affiliated Jewish congregation in Los Angeles, he as rabbi, she as cantor (a singer who leads the prayer services), before they met Reb Zalman and the Jewish Renewal Movement, which they both connected with immediately. Nadia is now a rabbi, ordained by Reb Zalman. When they moved to Boulder, in part to be closer to their teacher, they quite propitiously found the opportunity to work with the Lutheran community, and Reb Zalman has supported them at every turn, often appearing at the church for special occasions, giving talks, guidance, and healing. He also has been a valuable resource for how to handle controversy. "He called me up once and told me to check out a website that attacks him. I read it and it was scurrilous stuff. A couple days later I tell him the website was repulsive, and he chuckles and says it has been up for a long time and every once in a while he visits it to see what it says about him," Victor tells me. "What's he wasting his time for, I think. And then it dawned on me that it was his way of teaching me about how to act under criticism, how to act when someone challenges whatever it is I'm doing. For Reb Zalman it was just like water off a duck's back."

When Reb Zalman and I spoke about the different stages that students pass through along the spiritual path, he suddenly recalled a book written by Karl Stern titled *The Third Revolution: A Study of Psychiatry and Religion.*[14] (This is how Reb Zalman's mind works. It's an electrically charged treasure trove of references, theories, stories, and unfathomable knowledge.) In the book, Stern transposes Freud's developmental stages onto the unfolding stages encountered by a spiritual seeker. "The first phase is like the oral phase for a baby," Reb Zalman recalls. "When you get involved in a religion, it feels so sweet, so wonderful. It's milk and honey and I want, I want, I want. Feed me. Okay? Then there is the next phase, which is the anal phase. You've got to get your shit together and not do it all over the place. And it's like toilet training and discipline.

"The third phase (the phallic phase)—oh, everything is so symbolic. You're already in the practice and everything you do is fraught with boing, boing, boing—so symbolic, so rich, so beautiful. The dream life is full. You decorate the place where you are doing your *puja* [a Hindu word for the act of showing reverence to God]. You're hanging around your altar and it's beautiful. And then comes the fourth phase (the latency phase) where you say, 'I don't care if you have the decorations or not. What I care about is the *sangha* [the community]—the communion of saints.' You realize you can't do anything by yourself. You have to be embedded with the group and work with the group. The fifth phase (the genital phase) is when you say community is all right, but now you go deep inside yourself and you have to go through the dark night of the soul to get to the unitive experience. These are the stages. You will find many people who teach about stages that you have to go through," he tells me, and then launches into another explanation of the spiritual process that is just as intriguing.

In 1956, Reb Zalman accepted a teaching job at the University of Manitoba in Winnipeg, in the Near Eastern and Judaic Studies department. And then, in 1959, because of a growing interest in the religious implications of psychedelics, Reb Zalman decided to experiment with LSD. "Now, to my mind, this wasn't anything outside of the tradition. Judaism, unlike Islam, does not abstain from alcohol. The Jewish way is to sacramentalize alcohol. It is a powerful substance, so we use it in a sacred context and with a *L'chayyim* [a toast to life]. So, I felt it was the same situation with psychedelics. And, I wanted to know if it was like what was going on in deep meditation. This was serious to me," he told me.

Reb Zalman had met Timothy Leary while visiting Srimata Gayatri Devi's (the Hindu saint in the Ramakrishna Order)

Vedanta Centre in Cohasset, Massachusetts, and the good doctor agreed to accompany him on a "trip" there at the peaceful ashrama. On the appointed day he arrived at the Vedanta Centre dressed in *Shabbat* clothes and armed with Mozart records and Hasidic melodies. The time had come! "I drank down the holy draught and there was a silent moment of absorbing it. The record player was going and I was sitting there on pins and needles waiting for something to happen, but, a seeming moment later, I had danced through several sides of the Hasidic records and wasn't winded a bit—I felt as if even my bones were dancing. I kept saying, 'It's better than schnapps! It's better than schnapps!' "[15]

For Reb Zalman the "trip" was a reaffirmation of his need for spiritual experimentation. "For me, the empirical possibility that every possible construct was true, and could conceivably coexist, came with taking LSD. I began to see Hasidic Judaism as I knew it as one possible construct, but not the only necessary construct. I learned to wiggle my mind into other possibilities. I could see the unique possibilities of other religions, and other people."[16]

Though his Rebbe and the Lubavitch community were at first tolerant of his one foray into psychedelics—his Rebbe told him that taking LSD was like any other experience, but you still had to do the work yourself—that changed quickly when Reb Zalman gave a talk at a Reform temple in Washington, D.C., on the connection between Kabbalah and LSD. The talk was given in 1966 and was well received. A couple of weeks after his talk, a Conservative teacher of Judaism came to the Reform temple to give a presentation and asked what topic Reb Zalman had spoken on. When she was told of the subject, she went through the roof. The woman wrote an article on Reb Zalman's talk, and for her research she called the Lubavitch headquarters and asked if Zalman took LSD with the Rebbe's permission. The people at Lubavitch got spooked and told her that he certainly did not and that Reb Zalman had questionable credentials, inferring that his ordination was not authentic, which was a complete lie. But the woman put the "official disavowal" in her article, and Reb Zalman was effectively cut off from the Lubavitch community.

It was a very painful moment in his life. Over the years, however, he has put it in perspective. "I felt the more I reached out, the more I realized that it's important for the Lubavitch community to hold the fort, but it wasn't important for me to hold the fort. It was important for me to go and help the people outside of the enclave," he told me. "Sometimes you have a pimple and it has pus. The body pushes that out. I was pushed out more by the Hasidic body than anything else," he said.

"There are certainly areas, especially in Judaism's social constructs, where we have limited ourselves; thinking of ourselves as a tribe rather than in universal terms, for instance," Rabbi Tirzah told me. "We've limited ourselves in our misogyny and by cutting ourselves off from the body. What Reb Zalman has done is given me the permission to peel back the layers of overgrowth that have obscured this beautiful live tradition."

Being "kicked out of the nest" to one degree or another is a necessary process in the teacher-student relationship. At some point students must go and test the waters themselves, to make their own mark in the world and carry on the soul-work that they were called to do. Some teachers need to slam the door in a student's face, while others do it with gentle nudges, but they're both pointing to the same end. Reb Menachem Mendel Schneersohn died in 1994, but Reb Zalman had managed to see him a few years before his death and receive his blessing in friendship. "He cared for me and I cared for him the same way. But it just didn't work anymore for me to do the same thing," Reb Zalman said.

In 1974, Reb Zalman accepted a job as professor of Jewish Mysticism and Psychology of Religion at Temple University in

Philadelphia. It was during his years there that the Jewish Renewal coalesced and became a genuine movement with certain structures and forms (though much looser than traditional ones). In 1995, Reb Zalman took a position at the Naropa Institute as the World Wisdom Chair. Though he is retired from academic life, he still works hard within the Jewish Renewal Movement and still trains students and rabbis. When I asked him about his legacy, he said, "Stem cells of Judaism. That's the short answer. I don't want it to be just this or that. I don't know which way it should go. You know time is going to tell, situations are going to tell. I just want it to be alive.

"Sometimes, somebody asks me about tradition and culture. So I say, 'Let me tell you what I believe about culture and tradition. Imagine I have a culture for making yogurt. I'd like to save that culture but I don't have cow's milk. I'm going to take some goat's milk and put the culture into the goat's milk. The same yeast is still going to be there. It's going to be using a different kind of milk.' What I'm trying to say with that is there was Judaism in Spain and it was in that culture, and in the Ukraine it was another culture, but somehow the bugs are the same bugs. I needed to make sure that between pre-Holocaust (the earlier paradigm) and the new emerging paradigm, a bridge was created for that culture. Once that happens it's out of my hands, I'm not worried about it. There is a beautiful sentence where Pharaoh says to Moses, 'What are you going to take with you? I'm going to let your people go for offering sacrifices. But leave stuff at home so I know you're going to come back.' Moses says, 'We can't do that.' And he gives him a line, 'For we know not how we must serve God until we get there.' That's the capstone for this thing about legacy."

Gratitude

I was speaking with a friend who has been a Zen practitioner for nearly fifteen years, and she told me that when she first started doing meditation retreats at a Zen center, she kept hearing how grateful everyone was. People were grateful for the teacher, for the teachings, for the meditation cushions, for the food. "They were grateful for being able to share their gratitude, for God's sake," she said, laughing at the memory of how annoyed she had felt upon hearing their appreciation. My friend had started Zen practice because she'd lost her sixty-year-old mother to cancer; in the beginning, gratitude was the farthest thing from her mind. But she used her initial annoyance as a productive irritant in her practice. She began to think about gratitude—where it comes from, and what it is. "I used to think that gratitude was a by-product of practice, but it's not. Gratitude *is* Zen. It's always there, waiting for us. You stir a pond and it gets muddy, but that doesn't mean the pond disappears. If something bad happens to us, gratitude is still there. I guess what I'm saying is that appreciation has a lot to do with patience," she told me.

Maezumi Roshi said, "What is this treasury of the true dharma eye and subtle mind of nirvana that Shakyamuni Buddha transmitted? All the Buddhist teachings deal with this most precious treasure. It is your life. It is my life."[1] Gratitude is a part of that treasure. It is a natural flow in our lives. The title of the book that contains this quote is *Appreciate Your Life.* Maezumi Roshi used to say these words again and again to his students: "Appreciate your life." Gratitude, as my friend said, is at the heart of Zen. When we appreciate our lives, we shift the focus from ourselves, from our own suffering, to how we are supported by the world. If we hit our thumb with a hammer, our awareness shrinks to the intensity of that pain. In our mind, the rest of the world disappears. The practice of gratitude continually reminds us about the "real" world beyond the border of our self-involvement. At any moment during the day or night, we can pause and take stock—if we can suspend our internal dialogue for a short minute—of how much we are given.

When I took an undergrad writing course with the poet Gary Snyder, the first assignment he gave us, in hope of raising our ecological awareness, was to trace how the water got to our tap. I immediately saw the environmental implications and difficulties involved in California water issues, but I was also struck by something else. Just the simple act of running water in my sink would not have been possible without the help of thousands of people and machines, not to mention the sun, the Pacific Ocean, and the Sierra Mountains, which act like great sails to catch moisture, and the rivers that fill the lakes and reservoirs. It struck me as a great blessing. I had a friend who made up his own first line to Genesis—"In the beginning, gifts."

As a society we have perfected the art of complaint, which is to say we have narrowed our vision. Spiritual teachers are here to pull back the blinds. "Look at every act of service that we do as a tremendous privilege, as an act of worship. We're all debtors in this world. Life doesn't owe us one single thing. Every act of unselfish service that we give awakens Divine power in us," says Sudha Puri.[2] Every teacher in this book teaches from a deep appreciation for life. This is their authenticity. When we talk of what is "transmitted" from teacher to student, we talk of that sense of gratitude. "Being humble and aware of our interdependence makes us see how grateful we ought to be that we are able to gather together with friends to pray, and to receive from some guide who has preceded us on the way, knowledge of the signs that mark the route. This gratitude should extend through the whole of our life—in order that through blessings received in various disguises, we are in this moment in the possibility of receiving more," writes Murat Yagan.[3]

The good thing about gratitude—particularly in this age of artifice and manufactured emotions—is that it is hard to fake. There is a palpable resonance in the lives of grateful people. I'm not talking about some sort of warm and fuzzy appreciation—certainly that can be a part of it—but something that is often hard won. How can we imagine gratitude when we're in the throes of great suffering, like my friend who lost her mother? Gratitude doesn't mean the absence of sorrow or suffering. "Gratitude requires attention and reflection," writes Gregg Krech.[4] Gregg is the head of the Tōdō Institute, which offers retreats in a Japanese therapy called Naikan,[5] a method of self-reflection that helps cultivate gratitude by uncovering, much like Snyder's exercise, the layers of support given to us by friends, family, nature, and the world at large—we count our blessings.

Reb Zalman makes a wonderful distinction between what he calls "commodity time" and natural, organic time—the sacred hours of the Sabbath, for instance. Though gratitude can certainly exist in "commodity time," it owes its origin to the deeper cycles of nature. That is why gratitude has space for sorrow and suffering, because it exists broadly, but can be found even in the tiniest details. Yet gratitude is not something we "get." It is already "here" and is cultivated within the existing soil of our life, and it often takes practice.

"To me, grace comes from an examination of one's life in which you realize that you don't deserve what you're getting, yet you're getting it anyway. That is the experience of grace, both practically and spiritually. If you want to put it in secular terms, it's the difference between seeing life as an entitlement and seeing it as a gift," writes Gregg Krech.[6] Gratitude is a powerful and intrinsic quality in spiritual practice, yet it doesn't happen overnight. In Kebzeh (Murat Yagan's practice) they say, "He who knows he has enough is rich." Sometimes this takes a lifetime to realize.

6

MASTER OF THE ORDINARY

Gehlek Rimpoche

To the Gurus, Guru om! Thanks to the teachers
Who taught us to breathe[1]
— ALLEN GINSBERG

Aura Glaser first met Gehlek Rimpoche in front of the Tibetan library in Dharamsala, India, in December 1980. She was with her friend Bruce Wilson and they were talking with Mel Goldstein, the author and Tibetologist. Gehlek Rimpoche, who knew Mel, ambled up and began chatting in English. He was warm and friendly and wore a Western suit. Aura had no idea he was a lama. All the Tibetan monks Aura had met came with a "full retinue complete with bells and whistles." Gehlek Rimpoche and Aura spoke briefly; he invited her to New Delhi; she declined. When they said good-bye, Aura shook Gehlek Rimpoche's hand.

"The moment he put his hand in mine my conceptual mind dropped away," Aura told me, laughing at what she had just said.

"All the hairs on the back of my neck stood up and I couldn't fathom what was going on because I thought I was having a conversation with a Tibetan businessman. But my experience in that moment told me something singular and extraordinary was taking place. All I could manage to do was look at him and ask, 'Who are you?' I had a profound and unmistakable sense of connection and recognition and mystery when we shook hands. He smiled and said, 'Ah, he'll tell you,' and pointed to Bruce as he began to walk away. I turned to Bruce, who was having a good laugh because he knew Rimpoche, and asked him, 'Who was that?' I then looked over and saw Rimpoche smiling and waving at me from across the courtyard."

Nawang Gehlek Trinley Namgye or, less formally, Gehlek Rimpoche, or simply Rimpoche (*Rimpoche* is an honorific title for reincarnated lamas; it means "Precious One") is a very tender-hearted and humble man with an incredibly piercing and analytic mind. One wants to call him ordinary but he's not, yet he gives people the sense that in ordinariness one can find complete spiritual truth—this makes him extraordinary. He was born in Lhasa, Tibet, in 1939, recognized as an incarnate lama at age four, attained Geshe Lharampa, the highest Tibetan scholastic degree given, at fourteen (an exceptional feat considering the process usually takes twenty-five years), was able to memorize five thousand pages of text (thousands more than any other person designated for such duties), and discovered, at nineteen, weeks after the Chinese Communist invasion, an escape route from Tibet into India over the Himalayas, which was eventually used by tens of thousands of refugees. Yet, when asked what he knows, he'll say "not much," and suggest you might want to study with some other great lama.

Aura's first meeting with Rimpoche is, for spiritual seekers, an affirmation of how some of us imagine a connection with a teacher should be, the instantaneous electricity, the concomitant profound insight upon first contact, the unbounded possibilities for the future. It's beautiful when it happens this way, but by no means common. For Aura, the likelihood of such an encounter was dramatically increased by her lack of expectations of profundity (my apologies to businessmen). Preconceived notions are generally *not* the fuse for spiritual fire. The more interesting aspect of Aura's story, however, is not that she was "jolted" in the first encounter with her teacher through a wordless and energetic exchange—that is a mystery that cannot be dissected—but that the experience enticed her to stick around and clarify what had happened.

Aura became Rimpoche's student that day in Dharamsala and is still his student twenty-five years later. The kinetic rush she felt upon first meeting him wore off, and, as in the sobering, post-honeymoon years of marriage, Aura got down to the real work of relationship, namely how to live life between the peaks of spiritual buzz and the valleys of its shadow. Constancy is the oft-hidden jewel of the teacher-student relationship; though rarely glamorous, it fills in, like a reliable understudy, the gaps of faint hearts and weakened spirits. It reminds us, quite appropriately, that we're in this for the long haul. Today, Aura is an author, psychotherapist, dharma teacher, and co-founder (with Rimpoche and meditation teacher Sandy Finkel) of Jewel Heart Buddhist Center, the international organization headed by Rimpoche and based in Ann Arbor, Michigan.

Aura and her childhood friend Sandy Finkel had been traveling together in India when she met Rimpoche, and they would eventually sponsor him to live permanently in the United States. Weeks after Aura's meeting, Sandy had a similar encounter. Though her meeting was less electric, she had an immediate resonance with the undercover lama and the same attraction to Rimpoche's complete lack of pretension and razor-sharp insights. "He can chat about this and that and then nail you to the wall within the same sentence," Sandy told me as we sat in her living room in Ann Arbor.

"When I first met him, I knew he was different. His facility for the English language was part of it, but he also had a familiarity with Western culture. You have to understand that in Dharamsala the relationships between teachers and students were much more formal. I could talk with Rimpoche about subjects that I wouldn't have broached with some of the other lamas—the whys of the practice, questions challenging the status quo."

There's a story that Rimpoche likes to tell and that his community often repeats. In the early 1990s he attended a workshop given by Allen Ginsberg (one of Rimpoche's students and a good friend) called "Spontaneous Poetry." In the workshop Allen would ask people, "What are you thinking? Say it now." Eventually he turned to Rimpoche with the same question. "I don't want to end up in the shoes of Jim and Tammy Faye Bakker," was Rimpoche's response (Jim and Tammy, as you may recall, were involved in a religious scandal at the time—embezzlement from the PTL Club, hush money for Jim's affair with Jessica Hahn, etc.). Allen said, "The way not to fall into that trap is to make sure you keep nothing hidden in any closet. No matter what it is, don't hide it. Keep everything out in the open." Rimpoche took Allen's words to heart. "I followed his advice, which was really great. He was totally and completely himself, and he showed me how comfortable I could be in my own skin." Rimpoche carried this transparency into everything he did, openly sharing his life with his students. In many ways it was a complete break with traditional Tibetan teaching etiquette.

"Rimpoche often shares stories from his personal life that are less than exemplary, even embarrassing," Sandy told me. Rimpoche's message is "Look, I have faults just like you, and I can still be compassionate and kind and enlightened, just the way you can." True spirituality is not about perfection—or, put another way, "perfection" is realizing our God-ness in our imperfection. "To be casual is my personality. I invite people over to dinner and talk with them because I treat students as friends. I drink wine sometimes because I like it. People don't want to talk about certain things, and sometimes it's easier to talk after a glass of wine. Or sometimes, when I have to say something difficult, I can have a glass of wine," Rimpoche explained. His candor is refreshing, but in many respects hard-won.

Gehlek Rimpoche gave up his robes (his monastic vows) while living in New Delhi, a few years after escaping from Tibet in 1959. He was in his early twenties at the time, and the air was full of rebellion—it was the sixties, after all. But it wasn't just zeitgeist; for years a troubling doubt had been coursing through his mind. Although Rimpoche had an exceptional memory, unlike most other incarnate lamas he could not recall any event from his previous lives, an omission that had caused him to question his incarnate status. "When I tried to remember anything regarding my previous lives and circumstances, conditions, and friends, my vivid, reliable recollections equaled zero. Then I wondered, What am I? A fool?"[2] These misgivings mixed with the horrors of expulsion from his homeland, ragged and penniless, and the shock of entering a new culture tipped him headlong into lay life and an entirely different type of exploration.

"I tried everything, smoking, drinking, sex, looking for some kind of kick that I thought I couldn't get from dharma [the Buddhist teachings]." Giving up a way of life that was the only one he had known shook Rimpoche and caused him great suffering. He had lost everything materially, and now he questioned his very identity—yet it was also a time to purge some of the nonessential parts of his spiritual practice and feel the absence of rank. His spiritual garments were gone, the external exoticism transformed into the ordinary. The circumstances of Rimpoche's life have, contrary to what one would expect, fed his Buddhist practice in a positive and openhearted way. His trials, like layers of geological strata, have given a rich shape to Rimpoche's personality and lay teaching style and, perhaps more important, have made him a more approachable, maybe even a more honorable, figure to his Western followers.

"I think that's why I respect him," said Greg Supa Corner, a student of Rimpoche's for eighteen years. "He's had his rebellion; maybe that was his training when he came from a monastic model and was thrown into India where he had to get a job. I respect that he had to do that. He came from a very wealthy family and probably owned four of the six cars in Tibet. He went from being this nobleman to riding in a garbage cart—he reflected on that, on how amazing life can be, from being on top to being on the bottom, and he was okay with it. Most of us would have freaked out."

In becoming a lay teacher after so many intense years of monastic training, Rimpoche created, in his person, a new platform of Tibetan practice. To study with Rimpoche is like entering a mansion through the kitchen door. It's homey, comfortable, friendly, and, above all, funny—easy to let your guard down. Much of a teacher's "business" is simply getting his students to relax and open up. As Tibetan scholar Robert Thurman observed, "Over the years I have probably had more fun with Gehlek Rimpoche than with almost any lama I have known."[3] Spiritual practice can be an overly serious occupation, but it doesn't mean we have to take ourselves seriously. In fact, to be light and poke fun at ourselves is, I think, essential—there's nothing worse than the droning melodrama of "My Spirituality." Rimpoche has a healthy dose of respect for his teachers and his tradition, but he can also be refreshingly irreverent. "I have no idea about Tibetan medicine; in fact I don't even like it. These Tibetan doctors give you pills until you die," he told me, laughing.

Rimpoche's power simmers neatly below his lighthearted manner; he is, after all, a Tibetan master well versed in all the intricacies his high calling demands. "One thing that's interesting about Gehlek Rimpoche is how traditional he really is," the composer Philip Glass—a longtime student—told me. "And that becomes apparent when you've been around him and seen the way he conducts his teachings. He's actually a very traditional lama in disguise." Rimpoche invites you into the kitchen, and there's usually a pleasant stretch of time before you realize that you're the one being cooked.

On one occasion, Kathy Laritz, a student of Rimpoche's for nearly twenty years and his assistant at Jewel Heart, sat crying after a good-bye party for her boyfriend, who was returning to Europe. She knew the relationship was most likely over. Rimpoche walked in and asked what was wrong, and she told him. "He took my hands—he is short and I was sitting up on this countertop and he's standing down in front of me. He took my two hands and started swinging them. I'm sad and I'm not in the mood for joyous movement and then he started dancing and he's moving his body and he started singing, 'Don't take impermanence personally.' I couldn't remain wallowing in self-pity with this beautiful man acting silly, wanting me to smile, and then hitting me with such a profound statement," Kathy explained, smiling.

Rimpoche's teaching method is particularly unusual among other Tibetan lamas because of his facility in the English language and his broad understanding of Western culture, not to mention his genuine love for its people. I believe he knows more about American and world politics than most well-educated citizens. Hartmut Sagolla, a German native and a student of Rimpoche's for over twenty years, was struck by Rimpoche's "Western style" upon their first meeting. "I thought, here's a guy I could probably ask anything and he would try to respond and try to accommodate my shortcomings and my cultural background and try to work with it. For me this was very important." Perhaps not since the late,

great Chögyam Trungpa Rimpoche (the renowned meditation master) has an Old Tibet–born (pre–Communist occupation) teacher
better comprehended and genuinely appreciated the Western character. Gehlek and Trungpa were roommates for a short time in
India, and Rimpoche had great respect for his friend.

"I don't think Americans have any more self-hatred than anyone
else. Look at the Chinese people: they may not hate themselves, but
they underestimate themselves tremendously. I find it much easier
to deal with Americans than Asians, because in America you can
say what you think and can be straightforward and you don't have
to have this politeness and saving face," Rimpoche told me. He became an American citizen in 1995, a long-held dream. "I thought
about America way back in Tibet," he told me. "I always tried to
talk about it." This has given his teaching a home-grown quality
that is rare among foreign teachers. He is not so much trying to im-
port exotic religious and cultural forms as he is trying to draw out
preexisting spiritual qualities in his students. This is very important. The deeply personal spiritual experience, of course, can never
be of "foreign origin."

American Buddhists have always, on some level, been obliged to
negotiate cultural exoticism. For many who were long disillusioned
by native religious forms, the foreign flavor of Buddhism was the
main draw; for others the cultural baggage that came tightly
wrapped in the dharma was a turn-off. The traditional guru model,
though initially attractive, has lost much of its luster through scandal and abuse. As American Buddhists mature as practitioners and
as teachers, they continue to explore the parameters of the teacher-
student relationship. Some have dug in their heels and resisted
change at every turn, arguing that "traditional" Buddhism (as it
was practiced in foreign countries) needs a long arc of time to establish itself in a new country before introducing adjustments to

forms and structures. Others have called for a true American Buddhism that embraces feminism, psychology, and social activism (particularly environmental issues)—components that have been largely absent in Eastern Buddhism.

The writer and longtime Tibetan practitioner Alexander Berzin, in his book on the Tibetan mentor-disciple relationship, writes: "Any approach at restructuring the teacher-student relationship needs to avoid two extremes. The first is justifying the deification of the teacher to the point that it encourages a cult mentality and whitewashes abuse. The second is justifying the demonization of the teacher to the point that paranoia and distrust prevent the benefits to be gained from a healthy disciple-mentor relationship. In trying to prevent the first extreme, we need great care not to fall into the second."[4]

It must be remembered that at its heart Buddhism, at least in its original intent, is devoid of any cultural authority and has fluidly grafted itself onto a variety of different societies, absorbing their flavors and vitality without losing the Buddha's central message. There has always been a tension, as Buddhism moved from country to country, between maintaining tradition and integrating new cultural forms. Rimpoche was quite aware of this dynamic and from early on worked to demystify many aspects of Tibetan practice and transmute those qualities into the vernacular without losing their core. "I emphasized that people didn't need to fold their hands in a certain way or anything like that," Rimpoche told me. "I was just a simple guy coming to talk about the teachings. Then gradually people began to appreciate the message and when they found it helpful they were able to develop some kind of a profound relationship to it."

Tony (last name withheld upon request), a longtime student of Rimpoche's, found this new approach invigorating. "He did away with *gassho* [placing hands together palm to palm] and bowing. He doesn't tolerate that. During some ceremonies bowing is allowed, but generally he says, 'Look, get off that trip.' He says, 'You're an American. Let's not bullshit ourselves, let's not ape some other culture.'" *Buddha* means "Awakened One," and the role of a Buddhist teacher is to be the shrill alarm to our sleepwalking, even if our dreamy heads are lost in the fanfare of religious form. For spiritual seekers, attachments to the accoutrements of religious practice—particularly in their exotic emanations—are often the hardest to perceive, though they can become as empty-headed as a commute to work.

Though a teacher might consciously steer the focus away from the foreign aspects of Buddhism, students are often resistant. Rimpoche never felt comfortable using the traditional "throne" or platform that Tibetan teachers sit upon during talks and ceremonies. He just sat on a cushion. Many of his students, however, preferred their teacher, if only in theory, at a different height. "There were times when I went into Jewel Heart centers and they made something funny: on one of the cushions they put a scarf on the back, tried to make it look like a throne. I started sitting on one cushion and then gradually more people came, so we had a stage. I put one cushion on the stage and then the cushion kept getting higher and higher. I don't know who did it, but I had to keep taking the 'throne' away. Now I have a pain, so I sit in a chair," he said, laughing.

One of the major contributions of Western culture to Buddhism has been feminism; the inflexible patriarchy of many Buddhist schools has been a continuing sore point among Western practitioners. Rimpoche, though very flexible in his approach, initially struggled with many feminist ideals. When he first arrived he had a habit of pinching women on the behind—he was quickly dissuaded from that cultural pattern. His "enlightenment" in this area was a group effort. Aura and Sandy are both feminists who hosted Rimpoche in their apartment upon his first visit. "We didn't let up on any of these points: Why is the lineage completely male? Why aren't there female reincarnated lamas? And on and on," Sandy told me. "We were his main gateway into the culture at large. He had very strong ideas about certain things, and we would have hours of conversation and heated debate," added Aura.

"We worked on the language in prayers and changed it where it needed changing. Just bringing awareness of these issues to the fore was essential," Aura said. The main thing was that Rimpoche was willing to engage in the debate and listen to his students' concerns. "Rimpoche eventually stated that these things were due not to any spiritual qualities, but to the imbalances in society, and he encouraged us to work for change," Sandy said. This is a case of the community teaching the teacher and of the healthy shift from the old guru model (where the teacher held all the power) to a less centralized authority. "The challenge that we face in the West with the introduction of a practice from a different culture is our tendency to honor external power instead of experiencing the nature of power growing inside of us," Kathy Laritz offered.

"Rimpoche feels strongly about staying close to the tradition and planting something in this new Western soil that he knows to be authentic and reliable. For some, these practices as they have been passed on fit quite easily and require little or no adaptation. Then there are those of us who hold a paradox—we feel deeply connected to the living wisdom lineage of Tibetan teachings and to the depths of practice within the tradition, while simultaneously feeling deeply committed to honoring our own inner wisdom. This can create heat or friction as one questions, on the basis of personal experience, some of the tradition's accepted norms. Bringing those different perspectives into conversation—both within oneself and with one another—is, I feel, an essential part of an emerging Western dharma," Aura said. It must be remembered that Buddhism is still relatively new to the West. It had spread from India throughout Asia over centuries, but never has it met such a foundationally different culture from its origins as it found in Europe and North America. The work of integration requires patience, caution, and respect.

We, as Western students, should also realize that foreign teachers are inherently limited (they can never know the culture as well as its inhabitants) when it comes to implementing change, which inevitably—if the natives are going to make the new religion personally relevant and vital—must happen. Much of the responsibility lies with the upcoming generation of students and the generations after that. As much as Aura and Sandy pushed Rimpoche to expand his concept of the feminine, they also accepted his limitations. "Rimpoche is still very much an Asian man; he's from Tibet and embodies many of those cultural characteristics—that's a reality. It is also true that his attitude has shifted significantly. He now recognizes many of the culturally embedded limitations and truly supports the empowerment of women in the dharma. Nevertheless, there are aspects of feminism and the emerging voice of the sacred feminine that, at the end of the day, are not really his to uphold, they are ours," Aura explained. "There are just so many cultural differences and Rimpoche has been amazing, staying open to it. It takes respect on both sides to figure it all out," Sandy added.

Western psychology is another example. Rimpoche has no past cultural context to make sense of it. "I don't know anything about psychology myself, so I cannot incorporate it," Rimpoche told me. "This I leave to those who are psychologists. It is for them to combine Buddhism and psychology together. What I do is what I know. This practice is so much like gambling—if you lose, you lose somebody's life, so I don't want to gamble on that. Those psychologists who are with me started calling it Buddhist psychology. I don't. If they call it that, I don't object because I don't know and I don't endorse it because I don't know. That's for them to figure out." Once again the important point here is Rimpoche's openness to the idea of integration, even though he might not understand it completely. This takes trust in his students, something that teachers, both foreign and not, must ultimately embrace. If teachers cannot trust their students, then the full measure of their wisdom will not be passed to the next generation.

With trust comes responsibility, and we in the West have to take great care—within all religious disciplines—in melding psychology and spiritual practice. Aura, a depth psychologist, has made the weaving of these two disciplines her life's work, accepting both her role as a westerner and her role as a practitioner of Tibetan Buddhism. "On one hand I don't draw a big distinction between psychology and spirituality. The practice of psychology, although it is young in many ways, is geared toward helping people move from suffering to freedom, and that is completely in harmony with dharma," Aura tells me. "But there is another way to look at it—within the psychological, you're dealing with personal material and your own unique way of encountering the world; whereas within the spiritual, insights tend to be universal in nature. Really, the two work in tandem. A lot of us have great insights but are not able to integrate them, partly because it's a matter of practice and deepening and steadfastness but also because there is such turmoil going on inside of us. Unless we clean up the mess in the basement, heaven's gate will never open up. An addiction to transcendence keeps us stuck between insight and embodiment. So I see psychology and spirituality working in very complementary ways, attending to the personal and allowing the universal in."

Ultimately we must rely on our own experience and trust that connection. But realistically who among us has not, at times, been confused as to the reliability of our own version of reality? As Johnny Cash so aptly sang, "It was patently unclear if it was New York or New Year." We need, more than occasionally, a standard of clarity, a litmus. The experience of the Buddha is that rock upon which all Buddhists depend, and it is his words—memorized during his lifetime and put into writing some years later—that are the roots of Buddhism's heavily grafted tree.

Tibetan Buddhism includes both sutras and tantras. The sutras "present the basic themes of practice for gaining liberation from uncontrollably recurring problems (*samsara* in Sanskrit) and, beyond that, to reach the enlightened state of a Buddha, with the ability to help others as much as is possible."[5] The sutras are generally where students start in Tibetan practice. The tantras are considered to be the more advanced and are, in many ways, the heart of Tibetan religion. The word *tantra* comes from the Hindu religion of India and has an etymological connection with the word *loom* and denotes an "extension" or "expansion" and a weaving together, underscoring the interconnectedness of all things. The word also relates directly to "text" or "textbook," meaning that there were sacred texts added to the Hindu body of work to extend its scope. The Hindu canon comprises many tantras or texts. In Vajrayana Buddhism (Tibetan), tantras (both of Hindu and Buddhist origin) constitute the root scriptures of the religion, and there is much emphasis placed on study, scholarship, and the memorization of sacred texts, whose numbers are vast. "The Buddhadharma [Buddhist teachings] is traditionally said to consist of eighty-four thousand collections, and each one of these is said to contain as many texts as could be written with all the ink an elephant can carry on its back."[6]

Because all is intertwined, tantra asserts that everything—all the energies of the mind and body—can be used to further our spiritual growth. And because all our human attributes are available for use in an alchemical process of transformation, Tibetans believe that we are capable of reaching nirvana in a single lifetime. In this regard, Tibetan Buddhism has created intricate and exhaustive maps (initiations, empowerments, visualizations, movement, chants, meditations, and so on) that take us through the step-by-step process of transforming our coarser energies into subtler ones. Unfortunately, westerners have a decidedly myopic view of tantric practice, usually confining it to sex; but tantric practice is intrinsically much broader in its bodily approach—there is nothing the warp and woof of tantra does not embrace.

"The rationale they [Tibetans] invoke for engaging their bodies in their spiritual pursuits is straightforward. Sounds, sights, and motion *can* distract, they admit, but it does not follow that they *must* do so. It was the genius of the great pioneers of tantra to discover *upaya*s (skillful means) for channeling physical energies into currents that carry the spirit forward instead of derailing it."[7] Whereas in Zen Buddhism stillness and quietness in the body leads to stillness and quietness of the mind and thus liberation, in Tibetan practice movement and sound can be used for the same freeing purpose. All human characteristics that can be seen as weaknesses (anger, nervous energy, depression) can be transmuted into spiritual strengths. The sheer numbers of human foibles and other energies of grander proportions have given rise, within the Tibetan tradition, to a multitude of different techniques.

Tibetan Buddhism is well known for its graded approach to enlightenment. Those 84,000 collections of teachings are matched to the human condition according to traits, energies, tendencies, and so on, and ordered in particular sequences to direct us to a life and death (reincarnation is a central armature upon which the teachings are molded) free from the bondage of suffering. There is a systematic and linear approach to Tibetan practice—baby steps, then a walking pace, then strides. Rimpoche began, of course, at the beginning and he did it with all the enthusiasm a toddler could muster for such serious business. Before he was sent to Drepung Monastery, Rimpoche lived with a learned teacher for two years of preliminary study. There he studied Lam Rim (literally "graded path"), the beginning teaching in the Gelug school, to which Rimpoche belongs—there are four main schools within the Tibetan system, Nyingma, Kargyu, Sakya, and Gelug. Bon, the pre-Buddhist Tibetan tradition, is often included in the mix because it shares common traits with the previous four.

In the evenings, young Rimpoche (he was only four years old) would meditate facing his teacher's room. "The guy to the left was from northern India and had a body odor. Tibetans don't have much body odor. So you get this huge strong smell from that side and he's sitting there in the posture and won't even move. And I look to my right and the business guy sits hunched over and maybe he's drooling," Rimpoche recalls, laughing. "No matter what you did, they wouldn't move, and I kept thinking we sat until midnight but it must have only been two hours, a little more. I told my teacher they may have a lot to think but I don't. And he said, 'No, you can just sit there and think, "Guru is Buddha, Buddha is Guru, Guru is Buddha, Buddha is Guru." Don't say the words, but keep on thinking them, and then move to "life is precious, very precious," and then "difficult to find, difficult to find, easy to lose, easy to lose, impermanent, impermanent." ' "

At age six, Rimpoche moved to Drepung Monastery, where he began to memorize the root texts and work on speed reading, so he could quickly read and absorb volumes of sacred texts. His previous incarnation belonged to the speed-reading group and, according to the Tibetan system, he naturally continued that track. From there, Rimpoche moved to the debate system and the logic system. Getting a start on the spiritual journey in infancy, particularly in such earnest fashion, is a rare process in the modern world and creates an entirely different teacher-student paradigm from that found in the West. Gehlek's many managers, attendants, and teachers (this entourage was common to a young incarnate lama) became his extended family, most taking, in some fashion, the role of parent— though he remained close to his mother and father and had frequent contact with them.

With nearly ten thousand monks in residency at its height, Drepung Monastery (the largest in Tibet and located in the capital, Lhasa) was part kindergarten, part boarding school, part religious temple and university. Buddhist teachings were entwined with the lessons of daily living in a highly structured way. "When I was a kid, I was badly beaten by my manager, by my attendant, by my teacher, because that's how kids, especially young lamas, were disciplined in Old Tibet," Gehlek writes. "It was not right, but it was what people did. I used to get all kinds of bruises. Sometimes when I rode a horse, I had to stand in the stirrups. My last beating might have been at the age of seventeen."[8]

For us here in the West this may seem outrageous, particularly in the present-day climate of religious scandals and abuses. Yet, without excusing the abuses, we must consider the cultural context. Tibetan Buddhism grasps its cultural roots tightly. In Tibet there was no separation of church and state, and as a population in exile, Tibetans have a strong desire to preserve their heritage in its native form. They will always have a different view of their religion than we do here in the West, and rightly so. Gehlek is savvy enough to recognize that his treatment was harsh within the modern Western paradigm, yet he approaches it differently.

"I never thought those people abused me, and I don't think I carry the scars of that today," he continues. "I certainly never thought I was a bad person or unworthy because they beat me. Don't put yourself down because something bad has happened. The bottom line is that the life the Buddha had is the same life that you and I have today. There is no difference in capability or body or mind. Only effort makes the difference."[9]

At age fourteen, Rimpoche's keen mind hit its stride. "When I reached the end of the Vinaya study [rules of discipline concerning the monastic vows], I began to think, and as soon as I began to think, I reached the top level of my class, immediately," he told me. He began teaching younger students, but soon everything changed. When the Chinese invaded, he escaped from the monastery to save his life, traveling with a group of other refugees. They were subjected to deadly strafing by Chinese planes along the entire route to the Indian border. When they reached the seemingly insurmountable Himalayan range, they sought advice from Rimpoche, the only incarnate lama in their ranks; he was nineteen years old. "I sat there and looked at the situation. I don't know if it was a coincidence or the effects of a flu shot or common sense, but I saw the range had four peaks, and I thought we should zigzag across to the farthest one on the right. So I happened to be the one to suggest that route, and the people began to follow me," Rimpoche said in his understated way. Tens of thousands of Tibetan refugees used that route in the decades that followed.

Rimpoche's sudden arrival in the bustling modern world of New Delhi was, in his words, "like being picked up by a helicopter in the seventeenth century and carried over and dropped in the twentieth century." Much of what he left behind he would never see again, including his parents. Because Rimpoche's family held high status (they were like the Rockefellers of Tibet), his mother and father were singled out by the Chinese as "troublemakers" and they were arrested and tortured, eventually dying untimely deaths. Rimpoche has shown an amazing resilience in the face of such horrors.

"Thanks to my teachers, to the training they transmitted to me, my struggle with anger has been much simpler than it might have been. Anger didn't overwhelm me. But I did notice a little hitch later on. I didn't have a problem with the Chinese in general, but in 1998, on my first trip to China, I discovered I had a problem with Mao. When I changed money to Chinese yuan, I saw Mao's picture on every single bill. The thought of putting his face in my pocket gave me the creeps. It was a strange feeling. Under the circumstances, I had to forget about Mao. In order not to be bothered ever again by the idea of Mao's image in my pocket, I took refuge in patience. Patience here means exactly this: not submitting to hatred."[10]

When Rimpoche gave up his robes, it wasn't taken lightly. "It was disgraceful—a very bad thing for me. However, it might have helped a little bit to understand the American life and what people go through," he exclaimed. Yet he found the dharma was not something that could be switched on and off with the flick of a wrist or the shaky feelings of doubt. "Buddhist practice was such a part of my life that it didn't matter whether I believed it or not," he said. The "practice," for Rimpoche, was no longer something he performed, it had become who he was.

In fact, even during his years of personal struggle he never stopped his practices or ceased studying with his many teachers, such as Lingstang and Trijang Rimpoches—the senior and junior tutors of the Dalai Lama. Nor did he alter his dedication to preserving and promoting Tibetan culture through his work with Tibet House—editing, translating, and publishing nearly two hundred rare Buddhist manuscripts, works that would have been lost but for his efforts. His teachers, to their credit, never lost faith in their wayward student. "First, when I was running crazy, my teachers asked me what I had found, was it something wonderful. They were sort of half-joking and half-serious, trying to bring me back to my senses. But they did it in an extremely gentle way—never, ever, trying to drag me back, always joking."

Rimpoche has continued that light approach to teaching, but he has needed to invent a practice form for lay students who are often saddled with householder chores and the frenetic distractions of the Western world. The upheaval in Rimpoche's life has taught him a great deal of flexibility. "Adapting is not that difficult, provided you don't have so much pride," Rimpoche told me. "Pride is the problem—you know, 'I'm the king! I'm the king!'—that sort of thing. But if you let go of that, then it's not too hard."

"One of the things Rimpoche does marvelously well is help Western students develop serious practice in the midst of complex and busy lives," Aura offered. "He's much more interested in people putting in a steady effort over a long period than in some kind of heroic sit-on-your-cushion-sixteen-hours-a-day-and-then-go-mad thing or running away from your home, your job, and your family in the name of dharma." Tony adds, "One of Rimpoche's favorite phrases is 'Don't fly in the air; walk on the ground.' Rimpoche talks about being a good person, a kind person. Before you can hope to be a bodhisattva—the mystic, flying in the air—you have to start at square one. Rimpoche is always saying how important a job it is being with one's family and attending to life in society, attending to the household, to parents and children—being normal."

Rimpoche is very traditional when it comes to the formal aspects of the Tibetan practice, although he recognized early on that the teachings on the guru-disciple relationship (particularly the devotional qualities), which is a major component of Lam Rim (the starting point for all students), is, for westerners, best postponed until practitioners have gained a fair amount of experience. "I hold back for a long time because of the guru scandals and all kinds of things. In the Eastern culture you don't talk about scandals, but in the Western culture you only talk about the bad things that happened, the dirty laundry. So that is the reason I don't talk about the guru-student relationship until a long, long time," Rimpoche told me.

When it comes to offering Buddhist teaching, Rimpoche is exemplary in his explication; he breathes life into the ancient words. He makes the teachings real through his interpretations and insights and also through the way he embodies them in daily life, which, perhaps more than anything else, helps impart the Buddha's message directly to the Jewel Heart community. Rimpoche has loaned students money, let them live at his house rent-free for months while they recovered from a bout of depression or an illness, cooked for them, and the list goes on. He has shown his students uncomplicated kindness, treated them as friends. When Supa first came to Jewel Heart after years of study with a foreign Zen teacher, he was burned out with the "I am the master, you are the student" model, and Rimpoche, sensing his discomfort, invited him over to his house and made him dinner, and that plain act of treating Supa as an equal had a profound impact. "If Rimpoche had been a plumber, I would have taken up plumbing," Supa stated plainly. "You know the Dalai Lama once advised, not to me personally, but he said you should begin the dharma as a discussion rather than a teacher-student relationship," Rimpoche said. "I took that to heart. I start always with a discussion."

Guru devotion within this style of teaching is not absent; on the contrary, many of Rimpoche's students demonstrate strong devotional attitudes, but they have a decidedly democratic flavor. "In the beginning I saw everything that Rimpoche did as something that helped people, and as an expression of skillful means," Aura said when I asked her about the devotional aspects of her practice. "What I would say now is that my devotion has gone to a deeper place. I can't say that everything Rimpoche has ever done has helped people. I don't know. What I can say is that I have been profoundly helped by the relationship I have with him—a relationship that is fundamentally about love and awakening the wisdom of the heart. Within the Tibetan tradition, you are encouraged to see the teacher as fully awakened, but it's not just the teacher you see this way. Your own deepest nature is understood to be no different from the teacher. Ultimately every being, and, in fact, every atom of existence, is seen as an expression of full awakening. In my case the relationship with a teacher has been central to opening my heart and mind in this way."

It is always fruitful to explore our motivations for studying with a teacher and doing a practice. The *idea* of devotion changes to the *act* of devotion, but only through honest examination. We then, slowly, make spirituality our own. "Rimpoche will remind us of the importance of motivation, what you expect to gain. You're here because you want to be benefited—good old Americans—'What can I get out of it?' My process boils down to not trying to sort out Rimpoche's motivations, but recognizing my own," Kathy told me. Our "noble" reasons for being "spiritual" are never black and white. They always include an array of emotions that run the gamut from exalted to base. The teacher is a mirror for our motivations, and the community has much the same function. We are often thrown together with people we would never mingle with in our "regular" life. Community rubs down our jagged edges.

In Buddhism, one of the three treasures (Buddha, Dharma, and Sangha) is community (Sangha). It shows us—and this is a recurring theme in previous chapters, but one that cannot be emphasized enough—that spiritual practice is never an isolated event; it teaches us connection and humility. Above all, it teaches us the constancy of change. A healthy community is always changing, always wrestling with identity, personality, function. Some students wonder if the Jewel Heart group is put together too loosely, while others bristle at any defined boundaries. People don't get along, jealousies arise—all great opportunities to learn more about who we really are. "There was a period of time in the early days that I thought people wanted me out of the way because they imagined this would give them more access to Rimpoche," Aura recalled. "And I felt really hurt. Here I was doing everything I could to bring Rimpoche to people, and what kind of thanks was I getting in return? This gave me a great opportunity to reflect on the meaning of generosity. Expecting appreciation or gratitude meant my giving had a lot of strings attached. I wanted to open to the experience of giving freely without hope of reward. Sangha held up this precious mirror."

The "practice" of being a student is always unfolding. Inquiry is never unfashionable. Sandy is still questioning aspects of the tradition. "You know, I've been doing this practice for a long time according to tradition and then I've had all these life experiences and sometimes there are conflicts between the two. I'm in an ancient tradition, but I'm also of another culture. The Buddha taught not to blindly believe his words, but you must experience it yourself and ask questions and use all your faculties as if you were buying gold; you've got to test it and rub it and make sure for yourself that it is real and authentic," Sandy said. Authentic questions are always part of practice. If inquiry is completely discouraged, run the other way.

Rimpoche teaches on many different levels, formally through textual analysis and interpretation, through description of visualization and meditation, through assigning mantras and bowing practice, and empowerments. He teaches casually, giving the medicine of the daily, yet his lessons do not always come candy-coated and easy to swallow. Because Rimpoche is such a likable fellow and his students often want to be around him, he will frequently use avoidance as a teaching tool. Hartmut traveled to Ann Arbor from Australia, where he was living at the time, for a three-month stay at

Jewel Heart in order to test the waters and see if his connection to Rimpoche was genuine. Rimpoche ignored him for the entire period of his stay.

"It was just before I left and he said, 'Oh, when are you leaving?' I said, 'In a few days,' and he said, 'Wow, why didn't you tell me? I'm sorry; we must get together.' Don't tell me he didn't know what was going on. Then we had a dinner with everyone and he said, 'It was nice that you came. Now good-bye.' And, 'When are you coming back?' I said, 'I'm trying to live here,' and he said, 'Oh, if you want, that would be nice,' and nothing else. So I had to work with that. He knew why I had come, and so I had to go back and look at myself. Do I want to live in the lama's lap and be around him and do what he says? Do I want to be like a kid and he my father? Is that what a lama is supposed to do? Is that his job? No, obviously not. It confused me, it shocked me, and it hurt me. I'd come all that way and Rimpoche totally leaves me alone. But it spurred me on to realize that this is authentic, this is real, he does work with my ego, with my nature—this will help me. It actually made me come back for more."

Every student I spoke with had similar stories, though each lesson depended on their personality type; for some, Rimpoche's approach was very gentle and encouraging, for others abrupt and cutting. Kathy, who is very shy in public, had Rimpoche continually blaming her, in front of everyone, for anything that had gone wrong, even if it wasn't her fault. "It was a big Jewel Heart joke that if anything went wrong it was my fault," Kathy said. "Occasionally he would say, 'Kathy, I'm sorry I'm being so mean to you,' and I would say, 'Rimpoche, you are not being mean. You're helping me,' and he would say, 'No, Kathy, I'm being mean to you.' " Supa, when he had been a practitioner for many years and had developed a little spiritual hubris, was expecting to be given an important job during a large retreat and was asked by Rimpoche in front of the whole assembly to catch the flies that were buzzing around everyone's heads and causing distraction.

"Rimpoche is tremendously skillful in setting up situations for people to discover where they are stuck. I like to think of Rimpoche in two ways: He's this amazing mirror which exaggerates a student's good and bad qualities. And he's also like the center of a cyclone, all quiet and powerful, but we in our stuckness are just swirling and crashing and destroying," Kathy said. "Sometimes he'll treat you like you're the best person at Jewel Heart and sometimes he'll treat you like nothing," added Supa. "I think you'll get that sentiment from most of the people at Jewel Heart. In hindsight, looking back at those times when I felt I was being punished, it was the best possible thing he could have done at that time. It was hard to take then, but after looking back on it I was so glad he did it, and that has happened over and over again. Now when he 'punishes' me I feel blessed, and I think, 'Wow, this is good.' That's quite a change."

The emphasis is on insight gained through rigorous and long-tested experience. "Rimpoche encourages people to investigate the teachings and practices for themselves," Philip Glass explained. "He stresses intelligent faith, not blind faith." Over time, Gehlek has come full circle and developed an unshakable belief in reincarnation and accepted his role as an incarnate lama. This comes, he says, "from a deeper consciousness that lies at the heart level, a kind of pervasive understanding. Not a voice, but a comprehension coming from inside rather than outside. That's why I believe in reincarnation—not because Buddha said one should." This realization translates into a deeper way of perceiving how to live this life and die this death, in a real and palpable relationship to our inner and outer worlds.

"Traditional teachers tell us that each of us has committed every kind of good and bad action in this life or another. Bad actions lead to more suffering and to a lack of freedom, and that's why it's so important for us to correct our negative habits. Good actions lead to freedom and a good life," Gehlek writes. "That's why it is so urgent that we develop good qualities, since we are expert at making mischief."[11]

Drawing Boundaries:
Community, Cliques, and Clubs

A spiritual community serves a number of purposes. At its best it supports, in a balanced way, our emotional, spiritual, intellectual, and physical development. Broadly, it reminds us that on the most basic level we are all part of one fabric spun from the Earth—nourished by its water, sun, air, and soil. Thich Nhat Hanh's famous line "There is a cloud floating in this sheet of paper" refers to this interdependence—the clouds drop rain to the trees and then wood is turned to paper and so on. There are clouds floating in all of us.

Beyond its mystical qualities, a spiritual community has more pedestrian but no less important functions. Among other things, it is a container (it gives us context), a forceful current (in which we can be carried in the combined power of many hearts and minds), a mirror (reflecting back our own sticking points), and a metronome (it provides a stable rhythm in our lives). To maintain a spiritual practice on one's own, without the support of community, is not only very difficult, but in many cases impossible. "The form carries you when you don't have enough spirit to carry you," said Joan Chittister, referring to the Rule of Benedict and its communal function. Community creates a space to practice and the pull of regularity to keep us on track. For we cannot really learn anything, though we often wish it were otherwise, without repetition. "Entering" the spiritual life takes dedication and sweat, and usually a supporting cast.

Yet groups, as we know only too well, have their shadow sides—even groups whose purpose is noble and godly—and can cause more division than unity. They can become a crutch instead of a freeing helpmate. Trungpa Rinpoche writes, "I am willing to share my experience of the whole environment of life with my fellow pilgrims, my fellow searchers, those who walk with me; but I am not willing to lean on them in order to gain support.... There is a very dangerous tendency to lean on one another as we tread the path. If a group of people leans one upon the other, then if one should happen to fall down, everyone falls down.... We just walk with each other side by side, shoulder to shoulder, working with each other, going with each other. This approach to surrendering, this idea of taking refuge is very profound."[1]

Spiritual communities are our teachers, and as with the teacher-disciple relationship, we must hold to the realization that we are working toward interdependence, not codependence. Healthy spiritual communities are particularly unique in that their boundaries are necessarily porous and inclusive. "There are so many things in Zen training that are, in a way, artificial. We draw a box around a place in space and we ring a bell around a period of time and we call them something— zazen, *dokusan* [the private meeting with the teacher]," said Bonnie Myotai Treace, a Zen teacher and founder of Hermitage Heart. Myotai further explains:

> In *dokusan* when we're with another person and we quietly drop the barrier, consciously put nothing in between one another—what is that? To speak about it is kind of absurd. To make that something other than the bread and butter of every moment can be the folly of Zen students. Zen poetry often speaks of that moment when the med-

icine becomes sickness. The structure of training can be medicine, and then there's a moment when it can become sickness. We should realize that when we are in the grocery store or the kitchen and having a conversation that we *are* in *dokusan*, that we *are* in the "great meeting," and that the person we are with is the great teacher and the bell has rung and we need to serve.

Joan Chittister writes, "And those things in me 'born of the spirit'—meant to be idealistic, 'spiritual'—have just as many times been corrupting. I was a 'good Catholic' and so became disdainful of those who weren't Catholic."[2] When I asked Mary Anne Kingsmill (Murat Yagan's student) about the particular challenges that women face in a spiritual community, she said, "Forming cliques. They often create difficulties and you have to work at finding positive support from women and not letting the negative aspects grow and become hurtful and divide the community into separate little islands." She added that she didn't know if this was a problem for men within the community as well. I told her I thought it was. As humans we love to run in packs; they can be called cliques, clubs, organizations, or religions, and if we keep their boundaries rigid, then we've squandered important communal gifts—the act of acceptance, the need for flexibility and understanding.

The solid container that is community, however, can just as easily be the proper medicine. Before I moved to Zen Mountain Monastery for a year of residency, I had a quaint fantasy of the spiritual life: most of the time spent in quiet meditation, reading sacred books, hours of reflection, a shared respect for service. My delusion lasted a day. There existed all I had imagined, meditation, reading, and so forth, but I'd blanked out eighty-five percent of reality, namely thirty-five other personalities. "In community you're with people of different religious backgrounds, different socioeconomic backgrounds, everything across the board, even different table manners," said Kathakali (Gayatri Devi's student).

When asked what part of spiritual practice they found the most difficult, nearly every student I spoke with said "community." Whether we live in a spiritual group, attend retreats, or work out in the world, our tidy view of ourselves is continually threatened by the "other." People snore, they spend too much time in the bathroom, they have little sense of personal boundaries, they're obnoxiously self-inflated, consciously humble, and boring. How can we be "spiritual" surrounded by a bunch of jerks? we ask ourselves. I remember going into an interview with a senior teacher and complaining about one of the monks' dharma talks: "He doesn't know what the hell he's talking about." And the teacher responded, "What's that got to do with you?" It was a beautiful moment that stopped me right in my tracks. Did I have a spiritual standard? Did people in certain positions in the monastery have to act a particular way? Was I trying to get some sort of dharma money-in-the-bank by rubbing elbows with "spiritual types," or was the other person's perceived lack of "spiritual knowledge" some sort of guilt by association?

Murat Yagan posited that if a group of enlightened beings came to Earth from elsewhere in the solar system to hang out with earthlings, they probably wouldn't search out the self-defined "spiritual types." Rather they'd frequent pubs and laundromats and flea markets. If spirituality is worn like a badge, then it's just another commodity.

It takes effort to resist spiritual materialism, it takes effort to resist forming factions, especially within the rarified atmosphere of a spiritual community where emotions generally run at a higher temperature. It takes effort not to be disdainful of other sects and religious practices, not to raise ourselves above others. Like racism, these attitudes can be very subtle, and a skillful teacher will use the communal atmosphere to root them out.

But perhaps the most difficult challenge we face, particularly in this secular age, is integrating the stability and regularity of a spiritual community into the architecture of our own being—taking the monastery or the temple or the zendo with us wherever we go, making the external internal. There are many reasons people leave spiritual communities, from scandal to burnout. Occasionally though, people simply no longer recognize a community's borders. They haven't left, really, they haven't grown out of a spiritual community; it has quite naturally grown into them.

7

A BRIDGE HOME

Reverend Mother Sudha Puri

*We have, each one of us, our part to play in human
destiny, and if we are fulfilling our part, that much
of the world will be made better because of our
existence, because of our love.*[1]

—SWAMI PARAMANANDA

When Susan Schrager was fourteen years old, she had a vision of the face of Saint Teresa of Avila. Susan wasn't
raised a Catholic. In fact, she had no particular religious upbringing,
but her family, through the guidance of her mother's friend Edith,
had ongoing Friday-evening discussions on Eastern religions and
mysticism—this was in Marin County, California, at the threshold
of the sixties, and the atmosphere was ripe with spiritual yearning.
The dialogues sparked a fire in Susan, and when she read about Saint
Teresa in a high school Spanish class, she felt the passion of the mystic, as only a fourteen-year-old can, course through her veins.

Twenty-four years later she was living in La Crescenta (sixteen miles from Los Angeles) working as a vice-principal at Clark Junior High School, as a consultant on education, and teaching part-time at the University of Southern California. It was a hectic but rewarding life. Through all of this, she had kept up her interest in spiritual matters, meditating on her own, and reading in a broad variety of religious disciplines. Then one day she had an urge to connect with a spiritual community. She had heard of an ashram right up the road from where she lived. It had been there since the 1920s, her students had talked of it, said it was strange, that weird people lived there, and an eighth-grader guaranteed it was a nudist colony. During Easter week Susan went to Ananda Ashrama, as it was called, on a Thursday evening for service and sat in one of the wooden folding chairs near the front of the shrine in the temple, waiting for the teacher to come and give a talk. There was a bowl of fresh fruit as an offering and flowers and red candles. When Gayatri Devi, or "Mataji," as her students called her, the spiritual leader of the community, walked between the rows of chairs and sat down on the platform, Susan saw the face she'd seen all those years before—assuming that it was Saint Teresa. She was surprised, but not overly so. Mostly she felt as though she'd come home.

Two days later, on the Saturday before Easter, Susan was in her apartment, sobbing with grief. She was saying good-bye to her life. It was quite odd, but she knew that eventually she'd be giving up her apartment, her profession, all her worldly goods and freedoms, in exchange for living in the ashrama in a small room and walking down an outside hallway to use the toilet. She had spoken to Mataji that first evening and had been invited to return the next day, on Good Friday, for a private interview. Susan had told Mataji about her vision during that meeting and asked for a blessing. "You don't need my blessing," Mataji had said. "You have my love." When Susan heard those words, she was touched, but there was something beneath them that pulled against some part of her that she hadn't felt in years. There are times when we think we have complete control over our lives, but then we are shown otherwise.

Srimata Gayatri Devi, who died in 1995, was a successor of Swami Paramananda (1884–1940), who founded the Vedanta Centre in Boston in 1909. Swami Paramananda (Swamiji) was a disciple of Swami Vivekananda (1863–1902), who represented Hinduism at the Parliament of Religions at the Chicago World's Fair in 1893. Vivekananda became the spokesperson for, and the shining example of, the Hindu religion and Indian culture—particularly in relation to Vedanta philosophy—as he traveled throughout turn-of-the-century America. He later founded the Ramakrishna Order (contained within the larger vehicle of Vedanta), which Swamiji passed on to Mataji.

Vivekananda's teacher, Sri Ramakrishna Paramahansa (1836–1886) is considered one of the greatest Indian sages of all time. He worshipped the mother goddess Kali and taught that all paths, all religions, lead to God. He considered his wife, Sarada Devi or "Holy Mother" (1853–1920), to be his spiritual equal, and she continued to teach his disciples long after his death. "Ramakrishna simply responded to the stream of Ultimate Consciousness, which has no intrinsic form yet expresses itself fully through all sacred traditions and through manifest Being itself,"[2] wrote Lex Hixon. Ramakrishna, particularly through his personal connection with many sacred traditions, is attributed with revitalizing Hinduism and being the centerpiece of the Hindu renaissance of the nineteenth century.

Within months of that first meeting, Susan Schrager was initiated by Mataji into this storied lineage and given the name Sudha Puri. Though her official title is Reverend Mother Sudha Puri, her students call her Sudha Ma or just "Ma." It took two years for Sudha Ma to leave her apartment. Mataji wouldn't accept any monastic without the blessing of their parents—no matter the age of the aspiring disciple. Though Sudha Ma's mother was excited about her daughter's spiritual quest, her father was adamantly against it. Why give up a very good profession—which she admittedly loved—and the respect of her peers and relinquish her apartment for a complete unknown? her father asked.

Ramakrishna's lineage is Bhakti Yoga, in which the student develops a deep devotional attitude toward the Divine. By extension, those devotional qualities naturally and frequently permeate the guru-disciple relationship. Though Ramakrishna taught that all religious paths lead to the same end, he "never implied that we should ignore the diversity of spiritual moods and their contrasting cultural expression."[3] He was in no way advocating a New Age mix—which so often muddies more than it clarifies—but an appreciation for and recognition of each path's particular and powerful attributes. Every religious path has its own flavor and shape. In Vedanta the essential teachings are based on three texts, the Bhagavad Gita, the Upanishads, and the Brahma Sutra. Devotees practice various forms of worship *(puja)* that often involve meditation, chanting (mantra), the reading of scriptures, food offerings *(thaal)* to deities *(murtis)*, prostrations, and devotional song *(kirtan)*.

Out of all the teacher-student bonds presented in this book, the Bhakti path is the classic guru-disciple example—it's what we think of when we think of Hinduism and yogis, what we view as both the "highest" spiritual relationship attainable within that tradition and the one that, conversely, we assume is most prone to abuses. In fact, it was Vivekananda whose model became the window, for us in the West, through which Hinduism and its various practices were seen and continue to be perceived. The Hindu guru-disciple model, except for a few notable blips on the screen, has been, for thousands of years, no more abusive—and quite a lot less so in most cases—than any other spiritual teacher-student relationship. In Bhakti Yoga the teachings state that God-guru-Vedas (scriptures) are all one, yet, particularly within the Ramakrishna Order, it is made clear that devotion is always focused on the Divine and never on personality, whether channeled through a guru, a mantra, a song, a deity, or any other vehicle.

Five months after their initial meeting, Sudha Ma found herself alone with Mataji at a local Thai restaurant. She was nervous. Generally an easy and confident conversationalist, Sudha Ma had been continually tongue-tied in her teacher's presence. Often when a student has a strong connection with a teacher, their usual ways of being, their habituated patterns, are jolted, laid bare, and it can be an uncomfortable process of adjustment. After ordering food, Mataji finally broke the silence. "She said, 'First of all, I'd like you to speak on the platform,' and I said, 'I have nothing to say. How can I speak on the platform?' and she said, 'You'll have something to say. Don't worry about it,'" Sudha Ma told me, smiling at the memory. "So that was scary and that conversation went on for about thirty-five seconds. Then more silence and then the next thing she said was, 'You have a very important role to play,' and in order to prolong this conversation I said, 'Oh, what?' Thinking in my mind, 'All right, I have my doctorate in educational psychology, school law, school administration, they have two schools in India, maybe I could help there, or maybe she's thinking I could sell books in the library, that would be good, I'd like to do that.' And Mataji said, 'I think of you as my successor.'"

In Vedanta, as with most Hindu traditions, when a student becomes a guru's disciple through formal initiation—given a new name, a mantra, and other instructions—the bond created transcends time. "The teacher, in our lineage, through the initiation process is committed to seeing the student through till final illumination, no matter how many lifetimes it takes," Sudha Ma said. "It's a very great obligation on the part of the teacher to do this, and the teacher is responsible in a karmic way at that point for every mis-step and imperfection in guidance." The responsibility, however, is—in a sense—a shared one because through initiation the stu-dent is not only creating a lasting connection with her teacher, but she is simultaneously tying a knot with the entire lineage. In turn, the teacher relies on the lineage for strength, guidance, and nourishment.

The Ramakrishna Order, as with Zen and Tibetan Buddhism and other mystical traditions, places a strong emphasis on spiritual ancestors, yet it differs slightly in its approach. Because of the order's devotional qualities, its interaction with lineage is much more active and present in a teacher's daily relationship to the world. Swamiji was never absent in Mataji's life after his death. Through prayer, she was in continual contact with her teacher, as well as Vivekananda, Ramakrishna, and Sarada Devi. The lineage was by no means simply historic. For Mataji, it was a direct and ever-present connection that she'd use as a "real-time" spiritual re-source to consult on decisions affecting students and the guidance of the ashramas. In studying with Mataji, you were also studying with the other great sages in the order—as they say in Zen, "meet-ing the ancestors eyebrow to eyebrow."

"Vedanta teaches that the soul is immortal, and when it sheds the body at 'death,' it simply proceeds to another plane. There 'free souls,' those who have been spiritually liberated during this life, can succor beings on that plane or on Earth, without limitations of the physical body or the personality. In the years since Paramananda's passing, many people have claimed to have been physically cured or emotionally helped through his intercession."[4]

Each teacher within the order is unique. They have their own personalities and teaching styles, yet it is explained from the start of the guru-disciple relationship that spiritual guidance passes *through* the teacher to the student and not *from* the teacher to the stu-dent. When Mataji left her body, and Sudha Ma became her successor, many of Mataji's disciples remained dedicated to their teacher. If you visit either of the Vedanta Centre's (the umbrella organization that Sudha Ma now heads) two ashramas (one in Cohasset, Massachusetts, one in La Crescenta, California) you will find a mix of both Mataji's students and Sudha Ma's students, though there is no prominent distinction between the two. Gordon Burnham (Jaidev), who became a student of Mataji's shortly after he met her in 1974, explained it this way: "I'm still Mataji's student. However, when Sudha Ma was empowered by Mataji, she took on the spiritual connection and power that flows through the whole lineage. Although I was not initiated by Sudha Ma, and she is not my guru in that sense, she is the open channel for my guru, who is the open channel for Swamiji, who is the open channel for Ramakrishna. My relationship with Sudha Ma is one of respect for that same channel of consciousness that Mataji held."

"Consciousness . . . transmitting only to Consciousness"[5] is the way Ramakrishna described the essential makeup of the guru-disciple relationship. Rita Burnham (Ravipriya), Jaidev's wife, came to the order through an instantaneous and deep connection with Swamiji after reading his biography. "I first felt that Swamiji was my teacher and that I was born at the wrong time," she told me. "It was very confusing and felt bizarre, but all I knew was that my heart was touched in a way it had never been touched before." When Ravipriya met Sudha Ma—after developing her connection with Swamiji—she was initially unsure as to the roles the different teachers should play in her life. Over time she came to understand that Swamiji was her *ishta* (ideal), the one to whom she prayed, and Sudha Ma was the successor whom she could connect with through personality and tangible presence. Ravipriya eventually became Sudha Ma's student, but often, through Sudha Ma's encouragement, prays to Swamiji for guidance.

"When I initiate a person, I give them the placing of Sri

Ramakrishna, Vivekananda, Paramananda, and Mataji. So they are not my pupils; they belong to the whole lineage of which I happen to be the dharma holder and spokesperson," Sudha Ma explained. Single-pointed devotion to the guru within this scenario is framed within the broad backdrop of lineage and the act of accepting its guidance. Spiritual power is attained through surrender, not through the accumulation of esoteric knowledge or mystical acts of grandeur. "A clear expression of Ramakrishna's intensely childlike attitude was his powerlessness, his refusal to perform miracles by exerting psychic and spiritual powers to which he could have had access. 'It is all up to the Mother,' he would ecstatically proclaim, 'I am simply Her child.' "[6]

The act of surrendering to the Divine is a central characteristic of the Ramakrishna Order. When Mataji was attending the second annual Snowmass Conference (Mataji was a founding member of the gathering that was convened by Father Thomas Keating to promote interreligious dialogue; it has been continuing for twenty years now), she was asked, along with the entire group, which spiritual practices had been the most effective in her life. "Surrender," was Mataji's reply. "Complete acceptance of what is happening in the moment," she said. Mataji was renowned for her warm and loving acceptance of everyone who crossed her threshold.

"Mataji—and it could happen across a crowded room—would look at you, right into your soul, and in that looking you knew that you were completely and unconditionally loved and accepted as you were," Sudha Ma told me. "You could be an axe murderer or completely self-righteous or whatever, she simply loved you." She embodied in many ways the Cosmic Mother figure that Ramakrishna held in such esteem. "Mataji was never attached to personalities," said Kathleen Hollum (Kathakali), one of Mataji's monastic students. "She had such a connection to God, and that's where she lived continually. I watched her go through serious illnesses and an auto accident and she never lost that bond with the Divine and to Swami Paramananda's work." It is no surprise that Reb Zalman and Timothy Leary chose Mataji's ashrama for their spiritual experiment with LSD; to them it was one of the warmest, safest, and most accepting places they could ever find.

When Mataji initiated Sudha Ma into the lineage, she gave her the practice of surrender and told her it was the most difficult one of all. It's tricky work, surrender—particularly within the context of the guru-disciple relationship in an order that sees no difference between God and guru. Sudha Ma:

> We all thought that everything Mataji did was spiritual. We were in love with her, so we were unquestioning. That's the danger of a spiritual relationship if you have an unethical teacher. In our tradition we're not after big followings. It's a very intimate practice. The whole reason for the ashrama is for the students to live with the teacher. We were all lucky here because we arrived with a lot of spiritual practice under our belts and we were so ripe that if we hooked up with an unethical teacher we still would have given our all. There is such a great danger in it, and we are so fortunate that our lineage is very pure so that we weren't taken advantage of. It wasn't until much later in my relationship with Mataji that I was able to distinguish between her personality and her inner spirit, to see that she's human. She is the most magnificent and extraordinary human being I've ever met, but she is human and she has foibles just as everyone does.

If there is an attraction to a teacher, a student shouldn't be frightened of that pull—how else can we learn?—but connection doesn't mean giving up our sovereignty. "Both Mataji and Swamiji encouraged people to test the guru, to not be blind. It wasn't like we were being asked to accept anything without question," Jaidev said. "I trusted my feelings enough to know that what Mataji offered was always benign. In fact, my trust in her minimized my response to other scandals because I didn't understand them. I had a real pain in my heart when I heard of the abuses with other gurus because I knew the teachings were pure. Mataji would say, 'A teacher, even a realized teacher, can fall at any point; if teachers believe they are immune to mistakes, then they're already off track.' "

Kathakali had no concept of what a guru should be, but like Jaidev she trusted her gut. If we can simply get out of our own way—beyond our projections and neurotic desires—and go with our instincts, nine times out of ten they'll be correct. "I just knew I was very attracted to what Mataji had to say and who she was," Kathakali told me. "When I look back on it, I would be very satisfied just sitting in the living room with thirty other people and watching her eat her dinner. The most important thing for me was living with her and seeing how she lived her life, above and beyond anything she ever said."

There are words that roll off the tongue in spiritual communities with an ease that is troubling—*humility, compassion, surrender, service, devotion.* We often don't really understand what our lips are proclaiming. But we should. I'm as guilty as the next person. We should know what the relationship with a particular teacher entails. We should constantly test our beliefs and our assumptions.

"I once asked Mataji what humility was," Sudha Ma recalled. "She said it's far from being servile. It's having a sense of proportion about reality and your place in that scheme; when you have that sense of proportion you are in awe. You have a willingness to do whatever needs to be done. And Mataji did everything—she cooked, she cleaned, she did bathrooms; there wasn't anything more sacred than anything else. That was our example. She served. She used to say that faith is experience, it is not belief and hope. The more you trust in the Divine, the more you see how it works."

Ramakrishna did not reject the world and its differences as meaningless. He simply saw the Divine in all existence. In the lineage there is no division between the sacred and mundane. "If someone came to Mataji and said, 'I had this most amazing dream,' she'd touch their forehead and say, 'You look pale, have you eaten?'" Sudha Ma told me. "Or someone would say, 'I had a vision of Swamiji last night,' and she'd say, 'You need a macadamia nut for *prasad* [an offering to a deity].'"

Swamiji, after founding the Vedanta Centre in Boston, opened his first ashrama in La Crescenta in 1923 and the second in Cohasset in 1929. Eventually the Boston location was closed and the Vedanta Centre headquarters was moved to Cohasset. In 1931, Swamiji opened an Indian branch of Ananda Ashrama, dedicated to the uplift and education of destitute women and children. There are now two ashramas in Calcutta that carry on the work. Originally, Swamiji opened the West Coast ashrama to escape the long, cold winters in Boston and to spread the message of Vedanta across America during his many trips by rail to and from either coast. He also was fulfilling a dream of creating a practice center closer to the rhythms of nature.

When Sudha Ma moved into the ashrama in La Crescenta, she managed to keep all her spiritual books that she'd collected in secular life and made shelves for them in her room. She liked things to be orderly and arranged her small library in alphabetical sequence by religion. Her altar was filled with favorite photos of teachers in the lineage, but she was particular and had opted for a different picture of Ramakrishna from the standard one, because she didn't like his ragged appearance in that photo. One day she returned from a trip to town and saw Mataji and another student leaving her room. They had rearranged her books according to size, and had replaced all her altar photos with ones she didn't like, including the one of Ramakrishna she had initially rejected.

"I thought, 'This is just horrible.' I could never find a book. And every morning I'd go to the shrine and think, 'Well, this is obedience,'" Sudha Ma said, chuckling as she recalled those early days. "I couldn't even look at those pictures, they were so off-putting. Finally, about six months later, I had a big rebellion. Most of the women in those days wore their hair long in honor of Mataji's Indian heritage, and it was parted in the middle. Mataji was gone in Cohasset, and not only did I cut my hair short, but I rearranged all my books and found my pictures and reconstituted my shrine, and then I waited for her to come back with great fear. I thought I was doing the most rebellious act, like the Boston Tea Party. I was so frightened, I thought I was the worst disciple, but I couldn't stand it anymore. When Mataji returned, all she did was smile and say, 'Your hair looks really nice.'"

Sudha Ma spends nine months of the year on the East Coast and visits Ananda Ashrama in California for two months in the winter and one month in the summer. The core community, both in Cohasset and La Crescenta, is relatively small, with five women monastic practitioners (only females take the monastic vows) and roughly the same number of men and women householders (students who live on the ashrama grounds but work in the secular world and do not take vows of celibacy, poverty, etc.). Householders, both male and female, and many lay practitioners take student vows, receive spiritual names, and live quite similar lives to the monastics. But generally the extended community has grown steadily since 9/11, and there is talk of adding a second service on Sundays in the Cohasset temple. Yet Swamiji's policy of no advertising or grandstanding, which he held to his entire life, still holds sway.

"We never advertise, we keep a low profile, we never charge for our teachings. They've been given freely to us and we give them freely. Our books are sold at the smallest possible price," said

Sudha Ma. "We feel very strongly that whoever will come will come and whoever we have at the time, that's the Divine intention. Mataji had spoken to two people in a New Year's Eve service, where Swamiji had five hundred. It doesn't matter. That is our path. It's quiet."

When Swamiji died and Mataji took over his role as the spiritual leader of the ashramas, she became the first Indian woman to be ordained to teach Vedanta in the West. Even though Ramakrishna devoted his life to the goddess Kali and always revered the feminine, the heads of the order, at the time of Swamiji's death in 1940, were quite uncomfortable with a woman guru and a largely female spiritual community. Just months after Swamiji's passing, they voted to discontinue their official relationship with Mataji's ashramas—they would no longer be recognized as part of the Ramakrishna Order. It was a painful blow for the thirty-four-year-old newly anointed guru, but it was just the beginning. "Mataji told me that when Swamiji left his body, someone said to her, 'He was the sun and you are like a matchstick.' For a very long time, people were tough on her," Sudha Ma told me.

As students, we often don't realize the process teachers go through—after years of arduous training as disciples—to become teachers in their own right. Even a profound enlightenment experience doesn't guarantee that a person will know how to teach. It takes hands-on training. Mataji needed time to grow into the position. The community needed time to accept her as the leader. Swamiji—even though he rarely advertised the centers or himself and kept a relatively low profile—was an internationally known and widely admired and venerated figure. After his death, Mataji stepped into an enormous vacancy filled with competing forces.

It's more than a little ironic, but none too surprising, that a number of Swamiji's students and other members of the Ramakrishna Order, whose task was to find their own spiritual center, felt so rudderless without him and even lashed out at his successor. But this reaction is not uncommon in many spiritual communities in upheaval, particularly ones with a strong devotional core. No matter the discipline, though, there are always politics, factions, infighting, and power struggles to deal with. That's why community is such a great testing ground for the application of what one has learned through meditation and prayer, ritual and service. "At some point Mataji refused to let the community make her feel miserable in her new role, and from that time on she didn't care what people said about her. But she never deviated in her behavior with the community or the order. She always treated them with respect and she never spoke badly of them, she just continued to be the same patient being," Sudha Ma said. "So patience wins out, if you don't dip to ignoble things, if you keep to the high road—that's the teaching."

When Mataji died, at age eighty-nine, Sudha Ma was faced with a similar situation. "You haven't lived until you've had to step into the shoes of someone like Mataji," Sudha Ma exclaimed. "I had a difficult time at the beginning. We all had a difficult time. Mataji was huge in our lives. Before she passed, we had no idea how we would ever live without her. In her frail state nobody wanted to hold her back, but it was a huge vacuum when she left us." Something extraordinary happened, however, when Mataji left her body. She had been in decline for some time and in need of much care, which was shared by a number of members within the community. But it was Kathakali who was continually at her side in those last months. She was holding Mataji at the time of her death. Kathakali and Sudha Ma had been very close over the years, and Mataji made it clear that she was counting on the two of them to help each other carry on Swamiji's work.

"Kathakali and I had a Pentecostal experience when Mataji passed. It was like some spirit came over us and stirred us up to incredible euphoria, literally for a couple of months. This spirit gave us so much enthusiasm and so much power that we felt no grief; I have never shed a tear for Mataji. Earlier I thought I wouldn't be able to survive her passing, so it was miraculous," Sudha Ma said. Kathakali confirmed: "I was her medical power of attorney and I thought when she moved on, maybe it would be time for me to go back into the world. Well, at the moment of her death I got such a buzz. It was instantaneous, like I had no control over my life. I'm just not the type of person [she's from a Boston working-class Irish Catholic family] who has these experiences, but the high lasted for weeks—I couldn't sleep, I couldn't eat, I had such enthusiasm for the work. All my plans of returning to the world were gone."

Ananda Ashrama comprises 120 acres in the foothills of the Sierra Madre Mountains, sixteen miles from Los Angeles. Originally a remote and rustic setting, the property's west flank is now bordered by the ubiquitous Southern California suburbs. Fortunately, much of the property opens to the steeply sloped chaparral canyons of the Angeles National Forest, and thus still feels like a quiet oasis. The semi-arid grounds are largely shaded by groves of poplar, oak, eucalyptus, palm, Himalayan cedar, acacia, and a luscious mix of evergreens. The Spanish Mission–style temple, main house, and large, two-story guest house are joined on the property by wood-sided cottages and cabins, narrow drives, a citrus and fruit orchard, and a dazzling array of colorful shrubs and flowers.

I met Sudha Ma and Kathakali and a number of other students at Ananda Ashrama in late August. Even in the summer smog, looking down the valley to the crush of homes and tangled freeways below, one could still feel the presence of something fresh and enduring. I sat with Sudha Ma in the library of the main house. Just across the large living room was Mataji's old bedroom, left largely untouched since her death. There is still a little wooden finger ladder attached to the doorjamb that Mataji used to exercise her hand after her debilitating car crash. Even though Sudha Ma had a profound spiritual transference at the time of Mataji's passing, the transition was nevertheless difficult and painful.

"Everyone suffered on different levels and in different ways," Sudha Ma told me. "So it was a great lesson for me. I had to live the life and go forward and pray and not be a big ego with big feet trampling on everyone's feelings, and I had to grow into this position and I had to grow into winning over some people. It took time, not with everyone but with some." Mataji had spent most of her last years in Cohasset, and the community at the La Crescenta ashrama had fallen into disarray. It was Sudha Ma's first real test as a leader. "There were all kinds of factions here at Ananda Ashrama. It was awful. I said, 'I don't care who you are, a monastic or a householder, whether you've been here twenty-five years or one, we're all leaving this place and giving the keys to a caretaker unless you get your act together and read Paramananda and start living the teachings again.' Luckily, they did, and most of them stayed."

"There always seems to be students, householders mostly, who have aspirations to be teachers—not consciously, maybe, but they seem to go in their own direction and get people who are disillusioned to follow them," Kathakali observed. "But I've been in community long enough to know that these episodes don't last, they blow over. When I was younger, I felt you had to protect the teachings and the teacher; there were no laws protecting them, so I thought they could get into big trouble. Now I know God takes care of them."

The most difficult transition for Sudha Ma, however, was a cultural one. Mataji had been the first Indian woman to teach in the West, and now Sudha Ma was the first American woman to carry on the tradition. On one hand, she was faced with the same dilemma as all first-generation Western teachers passing on a "foreign" spiritual discipline—that is, the ability to recognize where the skin of culture could be safely trimmed from the core of the teachings. Yet for Sudha Ma personally, the chore was simply to be herself under extreme pressure to act otherwise. "Mataji was very Indian, very grandiose. She had her own dishes and her own chair and nobody could sit in it for fear of sullying the vibrations," Sudha Ma said. "That's who she was, so refined and on a different level than we were, so it was natural for us to recognize that she needed special treatment. But I myself couldn't feign that I needed special dishes and that the chair needed to be roped off when I wasn't there because someone might accidentally sit in it. I don't mind if someone sits there; it's not going to sully my vibrations."

Not only did the community lose a revered teacher who had been their spiritual leader for fifty-five years, but her "replacement" came from within their own ranks: Sister Sudha, an American who grew up eating corn flakes and watching Walter Cronkite. It was a difficult yet beautiful lesson that forced many students to reexamine the essence of their own spiritual longings: Was their spiritual "progress" predicated on cultural standards? Did they believe that Mataji had made a mistake in choosing Sister Sudha, and if so, then what did that say about their faith and trust in Mataji? Was their entire inner life dependent on a particular guru? What does lineage really mean in the context of "losing" a teacher? Change, change, and more change, whether we recognize it or not, whether we like it or not, always forces us back to essentials.

In one of Swamiji's Sunday services he said:

Practical, practical, practical religion! That is my plea. And yet some of you say, "Why does he not give us practical teaching like the psychologists?" My friends, I am not on the market for sale, and never shall be. What are you seeking? Are you seeking

God, Truth, or do you want someone to think for you, and give you your salvation, your liberty, and your illumination? . . . It does not make any difference what you call yourself; be something that satisfies your own soul. Do not always look around to see whether your friend or your neighbor or the public approves; gain the sanction of your inmost being.[7]

Today both Mataji's students and Sudha Ma's students form a seamless group of practitioners among the two ashramas. This staying power is a testament to both Sudha Ma's leadership abilities and the strong lineage of the order. "We've all come back together again, Mataji's disciples, my younger disciples, there's no distinction among them, no separation between us," Sudha Ma explained. "Mataji's oldest and most dedicated disciples are completely supportive and loving. We always felt that Mataji wasn't the spiritual leader; she was the caretaker of these ashramas. We now have a great stake as caretakers so this place will be available to the next generation physically, emotionally, and spiritually."

What we see in the transition from Mataji to Sudha Ma is both an integration of Vedanta into American culture and an updating of the guru-disciple relationship. Mataji was of the "old school," in which gurus were perceived as more godlike and on a much higher level, as Sudha Ma explained, than us "regular folks." This model worked in its time and in its place, but within Mataji's lineage it can no longer function in the same way when channeled through an American teacher and existing in the American landscape. Mataji chose an American woman as her successor. She must have seen no essential difference between East and West, between an "American Vedanta" and an "Indian Vedanta." She used to say that spirituality was about "living the life," and she expected Sudha Ma to do just that, to live her own life, to be an American (how could she be otherwise?) and deal with this time in history. Still, the lineage is Bhakti and necessarily revolves around devotion. Sudha Ma's work is to mediate a student's devotion in the healthiest way possible.

"I find I have to reduce a student's devotional attitude so they are not dependent on me in that way. Their devotion is huge and it makes me very uncomfortable," Sudha Ma exclaimed. "The teachings state that God-guru-Vedas [the scriptures] are all one, but for a student to have me as their *ishta* [ideal] is, I think, awful for them and for me, too. I honestly don't feel swayed by somebody's devotion or when somebody tells me, 'You are Divine, you have changed my life.' I'm very grateful to God that their life has been changed, but inside I feel nothing about it. If somehow I've been used as an instrument, that's great, but I know it isn't me.

"I understand their devotion because it's the same way I felt with Mataji—that I had arrived home, that I'm accepted and loved and part of a family, and to have that unconditional love is a rare thing in life, it's a haven, so they become devoted. And maybe they've read about devotion here in our lineage, about our devotion to Mataji. So I try to be very honest and clear with them, to accept their love and their gifts and their appreciation. But the fact of the matter is that if they get caught up in personality, it's very damaging for them. So I really don't encourage that kind of devotion."

Mataji taught through sheer presence. "Her presence was such that it changed the energy in a group. She could walk into a room and do or say some simple thing and people could get so worked up. She had a way of stirring up the ego, she was a master at it," Kathakali told me. "She was very loving and she didn't like to see people suffering and she prayed for them constantly, but I think, truthfully, if it was a choice of someone being happy or moving forward on the spiritual path, then that person would just have to suffer, because Mataji's role was to move us to spiritual growth."

The role for Sudha Ma is the same, but her method is different.

"There is often sibling rivalry among the students. It's the same thing we felt with Mataji, and she encouraged it by playing off one against another. I can't play those games. It just isn't in me, I'm not smart enough or advanced enough or whatever it is. So what you see in me, that's what I am and I can't do magic," Sudha Ma said. "I can't take the role of guru as sort of a god. I'm happy to share freely. I will give you the guidance I can give you. It's just a different model, me being an American."

Sudha Ma is being genuinely modest. She has grown into a powerful teacher in her own right. In speaking with her students, I heard the same timbre of devotion and respect as is given Mataji. Warren Marr (Rishi), who was being initiated five months after my visit and who has been a part of the La Crescenta community with his wife, Diane, for eight years, said, "I've observed Sudha Ma being devoted to her ideals in an undiluted and pure manner. There's no PR agent, no big retinue; there's no desire for personal gain, there's no hint of scandal, there's no 'let's take some of my close disciples and take a ride in my Rolls-Royce.' She shows us an unadulterated practice of Bhakti, love in a pure sense."

Rose Sheldon (Lakshmi), a student of Sudha Ma's for five years, had a love-at-first-sight experience when she met her teacher. "When I first laid eyes on Sudha Ma, I knew she was my teacher, I didn't have to be formally initiated. She's like a mother that you always wanted, nourishing, loving. What I feel for her I can't put into words." Lakshmi was raised a Catholic, and for her, devotion comes quite naturally. She is still a practicing Catholic, and Sudha Ma encourages her to continue in her original faith. In fact, her practice of Vedanta has brought her closer to the Catholic Church.

Sudha Ma, like her teacher, treats each student individually. If someone arrives with a big ego, she might be tough on them, yet someone who needs nourishing will get warmth and encouragement. "Sudha Ma teaches in many different ways," Joan North

(Janapriya), a student for five years who lives at the ashrama as a householder, observed. "From the platform, in casual conversation, she makes it funny, there's psychology in there, too. And she's not just kind and compassionate and good, good, good. She can be strong, and I like that a lot."

Anyone who wants to be Sudha Ma's student must ask her for initiation. Usually Sudha Ma will spend quite a bit of time in prayer and ask for guidance from the lineage before she will give an answer. Sometimes she'll feel that the student isn't ready or that they already have a teacher—one that is in the future, the past, or the present. There is no set period for the decision to be made. It could take an hour, a day, or five years. Sudha Ma is very cautious about it and never in a rush, though the students often are. She treats everyone who comes to her with the same interest and compassion. "I don't see the distinction between souls. If someone asks me to help them or give them guidance, I will always do so, as I will with my disciples," Sudha Ma said. A student asking for initiation is actively seeking a teacher-student relationship with a little more fire beneath it. Sudha Ma: "If you live very close to the teacher, you get close to the fire and get burned. Part of becoming a student is the willingness to get burned."

Rishi was introduced to Sudha Ma by his wife, Diane. It took him eight years to ask for initiation. At first the devotional aspects of the practice were simply too overwhelming. "I had a hard time with the level of worship. I can remember a few years ago at morning service I just got up and walked out, not able to bow to anybody," he told me. "I don't know how, but I just worked through it and remained in the presence of doing it until it became normal and now I don't have a problem. My initial reaction was a visceral thing and involved my ego. Now I know there are processes that are way beyond my little world. I'm just thankful to have what little control I do have over my life. The practice is simply an acknowledgment of the Divine. It's much easier for me to give my devotion through my work and simply just by being—if I can personally embody the ideals as best I can it radiates out into the world. So for me my devotion is expressed by offering my service."

"All of us have personality problems. We are all like kinked garden hoses and the spirit of the Divine is flowing, flowing, flowing, rich and beautiful and nourishing. And here we are with a kink. Sometimes we cut it off entirely. Sometimes we have a trickle. We have a kink in our consciousness and we have parts of our personality that, as regular as clockwork, cut us off from what would make us happy and really peaceful," Sudha Ma said.[8]

"This spiritual process is like lifting up a rock and discovering something a little slimy that you hadn't thought was there," she continued. "That's what happens when you say yes to the universe. So there's a period of time when both the teacher and student must really discern and take the idea of a relationship very seriously. It's like a marriage, this guru-disciple thing, and the honeymoon period lasts only so long and then you are really into the serious work of inner transformation, of clearing debris. I never give direction to anyone about their life—should they get a new dog, should they get a new husband, a divorce, a new wife. That's not what it's about."

When I asked Janapriya, who has been involved in some type of spiritual practice for years, how her view had changed over time, she said, "Spirituality is so much more mundane than I originally thought. It is just doing the work, the ego work is nonstop. It's quite boring at times, but at least I know what's going on, so when I draw somebody close to me who pushes my buttons, I know it's me doing it." This "nothing special" attitude has been a recurring theme throughout these chapters with mature practitioners—they reach a point where all the blinding glitter and glamour of a "spiritual life" has worn away and what's left is plain life. So watch what you wish for.

I asked Rishi why after all this time he had decided to get initiated. "I never thought of having a spiritual teacher. I'm not sure I was even aware that there was such a thing in this day and age, so just over a period of time, seeing it function here and having so many friends who went through the process here, it seems like a logical next step to carry it to another level," he said. "There's a sense that maybe it will be a help in the afterlife and that it would be an absolutely incredible waste not to take advantage of this opportunity. It seems that initiation is another bit of wisdom that presents itself as an unknown in this relationship with Sudha Ma. I would just like to know more, sort of like a moth getting drawn to a flame."

Sudha Ma was put in a unique situation early in her relationship with Mataji. Within five months of meeting her teacher, she knew that she was designated as her successor. But you cannot become a teacher unless you have fully realized what it is to be a student.

"Mataji said, 'Everybody wants to be a teacher but no one wants to be a disciple.' And 'disciple' means to have a certain discipline. She said that truthfulness is extremely important in discipleship. You should be so truthful that the light of it shines until you're bare. It doesn't require the teacher to do that, but it requires desire in the student to do that, to let go of what you are hiding behind and to have humility and be willing to know you know nothing. I'm always starting from kindergarten, and I tell everybody that if you think you know and that you're pretty advanced spiritually, you've shot yourself in the foot. That sense of humility can't be simply proclaimed—'I'm humble!' You really have to pray for that position.

"In our tradition, freedom is the ingredient for growth; it is an amazingly delicate process. Vedanta embraces all paths actively. It realizes that the soul is truly the teacher and to interfere with the destiny of the soul is just not done. A teacher is simply a midwife; the creation part is up to the student and the Divine."

The Healthy Diet of Disillusionment

"Disappointment is the best chariot to use on the path of the dharma."[1]

—CHÖGYAM TRUNGPA RINPOCHE

The question is not *will* we become disillusioned by spiritual practice, it is *when.* Our disappointments can be broad and shallow or pointed and deep. Their circumference will often include the teacher, the spiritual community, and the very practice itself. Inevitably, at the beginning of the journey we have an idea of what spirituality is, but spirit can never be contained in an idea. So what we think it is and what it really is are continually at odds. We want to keep packing our bags for a trip, but in reality we need to empty the luggage and stay home.

Most disillusionment is a good sign. Like a mileage marker on the highway, it shows we are making progress. Of course, if our teacher really screws up, then that can lead to a destructive and unhealthy disillusionment, one that shrinks hearts. The type I'm talking about here is the necessary and fruitful kind; this disappointment shines a bright light on delusion. Yet the glare can burn.

My first spiritual disillusionment came almost a year after I'd left Zen Mountain Monastery, where I'd spent thirteen months in residency. I was living in nearby New York City and had decided to become Daido Roshi's student—I had been a provisional student at the monastery but hadn't formalized the relationship. I wanted a deeper connection and was required, as everyone was, to go before the Guardian Council (a group of senior monastics and senior lay practitioners) to clarify my reasons for taking such a step. It's a serious matter, and the Council was there as a test of my sincerity. The first question the group asked was *why*. Why did I want to form this relationship? I'd answer and they'd ask again. I'd answer and they'd ask again. "I want to strengthen my commitment," I said. They asked again. "I want to dig deeper into what it means to be alive!" They asked again. This went on for some time, and I kept coming up with answers that I thought would satisfy them, but nothing worked.

Then Shugen Sensei, the head monastic of the monastery, turned to me and said, "Look, John, you spent over a year here, and nobody really knows who you are." His words were like a punch to my stomach. Before coming to the monastery, I'd gone through a painful divorce and I spent the year in residency trying to heal those wounds, largely by keeping to myself, doing what was required of me but nothing more. Though I've always had a problem being emotionally available, during that period it was intensified. In many ways I'd come to the monastery to hide and had equated spiritual practice with this solitary course. For the most part, the monks and Daido Roshi left me alone during that time, realizing, I think, that I did need time to heal. But now, when I was asking to move to the next step, they were making it clear that "hiding" was not part of the practice.

The fact that I had been "trying to disappear" was pretty obvious to everyone around me, but for some reason I'd convinced myself that I was quite "open and spiritual" when I lived there. Getting "exposed" was painful. When Shugen Sensei made his statement, I just stammered, but finally broke down into honest dialogue. I drove back to New York City (a three-hour drive) with my friend Carol Dysinger, who had gone through the Guardian Council that same day. We compared notes and licked our wounds. Later she said, "Going in front of the Council is the beginning of exposing something very specific and personal. That's why it's so painful, because everything you thought was hidden is written backward across your forehead and suddenly you see it through someone else's eyes. But that is the beginning of freedom in a lot of ways." Finally my spiritual romanticism began to crumble. Spirituality had become personal.

"Disillusionment is an important part of the spiritual path. It is a powerful and fiery gate, one of the purest teachers of awakening, independence, and letting go that we will ever encounter. To be disillusioned is to be stripped of our hopes, imaginings, and expectations. But while it opens our eyes, the resulting pain all too often closes our hearts. The great challenge of disillusionment is to keep our eyes open and still remain connected with the great heart of compassion."[2]

—JACK KORNFIELD

"I often say that Zen actually provided the place for me to fail, which was what I really needed. I didn't know it at the time, but I needed my personal will broken. I had a very competitive spirit. I needed to come up against something that I couldn't win."

—ADYASHANTI

"When I first arrived in the Kebzeh community, I thought I had to throw away everything that had come before. I was so determined to be Kebzeh, I kind of stopped everything else.

It took considerable suffering to realize it didn't work that way. I had to learn there were two reasons I was here. One was that I was going to learn and receive, and the other was that I had something to offer. That, in fact, by not fully manifesting myself as best I could, I was disallowing reciprocity, and therefore I was preventing any relationship to form."

—SHARRON ALLEN (MURAT YAGAN'S STUDENT)

We are all on this train and we all want to know what's around the next corner and since we don't know—because we haven't traveled this route before—we imagine a landscape and paint in its colors, its inhabitants. But disillusionment is always headed in the same direction, straight to the heart of unknowing. Our mantra should be, "It is not about control." Adyashanti writes, "I find that the core issue that keeps human beings experiencing themselves as separate is the desire and will to control."[3] I can tell myself this fact each day, but until the tenderness and persistent ache of that truth reaches through the thick mortar of my skull, I'm never going to "get" it.

"Disillusionment in itself is not the real problem. Awareness involves breaking through illusions, which, of course, is disillusioning. Often the real obstacle is being so attached to whatever emotions or meaning the illusions were feeding that letting go of illusions feels like a loss instead of a gain. To see how one's previous good feelings contained illusion can be a bitter pill at first."[4]

—JOEL KRAMER AND DIANA ALSTAD

"Maybe life is simply a going from light to light, from darkness to darkness till the last Great Darkness signals the coming of the First Great Light. That would explain why we are in a constant state of 'disillusionment.' I have come to understand that it is not protesting what we do not like that counts. It is choosing what we do which, ultimately, changes things."[5]

—Joan Chittister, OSB

"Buckminster Fuller pointed out to us that we can't learn without making mistakes. Biologically we are programmed to learn from mistakes."

—Reb Zalman Schachter-Shalomi

"The death knell for me is any kind of spiritual perfectionism. Everything gets frozen in that; it's a shame-oriented perspective. Trying to be clear is a lot different from simply telling the truth about *not* being clear. Often the very attempt to 'get things right' is an expression of fear. In a sense, letting things go awry allows them, strangely enough, to come back into harmony."

—Laura Mackenzie (Adyashanti's student)

Dogen Zenji, the thirteenth-century Zen master, said, "Zen is one continuous mistake." Spiritual practice is not a process of building perfect castles in a row so we can have a secure place to live. We are all going to lose these bodies we currently inhabit. How do we digest this grand disillusionment?

8

UNDISCOVERED GENETICS

John Daido Loori Roshi

Less and less do you need to force things
until finally you arrive at non-action.
When nothing is done,
nothing is left undone.[1]

—Lao-tzu

Zen is simple. People get into trouble trying to make it complicated. Hundreds of thousands of pages have been written to explain it, but it drops between those words like rain through open sky. "Things change" is one way of explaining it. "Doing not-doing" is another; also "We are perfect and complete as we are right now." Zen teachers have a difficult job—to convince their students that there is nothing to gain, nothing really to look for or acquire. It's like teaching a frog to be a frog.

John Daido Loori Roshi has been teaching Zen students since the 1970s. He is the abbot of Zen Mountain Monastery (ZMM), a majestic congregation of buildings—years ago a Catholic summer camp for boys—nestled on 160 acres of gently sloping forests and meadows in the Catskill Mountains of New York. Daido Roshi (students call him "Roshi," "Daido," or "Daidoshi") is tall, lanky, olive-skinned (an Italian American from Jersey City, New Jersey), with the requisite Buddhist shaved head. Daido is seventy-three years old, charismatic; when he walks into a room, people tend to stop talking. He's telling me a story about his late Japanese teacher, Maezumi Roshi.[2]

"I'd been living at Zen Center for a number of years," he said. "The practice was hard, hour after hour of zazen (meditation) and long days working to keep the Zen Center financially secure. But I loved it and came, after time, to have confidence in my own spiritual wisdom. At some point I figured that I'd come to understand death. So during a private and casual conversation I told Maezumi I'd 'sorted out the whole death thing.' "

As Daido is telling me this story he rubs the perimeter of a sun-faded anchor tattoo on his left forearm—a remnant of his navy days—as if tracing the outline of his life. "Maezumi looked me straight in the eye and said, 'So you've figured out the great matter of life and death, have you?' Before I could answer, he leapt from his seat, knocked me to the floor, and began choking me. At first I began to laugh. I'm big and Maezumi was a little guy, so I wasn't that worried. But quickly it got very hard to breathe and I could feel the ends of his fingers pushing deeper into my windpipe. I began to choke and sputter and I realized that Maezumi was serious, so I began to struggle, but he was incredibly strong. Without thinking, I managed a roundhouse right punch to Maezumi's jaw and knocked him to the floor. He didn't stop laughing for five minutes and then said, 'Conquered death! Ha!' I had bruises on my neck for a week."

The late Shunyru Suzuki Roshi, the Japanese master who

started the first Buddhist training monastery in America and the author of the classic *Zen Mind, Beginner's Mind*, wrote: "The teaching given by Shakyamuni Buddha during his lifetime was accommodated to each disciple's particular temperament, and to each occasion's particular circumstances. For each case there should be a special remedy. According to circumstances, there should even be teachings other than those which were given by Buddha. In light of this, how is it possible to interpret and pass down an essential teaching that can be applied to every possible occasion and individual temperament?"[3]

I've been Daido's student for eight years, and have been studying at ZMM for over ten, but I've never been choked by my teacher. In the beginning I was actually a little envious of that story. It seemed the epitome of "the Zen encounter," like the ones I'd read about in the ancient texts of old Chinese masters vanquishing their disciples' illusions. My relationship with Daido has been largely quiet and gentle, though I never asserted that I had conquered death. Most of us come to a teacher with a bundle of expectations, both conscious and unconscious, about how that teacher should be, how they should act. Usually the first few years are spent dismantling those preconceived notions.

"Working with a teacher has been quite a challenge," Bear Bonebakker (Gokan) affirmed. He's been a student of Daido's for ten years. "I still feel like when I come out of *dokusan* [a private, face-to-face meeting with the teacher], what is supposed to be happening in there isn't happening. And I think to myself, 'I don't know what everyone else is doing in there, but it must be better than what I'm doing.'" And he laughs.

The overused metaphor of a Zen teacher being like a mountain guide (an experienced climber who already knows the route and its footholds), though partially true in some practical applications, can obscure a very important teacher function—to keep the student off balance. In Zen, the spiritual guide is simultaneously mapping a path up the mountain while whispering in the student's ear that no such mountain exists. "Where can I stand in all of this thin air?" the student asks. "On your own two feet," says the teacher. The large brushstrokes we use to paint the picture of the teacher-disciple relationship in the beginning later change to finer details.

"I remember in the beginning when I thought Maezumi was boring and Tetsugen[4] told me you really have to tune into the subtlety of the way he teaches. So I began to notice how much stuff I was missing in the *dokusan* room and in the talks. I was missing a lot," Daido said. Any relationship we form—with a boss, a colleague, or a spouse—takes time to deepen and reveal its richness.

There's a refrain (almost a lament) at ZMM: "Daido never gives you anything." It echoes throughout every aspect of the training at the monastery, but most particularly it rises in response to the teacher-student encounter in *dokusan.* It is in this meeting, perhaps more than any other within the Zen structure, where the spiritual relationship between master and disciple is nurtured, tested, deepened, and continually redefined. It is a cave of mirrors and it is where, many students attest, Daido's genius shines. Yet it is very hard to describe; it's mysterious.

"Every time I've gone into *dokusan,* my heart has been in my ass because I was terrified," said Michael Grody (Yukon). He's a monk at ZMM, has lived there for over eleven years, and has been practicing there for over twenty. "For all these years, after every single *dokusan* I feel like something has happened, but I just don't know what it is. There is something that goes on in that room that is like no other relationship I have."

Carol Dysinger (Kyoryu) observed: "I had a sense that if I could figure out a way to walk into that *dokusan* room and tell the truth, my life would be much better. I felt that Daido wanted me to be able to do that, he was on my side but he wasn't going to open the door for me, and he wasn't going to move my mouth for me." Kyo-ryu has been a lay student of Daido's for eight years.

I asked Daido how he deals with a student's expectations and idealizations. "I don't consciously navigate anything. That's not my way of working. It's intuitive, and I'm always responding to the circumstances that are present in the moment. I never second-guess people. I never address what I see. I only address what they say, which is their reality, not my reality. I try to work with their reality." Shugen Sensei, Daido's student, second dharma heir, and a teacher in his own right, said, "You have to trust in the dharma and the students' ability to realize it themselves. For me it's not a personal thing. The most important thing I can do as a teacher is make it *not* about me. Because then, regardless of what happens to me, the student's relationship with the dharma will be strong and my relationship with them will be clear and straightforward—it's basically a meeting about the dharma. It's not a complicated relationship."

The *dokusan* room is just off the zendo (meditation hall), and its location defines much of its procedural function. The student brings all that arises in zazen (which literally means "seated meditation")—the problems and the understanding, the insights, confusions, sticking points—into the private interview with the teacher. Zazen is the bedrock of Zen training. "Thus they sit, hour after hour, day after day, year after year, seeking to waken the Buddha-mind so they may later relate it to their daily lives," wrote Huston Smith.[5] At ZMM, new students usually start by counting their breath during zazen—inhale one, exhale two, and on up to ten and then starting over, trying not to get lost in thought (which is extremely difficult). The next step is to take up either koan practice or *shikantaza.*[6] Zazen is where the Zen student reconnects, through stillness, with the "beingness" of the world, but there is much in the mind that gets in the way—boredom, lust, anger, and so on. If the Zen teacher can be likened to a doctor (the Buddha himself is often referred to as the Peerless Physician) then zazen is the body cavity of Zen practice. It is the teacher's entry point, both solid and ephemeral, where patterns, proclivities, and the rigid tendencies of the self are found.

"Zen's object is to infuse the temporal *with* the eternal—to widen the doors of perception so that the wonder of the *satori* experience [a mystical opening or awakening] can flood the everyday world. . . . The life of Zen . . . does not draw away from the world; it returns one to the world—the world robed in a new light. We are not called to worldly indifference, as if life's object were to spring soul from body as piston from syringe. The call is to discover the satisfaction of full awareness even in its bodily setting," writes Smith.[7]

This "awareness" is what the Buddha realized one night 2,500 years ago under the bodhi tree, and later called the Four Noble Truths. The First Noble Truth is that life is suffering—that is, everything in this world is impermanent, transitory (things change and we find this troubling). The Second Noble Truth is that the cause of this suffering is desire, namely the desire to pull away from the reality of impermanence, to separate ourselves from life. The Third Noble Truth states that there is a way to end our suffering, to be released from our separateness. The Fourth Noble Truth describes the steps required to end our suffering and is called the Eightfold Path: Right View, Right Intention, Right Speech, Right Action, Right Livelihood, Right Effort, Right Mindfulness, and Right Concentration.

The Buddha first transmitted the dharma to his disciple Mahakasyapa. In what is known as the Flower Sermon, the Buddha—in front of his assembly of monks—silently held up a lotus flower and Mahakasyapa smiled. That's it, the smile, the flower; this exchange designates the first transmission of the Buddha's teachings, the first turn of the dharma wheel. Mahakasyapa heard no words but simply understood, simply realized, when seeing the flower, the "satisfaction of full awareness."

As the Zen lineage unfolded, this "transmission" repeated itself down through the years in a feast of experiences. Awakenings came at the sound of a pebble hitting bamboo, at the sight of a teacher holding up a finger or a stick or waving a fan; it came from a shout, from a sob, from silence, or from a teacher's hands on a student's throat. When it did come from words, they were stitched together in such a way as to confound the intellect. "Things as it is," said Shunyru Suzuki when asked about the meaning of Zen.

Yet what is it that passes from master to master, from teacher to student? Daido likens the process of Zen transmission to his own family bloodlines. "Many of the things Maezumi passed on live in his disciples," he explained. "I can say the same thing about the qualities of my father. I hardly knew him [Daido's father died when he was eight], but I believe it when people tell me that I'm like my father. With my teacher it's not a genetic thing, it's mind to mind. But what passed between us, between Maezumi and myself, has, I think, an as-yet-undiscovered genetics all its own."

All of this talk about "transmission" is a little confusing because it sounds as though something is actually given to the student by the teacher. The answer is yes and no. Daido explained it this way: "The Chinese master Yunyan taught the dharma to Dongshan, who became a brilliant teacher. In various koans there would be three monks, and Yunyan would always be the one who wouldn't get it, or he was the one who came across the worst. I said to Maezumi that Yunyan doesn't seem very clear, and I asked him if he thought this was so, and he agreed with me. Yet Yunyan produced this extraordinary successor who completely outshines him. It's un-believable. How does this happen? It happens because if the teacher is successful, he or she awakens in the student what is inher-ently there. That's why we call it 'the wisdom that has no teacher.'

That wisdom doesn't come from someone else, it comes from within. At best a good teacher is a good facilitator rather than a conveyor of knowledge. This is important because it protects the dharma from individual personality flaws."

This is particularly pertinent to Daido's situation as well, because his teacher, Maezumi Roshi, was—depending on whom you talk to—an alcoholic or had, on occasion, a problem with alcohol. He also had a number of sexual liaisons with students. These admissions rose to the surface in 1984 and caused many in the Zen Center of Los Angeles community to leave. Daido himself was living in New York and working on establishing ZMM as a training center so he missed the heart of the storm, but it still affected him a great deal.

"What Maezumi taught me was to trust myself, to trust zazen," he says. "And that's what I teach my students. I cannot stress this enough: students must trust themselves. I really have nothing to give them. Maezumi gave me nothing. This doesn't cancel out the fact that his drinking was destructive; it caused a lot of problems. He admitted everything, apologized deeply, and checked himself into the Betty Ford clinic. For me that was good enough. Enlightenment is simply a way of understanding the nature of the self and the nature of the universe; it's not a prophylactic against anything ever going wrong. To me, ethical guidelines are very clear: follow the precepts. A teacher needs to practice what they preach. But no matter the situation there needs to be, in Buddhism, some place for forgiveness, some place to correct, to redress the wrong, and I think the precepts and moral and ethical teachings provide for that. The problem is we're a society that is so damn unforgiving."

Though it may seem that transmission of the lineage happens in a moment, it is really a long process. "In a very real sense transmission is always taking place, particularly being in residence all those years and sitting every day," Shugen Sensei told me. He received transmission (conferring upon him teacher status) from Daido ten years ago. Though the process is gradual, the "moment" of his "final" transmission (called *shiho*) is codified in a highly ritualized ceremony that has both private and public components. "*Shiho* is very dramatic," Shugen Sensei said. "The process itself is full of drama, the liturgy, the oral teachings that are taking place—some of the teachings that are handed down from teacher to teacher are only done at that time—visiting the altars and doing hundreds of bows each day to the lineage. Like a lot of parts of the training, you are aware that something is happening, but I was also aware that there was a great deal happening that would only become clear over time."

I mentioned this in the previous chapter, but it bears repeating: teachers don't become teachers overnight because they suddenly receive a new title. "Even with the finality of the ceremony, it has taken time to grow into this role. I would say that these last ten years have probably been the most fruitful period of my whole training, to have studied so deeply and intensely and exhaustively with Daido and then suddenly not have everything so clearly defined. It was difficult but also exhilarating. Now I can turn my attention to those things that were really calling me," Shugen Sensei said.

Losing his father at such a young age was understandably difficult for Daido, but that sorrow was, in large measure, the force that planted the seed of his spiritual seeking. This great loss and his upbringing—overseen by his mother and grandmother, in a tight-knit Italian Roman Catholic community—gave his spiritual inquiry a communal and cloistered context that, not surprisingly, manifested in his affinity with the monastic form. At the age of sixteen, in large part to escape the mean streets of Jersey City, he forged a birth certificate and joined the navy, returning five years later to enter college on the GI Bill. Trained as a chemist, Daido worked in the food industry, synthesizing natural food flavors into additives. After seventeen years he became "disillusioned by the slippery ethics of his employers" and returned to his first love, photography. It was through the camera that he made his connection with Buddhism.

During a workshop with Minor White—the famous photographer who incorporated Eastern spiritual techniques (meditation, yoga, etc.) into his teaching format—Daido had a profound opening experience. "I lost all track of time, and after I came out of it, all my questions and answers had disappeared," he said, describing the experience. His change in consciousness lasted for weeks, but then, as always happens in these circumstances, it began to fade. "Over time I realized that I was losing whatever shift it was I felt in the workshop and I started doing yoga, I was standing on my head, I was reading books on Gurdjieff, on Tibetan Buddhism, even on Christianity [he had long since left the Catholic Church]," Daido told me. "At one point I became a vegetarian. That's how far it went [he is now decidedly *not* a vegetarian]."

After a few months he called Minor White and made an appointment to speak with him about all that had come up in the workshop. Daido drove from New York to Cambridge, where White was teaching, and had dinner with the photographer and some of his students at White's house. After everyone left, Daido and White stayed up late talking about philosophy, Zen, meditation techniques, and photography, but though Daido had thousands of questions White could offer no spiritual recipes. After their talk, Daido returned to his hotel room, where he saw a poster in the lobby for a seminar at Harvard titled "The Visual Dharma," in which teachers from various religious disciplines were going to discuss the visual arts from a spiritual perspective. It was exactly the thing Daido was looking for, and he decided to return to Cambridge the next week to attend.

At the seminar there were a number of teachers including a

rabbi, a Zen teacher (Eido Roshi[8]), and Chögyam Trungpa Rinpoche, who sponsored the event. When Daido heard the speakers, he knew in what direction he should head. "There was no question in my mind when I heard the two Buddhists. What they said resonated with me completely," he told me. "After his question-and-answer session, Eido showed three slides of Dai Bosatsu while he talked about the training there. The slides were pathetic, underexposed, drab, and poorly framed. One was slightly out of focus. 'This man needs a photographer,' I said to myself. I *could* have said, 'I need a teacher.' But I just wasn't ready to admit that yet. Instead, I told myself that I was going to help *him*," writes Daido.[9]

Daido started visiting Dai Bosatsu on a regular basis and learned a great deal from Eido's teacher Soen Roshi[10] over a number of months, but it wasn't until he met Maezumi Roshi that Daido found his true teacher. They met in Boulder, Colorado, where Daido was teaching photography at Naropa[11] and Maezumi was visiting for a few weeks, filling in for the absent Trungpa Rinpoche. One evening Daido was invited to a party at Maezumi's apartment. The story of their meeting, which I had heard a number of times, has become something of a ZMM legend and is contained in Daido's recent book, *The Zen of Creativity*, but he retold it for me:

> It was late and I kept trying to leave the party and Maezumi kept saying, "Please stay." So I stayed and sat next to him and he would say to me, "Ask me." And I'd say, "Ask you what, Roshi?" And then he would go silent and then he would say, "Daido, tell me." And I'd say, "Tell you what, Roshi?" And he'd go silent again. This went on until two or three in the morning. And then I told him I had to leave because I was exhausted, and I started straightening the place up because I felt bad to leave it in such a mess from the party, but Maezumi said, "No, you go," and pushed me out the door. I went back to my room

and fell asleep on the couch. About two hours later, right before sunrise, there was a knock and it was Roshi and he was dressed in his formal robes and he was very authoritative and strong and he told me to follow him back to his room, which I did. Roshi was very somber and formal and he put out four teacups. He told me one was for Soen Roshi, one was for Yasutani Roshi—his teacher who had recently passed away—one was for me, and one for him. He poured the tea and when I put the cup to my lips and took a sip, I started crying. I felt my heart being pierced and I looked at Roshi and he was crying, too. I felt tremendous gratitude in that moment and tried to express it, but Roshi shushed me and took me to the door and gently pushed me out.

Though Daido would not have much contact with Maezumi for months after this encounter, a seed had been planted. After his summer Naropa teaching assignment ended, Daido journeyed home to New York, where he and his wife, Joan (Yushin), and son, Asian, lived in a primitive farmhouse along the Delaware River. Soon after his return he received a call from Maezumi. "He asked me if I had a teacher and I said, 'Not really,' and he asked if I would like to come and study with him and I told him I'd love to," Daido said. He and his family soon moved to California, where Daido immersed himself in the day-to-day duties and practice at Zen Center of Los Angeles and where he continued to explore the relationship between his photography and Zen. He had found his path, his teacher, and a practice that completely transformed his life.

"I trust zazen because I was probably the most deluded, confused, angry, antireligious person you could ever meet. There is no reason in heaven or hell why I should be a Zen teacher, sitting here, talking like this. All I know is I found out about zazen." Daido eventually received *shiho* from Maezumi Roshi in 1986.

For Daido, art and creativity have always been a gateway into Buddhist practice, and he has actively maintained that connection throughout his teaching years. "Daido Roshi understands that Zen training and creative exploration complement each other," says Kaz Tanahashi,[12] who has been teaching Zen brush workshops at the monastery since 1986. "The creative process is a way of uncovering our consciousness. Daido uses art as a doorway into Buddhism." For Daido, that doorway is nothing but the intimacy of our own lives. His writings and teachings continually dismantle the illusion of separateness—for him the worlds of art and Zen are an intimate realm of seamless movement.

"Reconnecting people with the creative process has been something that Daido has always stressed, and it's wonderful," Michelle Spark (Seigei) told me. She's a fine-arts painter, has been Daido's student for fifteen years, and is a senior lay practitioner. "It's very sad to me that people don't see themselves as creative, and I totally agree with Daido that creativity is central to the spiritual process." Daido writes, "Art practice was intimately woven into the fabric of Zen training. Zen arts, creativity, and realized spirituality were seen as inseparable, and a Zen aesthetic developed which expressed eternal truths about the nature of reality and our place in the universe. . . . Through our art we bring into existence something that did not previously exist. We enlarge the universe."[13]

When Daido founded ZMM in 1980 (Maezumi would act as abbot until Daido's transmission ceremony in 1986), it was originally called the Zen Arts Center, and to this day artists make up a large proportion of the community. Daido's use of art as a tool and expression of spiritual life builds upon an ancient tradition, and much of what he has created at ZMM does the same. Daido describes his approach as "radical conservatism," borrowing forms and teaching methods from the major schools of Japanese and Chinese Zen, as well as from the Christian tradition, to stitch together an eclectic fabric of monastic practice. The practice includes offering weekend retreats for nonresidents—aikido, ikebana, writing, Zen archery, yoga, to name a few—and a monthly (year in and year out since 1980) week-long meditation retreat *(sesshin)*. Both men and women practice at ZMM; celibacy is a choice, not a requirement, and there are a number of monks and residents in stable heterosexual and same-sex relationships.

Daido's main influence, however, can be traced back to Zen master Dogen.[14] Daido has incorporated many of Dogen's monastic training methods into the daily schedule at ZMM and, like Maezumi, has continually used Dogen's teachings as a model. In fact, the Mountains and Rivers Order (ZMM's umbrella organization) borrows its name from the title of one of Dogen's sutras.

"The reason I identify so closely with Dogen is that I have a sense that what we're trying to do here as first-generation American Zen Buddhists is similar to what Dogen was trying to do as a first-generation Japanese Zen Buddhist. He was bringing the dharma from a Chinese master and establishing it in Japan, making it Japanese. Basically, Dogen established the prototype of Zen monasticism in Japan," he told me. Often referred to as the "boot camp of Buddhism," ZMM is a rigorous and tightly run training center for monastics and lay practitioners. The core of the monastery's "training matrix," as Daido calls it, are the "Eight Gates." Daido describes them as "a modern statement of the Buddha's Eightfold Path." He lists them as zazen, *dokusan*, liturgy, the precepts (the moral and ethical teachings of Zen), academic study, work practice, art practice, and body practice (exploring the relationship between body and mind).

The monastery, its schedule, the retreats it offers, the monks and resident and nonresident sangha—who are an integral part of the organization's ongoing success—the buildings and grounds, all form the "container" in which students train. The rigid structure is both an abrasive and a comfort. When Gokan first came to the monastery, he struggled with lethargy and low-level depression and the simple practicality of the monastic schedule was of great benefit. "I was depressed, and one of the things that helped was just getting up and doing things. I like to work and I like to be active. There weren't any questions about what I was going to do, and it gave me a feeling of purpose," he explained.

For Yukon the ZMM schedule transformed his relationship to structure. "I was totally scattered when I arrived at the monastery. To me, structure was always ugly because my father was such a Boy Scout. He used to give us citations if we left our shoes out on the floor. So I rebelled," he said. "In this practice you find the same type of structure, but it is about mindfulness and attention and loving what is around you. The old idea of structure gets dismantled. It doesn't have to do with anal retentiveness; it has to do with taking care. In a sense, structure is no longer external. It is something real for me so I can enjoy being around things rather than detesting them."

There's a foundational paradox here, of course, and it points to the heart of Zen. Form is used, in a very conscious way, to teach formlessness. The Heart Sutra, a centerpiece of Zen liturgy, says, "Form is exactly emptiness, emptiness exactly form." When Joan Chittister states that "it is God that religion must be about, not itself,"[15] she is alluding to the same thing. If God is simply about form and structure, then we have missed the mark completely. Emptiness here does not mean lack, it means the fullness of nonattachment.

The "everyday" for students at ZMM (both residents and visiting lay practitioners) is filled with intricate details. Students receive training positions that entail doing very specific, often ritualized tasks. They must ring the *inkin* (a small brass bell) a certain number of times and make it sound a certain way, they must bow when entering the zendo, they must memorize chants, they must not move during a period of zazen, they must eat what is served, and learn a thousand other details. But these button-pushing qualities— this über-structure (nearly every minute of a student's day is scheduled) so inherent in the container of monastic training—are a genuine gift.

The students are able to see, almost daily, where they get stuck, to which parts of the self they attach. The "present" in "being present" is not a static thing. The present can mean making love, being trapped in a burning car, or hitting the *makukyo* (a wooden drum used to keep time during chants) horribly out of rhythm. Living in the "now" has a rosy ring to it, but "now" can be as painful as hell. The Zen teacher's job is constantly to rub the student's nose in this "now," in the particulars of life.

"You have to have an open willingness to do the practice and that means you have to be able to put up with a certain amount of spiritual pain—finding that you are 'okay' in all situations. Life isn't lived in neat little compartments," Alex McMullan (Nenshin) offered. He's been Daido's student for over thirteen years. Zen is not about perfecting anything. The idea of perfection in practice, in performing the tasks at the monastery, is what trips us up. *Oryoki*, for example, Zen's ritualized form of meal-taking done most often during meditation retreats, is a choreographed dance of bowing, chanting, eating, serving, and receiving. For new students it's a nightmare, like having to learn the tango in an hour. Students assume, quite mistakenly—I know I did—that learning how to do *oryoki* well is the goal of practice. Doing something well is satisfying, and certainly Zen training can help our focus, power of concentration, and teach us how to do tasks thoroughly and to the best of our ability, but these things are by-products. *Oryoki* simply shows us the state of our own mind. It functions, like a gifted teacher, as a mirror that helps bring us back to bright awareness (from that tumble of mind-spinning distractions). Pay attention, it says.

Each month ZMM holds a Zen Training Weekend (dubbed ZTW) where outsiders can come and live the life of a Zen monastic for two days and nights and receive instruction in all that the monastery offers—Zen arts, body practice, liturgy, interview with the teachers, and so on. For many of the retreatants, a taste of monastery living can be a bit of a shock—up at 4:00 a.m., sitting cross-legged on a cushion, bowing, chanting, the sight of the shaven-headed monks in their flowing robes. Consistently, however, what raises the most hackles with ZTW participants is getting the toilet-cleaning detail during Work Practice (an hour-and-a-half work period of monastery upkeep done after breakfast). I've seen retreatants utterly dumbfounded and livid that they had "paid 250 bucks to come to a monastery and clean toilets." But then, what had they come for? The practice of Zen is not to step out of our life but to step back into it. Master Unmon, when asked "What is Buddha?" said, "A shit-stick!" It's no different from everyday life. Of course, long-term practitioners often have the same reaction when they get a task they don't like, though the argument has gotten a little more sophisticated—"Toilet cleaning? Look, I've learned to do that without any problems so I don't have to do it anymore."

Daido, with much input from the sangha, has, over the last twenty-five years, refined the monastic format. Buddhist monasticism is still very new to the West and is an ongoing experiment. Daido has been very careful and patient about introducing new elements into the established Japanese-Chinese model—though ZMM, from its inception, has been decidedly Western in allowing a coed resident community and training women to be teachers, as well as promoting environmental activism, aspects largely absent in Japanese Zen. Yet Daido decided early on, partly in homage to his Japanese teacher and partly because of his own belief in the traditional system, to keep much of the ancient hierarchical format in place. There have been two trends in Western Zen: one has been to do away with hierarchy altogether—to get rid of the robes and any outward expression of rank and position; the other has been to keep all or parts of the hierarchical model. Daido opted, quite forcefully, for the latter (leaving behind the strictures of patriarchy), and has used it as a sort of pebble in the practitioner's shoe, as a background tension to training.

The reasoning behind his approach is that hierarchy is everywhere in the world: we have bosses, we have parents, there are weak countries and strong, animals feed on other animals, and so on. Why shouldn't we dive into that mess in our practice? At ZMM there are obvious outward expressions of rank. Non-monastic residents have gray robes, monastics have black. Postulants, novitiates, and full monastics are identified by particular aspects of dress, *jukai* students (ones who have taken the Buddhist precepts) wear *rakusus* (small biblike garments), and practitioners are seated in the zendo in order of how "far along" they are in their practice. For the ego it's quite a fiery setup.

"You sit in the zendo in a hierarchical space and you sit next to somebody and you think, 'What are they doing here? Why are they ahead of me?' " Seigei told me. "It happens to everybody and you can't understand it and you think it's wrong and you think it means something. But all it means is that you're not really dealing with where you are. It has been a wonderful thing because I've seen how it has worked on me in very positive ways." "Don't get attached to form," Zen keeps asserting, and every aspect of the training at ZMM is ultimately pointing us in that direction. I never had much of a problem with the hierarchal atmosphere because I didn't have the urge to "move up" along the ladder of the order. At least that's what I thought in the beginning. What I eventually found, however, was that I was feigning disinterest because I was ashamed of my competitive nature. My "idea" of spirituality didn't allow it, so I simply avoided it through "manufactured detachment." I rubbed up against the "system" in a different way, but it still helped me uncover some sticking points.

Much of the movement within this structure is ritualized and quite beautiful. Residents chant together, bow together, meditate together in particular forms that have been handed down through generations, and there is a palpable sense of all those who came before bowing as you bow. Ritual deepens meaning. One of my favorite service positions at the monastery was the morning timekeeper (jikido). As part of my job, I would get up before everyone awoke, make coffee, and then light the candles and offer incense on all the altars in the building in a prescribed order. When I bowed, lit the candle and incense, and bowed again, I felt a true connection with the ancestors, and with all the practitioners who had come through the monastery and those who were still sleeping.

ZMM's rigorous program is, most assuredly, not for everyone and there is an unfortunate tendency, at times overt and at times subtle, among some community members to look down upon people who find it unpalatable. This "spiritual jock" attitude asserts that because the practice at ZMM is so finely tuned structurally, it is therefore superior. This is ridiculous, and is akin to snubbing someone because they like strawberries instead of raspberries. It plays into another faulty assumption about Zen practice: that if you push hard enough—physically, emotionally, mentally—and you do your job well enough, then you'll be able to "break through" to enlightenment. Though we certainly shouldn't be lazy about our practice, being a jock, believe it or not, is mostly a liability.

Shugen Sensei came to Zen with that mindset. "It wasn't conscious, but the way I sat zazen was kind of a sport," he told me. "There was a lot of huffing and puffing and I was tremendously tense and doing what I knew how to do, which was push in a very physical way to get the end result. In the beginning my practice was a lot about endurance. I was in a lot of pain and I created a lot of pain in the way I was sitting and eventually it was winning and I was losing. I realized I had to shift my whole way of looking at the experience. But, for me, finding a different form of effort that wasn't so forceful was scary. Because I felt like I wasn't doing anything. I felt like I was giving up and being passive. That change was a long process and it was a great surprise because initially I thought all of that physicality was going to serve me well."

There is a classic image Zen students hold in their heads: the master strolling through the zendo yelling at the disciples to "push harder," "concentrate," "break through the koan," "die on the cushion!" It's a very martial vision, the rallying of the troops and so forth, but underneath all the frothing is the need for surrender and flexibility and, ultimately, connecting with something that is the opposite of "pushing."

Daido carries a very strong idea of what Western Buddhist monasticism should be. He is dedicated to laying a solid monastic foundation in American soil, but with many visionaries the need to create what you see in your head and what you feel in your heart often comes with the need to control. For the visionary, being controlling is an occupational hazard, and over the years the recurring knock I've heard against Daido is his "issue" of control, so I asked him about it.

"It depends on who is saying it. If someone comes into practice here from the world, they are used to doing what they want. They come home from work and they have their own house, they can go out to dinner, a movie, cook what they want. When they come into the monastery it's a culture shock: everything is defined, you can't stay up until eleven o'clock at night, meals are served at a certain time every day, there are specific periods to shower, do your laundry. Definitely that's controlling. Most coaches and trainers are controlling," he said.

"I don't tell people how to live their lives outside of following the schedule. If people are having marital problems, I don't say 'Well, you do this or that'; I help facilitate what they are feeling. As far as operations and the seniors [monks], it's once again about context and who says it. I'm seventy-three years old and I have a lot of experience. I'm basically the CEO of Dharma Communications [the publishing and retail wing] and Zen Mountain Monastery and I bring my business skills to that." There is general agreement among the students that Daido can be too controlling in certain circumstances, and I tend to agree, but the range of how people deal with his controlling personality is quite varied. Daido has never told me what to do. He has never meddled in any aspect of my life unless I asked him specifically for advice. With other students he has been much more hands-on, particularly, and understandably, with his monks.

The issue of control is a central one within the teacher-disciple relationship. Certain types of control can manifest as authoritarian power, which is never a good thing. At ZMM the rigid structure is a part of the bargain, and Daido has always been up front about its function. Is he too controlling as a teacher? Some students, as I said above, would say most definitely yes (and a number have left because of the strictness of the program), and others say that you can't so easily separate, in this case, the teacher from the well-oiled system that he largely put into place. And this is an important point. A good third of the students I spoke with said that they practice at ZMM not because of any particular teacher or monk but because of the structure of the training—they like the clearly defined boundaries (the control) and the stability.

And Daido is nothing if not stable, consistent, and dedicated to

ZMM and its community. "Daido doesn't travel much. He's not a teacher that's in every port. He's here," Seigei pointed out. "You know when he's going to be here and you really feel his dedication to the place and keeping the practice going." Gokan adds, "I think what has made me trust Daido all along, even when I was being skeptical and critical, was realizing his dedication and patience and that he just keeps showing up to do the work."

A teacher's personality can act in much the same way as the structure of Zen: it can be an abrasive or a comfort. Kyoryu, who grew up with a troubled father, said, "For me, Daido is the perfect embodiment of the medicine and the poison. I am from an Italian family and Daido is every inch the patriarch in many of his personality traits, yet he is not someone that I can easily pigeonhole in that way. If I had the guts to test my assumptions, which I did on occasion, he would totally surprise me."

How we "fit" with a teacher is secondary. The question is, what are we willing to learn? "Sometimes people come to me and say, 'So and so said such and such; is that a teaching?' And what they are really saying is, 'Was that intentional, did they really mean that?'" Shugen Sensei told me. "Which is code for, 'If it was a teaching, then I'll listen to it and learn something from it. If it's not a teaching, then screw them, I'm going to throw it away.' That doesn't make any sense to me. It often doesn't matter what the other person's intention is—sometimes it matters—but the main question is, 'What can I learn from it, how can I benefit?' And that's completely up to the student."

Though my family was not churchgoing, my father was what used to be called a "spiritualist," being an early theosophist and then an admirer of channelers. All the kids used to get *Seth Speaks* books (famous channeling books from the 1970s) for Christmas, and for years there were "spiritual" meetings at our house every Friday evening. Needless to say, I grew up with a strong ambivalence toward spiritual practice and "spiritual authorities," yet my father's lofty and often admirable spiritual desires planted deep seeds. Already a literary Buddhist from an early age, when my marriage fell apart in my mid-thirties, I ran like water down a steep slope into the arms of Zen practice. During my first *dokusan* with Daido, I admitted that I felt quite uncomfortable with him there in front of me dressed in gold robes like the Pope and me bowing before him. He told me that the robes, the bells—even him in his teacher role—was, in a sense, bullshit. "So let's cut through all that crap and get down to why you are here." I really appreciated him opening the door in that way, and it was one of the reasons I became his student.

"I've been stuck so many times and in so many places, and Daido has taught me over and over again to have patience. Zen is not for sprinters, it's for long-distance runners," Nenshin told me. "Now I'm much more relaxed. It's okay not to know. In this way I'm a lot more open and things become clearer and clearer."

Do we need a formal teacher to bring us to that place of realization and self-trust? Perhaps not, perhaps life itself is the best teacher and the only one needed. It is, however, a privilege indeed to be working with someone whose sole purpose is to entice and cajole you into opening your eyes and experiencing a saner reality.

"Zen teaching is like fishing," Daido told me. "Every fisherman has a technique. Some use flies, some lures, some bait. The key is to get students hooked. Genpo Roshi [Daido's dharma brother] uses Big Mind [a method integrating psychology and Zen], I use the arts, and Tetsugen uses social action. What counts is what happens when the students get hooked."

Yet, as Daido explains, "The attainment of our true nature is something no one can give; each person has to do it alone. Zen is a process for doing it. It wasn't invented yesterday. It is not a fad. It is simple and direct and very difficult. It challenges us to be with ourselves, to study the self, to forget the self, and to be one with the ten thousand things.

"Zen is not Japanese and it's not Chinese. It is American. It didn't come from Asia; it has always been here. It is a way of using your mind and living your life and doing it with other people. Unfortunately, nobody can supply a rulebook to go by because what it is about can't be spoken of, and that which can be spoken of is not it. So we need to go deep in ourselves to find the foundation of it. Zen is a practice that has to do with liberation, not some kind of easy certainty. The wisdom of that liberation not only affects our lives but all those who we come in contact with, all that we know, and all that we do."[16]

Leaving the Teacher

There are a thousand reasons to leave a teacher. If there is a scandal or abuse—a subject I explore in the final chapter—leaving can be quite traumatic but necessary. Perhaps, over a number of years of study, we realize that we need another teacher or practice. We might, and this is not uncommon, return to the religion of our birth after a time in another spiritual discipline. Sometimes we leave gradually, in a slow fade of diminishing interest, or we leave in a huff, slamming the door. Some of us flit from teacher to teacher, practice to practice, in the spiritual marketplace, never deepening our connection and never really gaining much insight. But for those who do stay long enough to sink roots, leaving a teacher and a spiritual community can be like leaving home. It is difficult.

How do we know if we should leave? If we have met another teacher who feels like a better fit, how do we know our desire to change is not buying into the "spiritual shopping" mentality? How can we tell whether we are not simply running away from some personal difficulty? "In my mind, trusting oneself means knowing those times when we are *not* trustworthy. Knowing when we need to stay put when our guts are telling us to get out and knowing when to do the opposite," Shugen Sensei said.

Often the need or desire to leave never arises; many people practice with one teacher and one community their whole lives. But even within this stable atmosphere our relationships change. We might not be as close to the teacher as we once were, we might not attend as many retreats or practice as regularly; in that sense we may feel like we've "left" in many ways. We can feel the often wide range of emotions that leaving brings—guilt, anger, sorrow, shame, relief, a sense of failure. There is a tendency to look upon leaving as a negative, and there is a long list of scenarios that support this, but leaving can also be positive and exactly what a student needs—that is, to graduate, to leave the nest and test his own wings.

Adyashanti had a student, for example, who felt strong enough to leave but couldn't make the break herself. "She said to me, 'You really need to kick me out of here so I don't keep pretending there's something to "get," ' because she already knew too much to believe that. She told me in front of a group of people and I said, 'Okay, that's it. I never want to have you come up in *satsang* [a public exchange with the teacher] and talk to me again. We're done.' And she got it. It was great," Adyashanti said. "But the amazing thing was that when I told her we were finished, this audible gasp went up in the audience. 'Oh my God! She's just been kicked out!' Even though she asked for it quite explicitly and I took her at her word. It was the talk of the day. In some people it brought up stark terror."

We usually come to a teacher with some kind of dependency, so the thought of "being on our own" is naturally frightening. This is the paradox, once again: we study with a teacher so we can eventually be free of the teacher (at least in some traditions). In a sense, our arrival knocks over the first domino of our leaving. Some teachers ask students to leave because they see an unhealthy dependency being created. Murat Yagan asked his student Jean Robillard to leave because he was spending too much time in the community and not enough time with his family, and his marriage was suffering. Jean stayed away for six years and got his marriage back in shape. On the other hand, it is not uncommon for students to stop studying with a teacher but still stay connected with the community. The nourishment and support found in a communal setting might be exactly what that person needs— they might be completely isolated in the "outside world."

It is impossible to make a list of criteria that would tell us when to stay with a teacher and when to leave. But we should fully explore our reasons for leaving. Daido Roshi told me he'd noticed that a good number of his students left after taking *jukai* (the Buddhist precepts), and he thought the reason might be that the process signaled a bigger commitment and made the practice, in many ways, more real. "More real" can be scary. According to the most recent data, forty percent of marriages in this country end in divorce. Maybe this means that nearly half of us are uneasy with commitment or maybe it means something else. According to my very unofficial sample, students, on average, have studied with at least two formal spiritual teachers for five years or more in their lifetimes. This adds up to a significant number of departures.

I've seen a number of monks and senior lay practitioners walk out the door for good (all of whom had either lived at or been associated with ZMM for more than ten years). It was difficult for the people who left and for the community as a whole. Often we don't realize the impact our departure has upon the ones we leave behind. If we can't be clear about our reasons for leaving, then we should allow time for the dust to settle. In finding a teacher patience is a virtue, and the same applies to leaving, barring the presence of abuse, that is.

Certainly we should refrain from beating ourselves up over our decision. There are many good and valid reasons for leaving a spiritual teacher and a community.

My friend Diana Hartel (Kosei) recently ended her formal relationship with Daido Roshi. She had lived at ZMM for three years, had been practicing there for over ten, and was considering becoming a monk. But an ill and aging father (who lived on the opposite coast) and a need to reconnect with her daughter changed her course—both very good excuses for leaving. Still, it has been a difficult process for her.

"When you want to turn away from something, even though it is not breaking the love that is inherently there and is simply changing how you formally relate, even that can bring up a whole storm of emotions. It's sometimes easy, under these circumstances, to go into anger, resentment, judgment, and blame—'gee, the place wasn't that good anyway,' and so on. I didn't want to do that. Those emotions did start coming, but I didn't let them overtake me," she said. What she did was talk to people about what she was feeling and seek out advice both from the community she was leaving and from other Zen teachers and sanghas. But, most important, she sat with her emotions and didn't try to suppress them or let them rule the roost. And she was patient, waiting two years before she made her decision.

After she had decided and was clear about the need to leave—she had moved across the country to be close to her parents and didn't want to have a long-distance relationship with a teacher—she met with Daido Roshi in person, in the formal setting of *dokusan* (which is the same process one goes through to become a student). He prodded her a bit to make sure she was clear on her reasons for leaving, she explained them to him, and they ended their formal relationship, but by no means their heart connection. "It was very clean on both sides and that was really great and it felt right. The door is always open to return if I want to," she told me. "I gave him a parting gift as well, just like when you become a student."

There is no one "correct" way to leave a teacher. There are clean ways to leave, and there are messy ways. In some cases our lives change and we don't see our teacher for years, but the relationship is still strong. My friend Emi Stanley has two teachers, Shenpen Rinpoche and Daido Roshi, yet her life is such that she rarely sees either of them. But the present distance has little bearing on the connection she feels. "Each of them has given me a dharma name. To think about what those names mean and what they saw in me when they named me brings me back to my heart and my practice. I have never felt like I've left either of them," she told me.

We shouldn't be afraid to leave a teacher and a community if those relationships are not giving us what we need, particularly if we've made a genuine effort, over a reasonable period of time, to make things work. There are times when banging our heads against the wall is useful—we might need to shake something loose—but then there are times when such effort is futile and it's advisable to change course. We must be careful of the temptation to leave just because we feel uncomfortable; in fact, that might be a valuable reason to stay. On the other hand, we should stay open to the possibility that our discipleship can reach completion. The main thing is to have an understanding of our patterns and peccadilloes. If we have had ten different jobs and two marriages in the last decade and we are feeling that our teacher is not up to snuff after studying with them for only two years, should we really trust our urge to flee?

9

TRAVELING WITHOUT A PASSPORT

Adyashanti

All that a guru can tell you is: "My dear Sir, you are quite mistaken about yourself. You are not the person you take yourself to be."

—NISARGADATTA MAHARAJ[1]

"I don't want to be in the role of 'wisdom guy' all the time. I like it when I do it, but all the time? I mean, who wants to sit around talking about the Truth for any longer than is absolutely necessary?"

—ADYASHANTI

Adyashanti *does* likes to talk. He's good at it. When he speaks, he brings clarity to the subject at hand, he provokes, he plays, and he turns things downside up. Yet being the "teacher" all the time doesn't appeal to him. Adya, as his students call him, when he does teach is interested in only two subjects—awakening and life after awakening. "No matter what I seem to be talking about, I'm really talking about one of these two things."[2] He's not interested in a spirituality that, he says, "manages your illusions and rearranges the deck chairs on the *Titanic*." The poet Ezra Pound said, "Literature is news that stays news." Shouldn't our spiritual practice be the same? When Adya speaks, his words "stay news."

"Move forward or self-destruct. That's what I tell people. I say, 'Don't get into this unless you intend to take it all the way, because you may end up worse than when you began.' People think spirituality is safe—we think it's warm, cuddly—it does have that side, but it's also dangerous and there are casualties along the way, like anything else in life," he says.

One morning when Adya was thirty-one years old (after thirteen years of arduous and unrelenting spiritual inquiry and Zen meditation), he had a profound awakening. The experience was triggered by the sound of a bird chirping outside his window. In Zen there's a long tradition of enlightenment stories, and his fits nicely into that canon. Yet a funny thing happened to Adya (then known as Steven Gray) a few minutes later: the thought "I just woke up out of Zen" popped into his head. After studying for all those years he gave up the idea of Zen, and in many ways the practice of it. "When you wake up, you realize that you wake up out of everything, including all the things that have helped to bring you there."[3] All the concepts of truth, tradition, wisdom, a teacher, a student are thrown out the window. You shed the skin of religion and become yourself. "I saw the whole Zen thing, right or wrong, and the teacher thing, as just an aid to get where I wanted to go. I didn't get into this to become Buddhist, to become Asian, to become anything. I just saw it as a tool I'm using," he told me.

A student asked Adya, "What is the teacher's role in life?" He said, "To be themselves. That is the teacher's teaching. The true spiritual teacher is a rare being who does not play roles." The student then asked, "And what is the role of a spiritual student?" Adya replied, "The role of the spiritual student is to seek the demise of the role of the spiritual student—as soon as possible."[4]

Adya studied with two Zen teachers, Arvis Joen Justi, a lay practitioner who studied with Taizan Maezumi Roshi, Yasutani Roshi, and Eido Roshi,[5] and Jakusho Kwong Roshi, the head of Sonoma Zen Center and a disciple in the lineage of Shunryu Suzuki Roshi.[6] When Kwong Roshi asked Adya to become his first monk, Adya was tempted. Kwong Roshi is very traditional, and it would have meant living at the Zen Center, wearing robes, giving dharma talks, lighting incense, and helping to run the place. Adya thought it would be a beautiful life, but ultimately he couldn't see himself within the strictures of such a cloistered form.

Having two distinct teachers suited Adya's personality. "Kwong Roshi is quite traditional, quite into form, and Arvis less so—although there are elements of her that are very traditional. These two aspects of masculine and feminine were really beautifully modeled for me and reflected energies within myself," he said. When Arvis asked Adya to start teaching, her lay practice style appealed to Adya's independent nature. She told him two simple things: "I trust you" and "teach only from your own experience." And that's what he has done, not worrying about form but concentrating on what worked best for his students.

"I started out doing exactly what my teacher did: meditation, and then I would give a talk, answer a couple of questions, and then do meditation again. What I started to see very quickly, within weeks, was that when I'd dialogue with somebody in these very short times after the talks, it was more powerful. People could make bigger leaps then than they did doing anything else. If I moved away from simply answering the questions to using the questions as a way to help take people to a deeper place, then the process gained even more strength. And so it evolved: there was less and less meditation and more time for engagement, even though meditation was certainly still happening."

Adya found that he had a gift for dialogue, and the more he moved in that direction, the less he looked like a modern Zen teacher. He didn't wear Zen robes, use Zen lingo, or teach any techniques. He talked, and when he talked people began to have awakenings. Students kept telling him that what he was doing was called *satsang*, which literally means "being together in Truth." The word and the practice come from the Hindu tradition. "I'd never heard the word. I only used the word because that's what people were more familiar with, so I thought, 'Well, why try to run against the wind?' You know, if that's what resonates for people, I don't care what I call it." Adya was learning as he went along. Whatever his students brought to the table, he met them there on an intimate level. "I'm not a visionary. I'm the guy in the back of the train holding on to the caboose, wondering where it's going to go. The community was very much teaching me, I was learning a lot of what worked, what didn't work. It was a great time," he recalled.

At some point, someone gave him a book called *I Am That* by Nisargadatta Maharaj, the great Indian sage, and when he read it, it was like taking a tour of his own living room. "I never felt anywhere else the click I felt with Nisargadatta. It isn't a total click because he's still a little more Indian, not so much guru, but 'your body is just something that's going to decay and then die'—he's a little bit more on that transcendence end than I am, but it was like finding a friend. This guy says what I've experienced. And I didn't find it as accurate anywhere else. Probably still haven't."

Soon Adya was being put in the Advaita Vedanta camp (Nisargadatta was also lumped with this group; *advaita* is Sanskrit for "nondual," which means realizing what you already are, not seeking spiritual experiences or states, not practicing any techniques), but he was also seen as a Zen teacher, albeit embodying more than the Chinese Chan school—looser, more folksy and humorous—than the Japanese school. But Adya doesn't care what you call the way he teaches. "I'm not teaching to transmit a tradition or carry on a lineage; I'm teaching to awaken whoever may be interested in awakening." Adya calls himself a "closer" because awakening is his starting point. "For me as a teacher, waking up to the absolute nature of reality is step one. For a lot of other systems, they're working up to that and it's almost the culmination. To me, that's the entry point. Until you've done that, we don't have much more to talk about. Wake up first, and then we'll see what you need to deal with. We'll see what's left, in other words."

I picked Adya to be in this book because I like what he has to say and the way he says it. But I was also interested in including a teacher who was outside of a tradition. Not too far out, though—I wanted someone who understood tradition and formal structure and opted for something else. Adya's "formlessness" calls for a different spiritual relationship, one that initially puts a lot more responsibility on the student. With Adya there is no guidance in the classic sense, no teaching of methods to attain a goal, no graded steps. He's interested only in stopping seekers in their tracks. And if there is nothing left to seek, then what? "If you look at your life, almost everything is in some way a subtle goal," Adya said. "You are always psychologically moving toward something, and when consciousness is no longer moving toward anything, then there is a whole different something that moves you. It's completely different from the personal, and it's not always immediately obvious to people. Very often it confuses them."

Contrary to common belief, awakening is not the end of the journey. Even though Adya will refer to his "birdsong awakening" as a final event, the label is misleading. "Awakening is the end of seeking, the end of the seeker, but it is the beginning of life lived from your true nature. That's a whole other discovery—life lived from oneness. Embodying what you are; being a human expression of oneness."[7] There is awakening and then there is embodying that awakening, making it real and integrating it into the world. These are Adya's "two things."

"I tell people I'm not in a babysitting program. I'm not here to crush your ego. I don't do that. Life's going do it for you. I'm not here to try to correct you. You better have your integrity together when you come here. I can understand the value of it for some people at some time and why teachers sometimes play that role and all that, but I'm just not interested in it," he told me. Some spiritual seekers find his utter lack of conformity difficult, particularly those who are just starting on the path. There is no ceremony to "become" his student. "I've had people tell me, 'I'm your student.' And I say, 'Okay.' Or they ask, 'Can I be your student?' I say, 'Well, you tell me, are you?' They say, 'I guess so,' and I say, 'Fine.' That's about it."

The same is true when it comes to his giving "transmission" to students and thus "making" them teachers. There is no ritual, no ceremony. Adya will simply know intuitively when and if he should ask someone to teach and then simply ask them. Bonnie Greenwell, one of Adya's older students, a longtime spiritual practitioner, a transpersonal therapist and author, was asked by Adya to teach when they met at a coffee shop. He was dressed in bicycle riding gear (bicycling is one of his hobbies) as he was on his way to a long ride. "Adya said, 'Well, I've known for over a year that I was going to ask you to teach, so why don't you go ahead and get started?' " Bonnie said. And that was that. Adya is very ordinary and he teaches through that ordinariness—if you think you are a "big deal" because you are now a teacher—well, get off it. On the other hand, Adya takes the teacher role seriously and he expects his teaching heirs to do the same.

"If they [his heirs] screw up, believe me, I'll give them a phone call. I'll tear them up one side and down the other if somebody screws up. It doesn't matter if they are eloquent or not. The most important thing to me is do they have integrity, are they screwing up on the integrity front? So far nobody ever has."

Adya doesn't have anything against structure and tradition per se. It's just that he thinks students shouldn't take it at face value. When I point out that structure and tradition in Zen are used as tools, as skillful means to force students to face their own ego patterns, he tells me, "That's the story about why the structure's there, and certainly that's a positive reason. But the structure's also there because Zen is an old-boys' school. We like authority and we like robes and we like hierarchy and it's a very male thing. It doesn't mean that kind of structure is useless—it just means, can we look at this thing completely? Can we tell the whole truth about tradition and structure? And not just say, 'Look, the structure is a place to come and confront yourself.' It's about that, and it's also about things that guys like to do. Guys do military."

As a Zen student, it's refreshing for me to hear a man say what some women have been voicing for years. Yet Adya is not completely formless and without any structure. During his retreats—he offers one-day, two-day, and on up to five-day intensives—his students are asked to meditate when *satsang* is not being offered. I asked Adya how he could have meditation without teaching any techniques. "It's the non-meditation meditation. You just sit down and if you notice yourself manipulating anything, just stop doing that. That's it. Because we're going after the natural state, and if we're going after the natural state we're not going to get there through unnatural means." His answer provoked another question. "Isn't that the same as *shikantaza*?" I asked. *Shikantaza*, as I noted before, is a form of meditation that is really non-meditation. You just sit and do nothing else. There are no koans to work on, no breath to follow, no thoughts to get rid of—"just sit," the Zen masters say.

"It's basically the same, but it depends on how it is explained," Adya replied. "That's one of the dangers of tradition. I have a great appreciation for it, but my appreciation has never gotten in the way of being willing to look at it again. What most people do is read what Dogen[8] said about *shikantaza* hundreds of years ago, which is about as relevant to people's experience now as a rat going down a hole. They read it and it's nice and it's elegant and then you just see on their face this 'Huh?' I spent fifteen years trying to figure out what the guy was talking about. Let's just say it in a way that's a little more relevant and you can understand it better. To me, either a teacher is restating tradition, or a teacher is, at the very least, reinterpreting it, making it so that someone can understand what it's all about. Each generation needs a voice that can present things so that people with them can actually hear. Otherwise we're just having to claw through lots of culture to get through to what's true."

I suspect that referring to a segment of Dogen's writings as irrelevant will ruffle some feathers, because in some Zen circles Dogen is equivalent to the Pope. But Adya is not simply being irreverent. He continually challenges his students and the world at large to look beneath their ready-made answers and somnambulist wanderings through conformity for conformity's sake. When I offered the comparison of *shikantaza*, he challenged its pat definition—fine, sure it's like that, but what do you really mean? Are you relying on the authority of someone who's been dead for hundreds of years or on your own experience? In Zen it is always said that the transmission of the teachings is "outside of words and letters." Adya is certainly not contradicting that essential message.

Being "outside" of tradition brings its own dangers. There is no lineage of authority to fall back on, no formal "certification" for teaching, and no board or its equivalent to ensure checks and balances. When Adya told Kwong Roshi that he was thinking of teaching, his teacher expressed concern for Adya's future students being outside of a lineage. In the end Kwong Roshi didn't encourage him to teach, but neither did he discourage him—the best he could do under the circumstances of a formal tradition. I asked Adya if he had any objective mirror against which he could check himself. "When I started to teach, really early on, I actually told my wife, Annie, and my mom, two people I really could trust—because Annie knew me before I started to teach and my mom knew me before I came into the world—I told them, 'Look, if I start to get whacked out or out of line or out of integrity in your eyes, I'm counting on you to tell me, to give me that feedback.'"

Integrity is, for Adya, the equivalent of lineage and tradition. He is relentlessly careful about his integrity and in no way rests on the laurels of his awakening. "As soon as you think that you'll never have to say 'I'm sorry,' you've already succumbed to your illusion, because you might have to. Enlightenment is no guarantee that you won't have to, that you won't do something that's a mistake or you won't do something stupid. I think, for me, never forgetting that is a safeguard," he told me. He is also explicit about the commitment he has to Annie, who is very active and visible in the spiritual community. "My commitment to Annie is absolute and I make that very clear, right up front. There's no room in there for anything," he said. "A lot of the younger women, they'd say, 'Oh, I'm in love.' But Adya is impeccable," Bonnie explained. "He's very clear that he's in a stable marriage and it's not in his conditioning to have his relationship mean anything other than commitment."

The Open Gate Sangha, which is Adya's spiritual community, has an office, a website, and a publishing wing that produces Adya's books, tapes, and CDs. They do not have a permanent building for retreats and rent the space when it is needed. Adya is not interested in creating an intentional community, not in any direct way. The sangha has evolved into a strong and supportive group quite naturally with little input from Adya—other than his teachings, of course. Since tradition and formal structure have little influence in the community and upon Adya's teaching style, every little procedural decision is an ongoing experiment. Things like what a teacher wears when teaching has no precedent. "Sometimes I'll show up in blue jeans and a halfway decent shirt and more often than not I'll dress a little bit nicer than that," Adya said when asked. "For me it's just enough to where I feel like I'm respecting what I'm doing, but not putting on pretense."

When Arvis asked Adya to teach she was doing so within a lay lineage, so there was no giving of a spiritual name as in a Zen monastic tradition. I asked Adya how he came to change from his previous identity as Steven Gray. "The name thing? Oh, a total, absolute embarrassment. Come on, I mean, 'Adyashanti!' Ridiculous. Big Sanskrit. Guru-ish," he laughed. "It was not what I would have really chosen." Actually, the name chose him. After he started teaching, a voice in his head kept telling him to find a name. He resisted for two years. He didn't want another name, he thought it a bit ridiculous. But the voice persisted, and then one day he was reading and two words popped off the page, *Adya* and *Shanti*, and they just fit themselves together and he knew that that was it. *Adyashanti* means "primordial peace." "I didn't want it to be the name. But it was sort of strange; it was not a drive, but something that just said, 'That's it, that's what it's going to be,' and then the 'no, no, no, no' back and forth for a while. One day I just realized that's it. Okay. I don't know what it's about, I don't even like it, but okay."

Many of Adya's students have long spiritual résumés; they've been through the mill or come from nondual (which tend to be less structured) backgrounds. Beginners, however, are not discouraged. Realistically the "beginner's mind," to borrow a phrase from Suzuki

Roshi, is exactly the proper attitude to have. Come fresh and open
and don't expect Adya to be a parental figure, a perfect teacher, or
even a "spiritual guy." Just don't expect anything and Adya will
meet you right there. "Whether anybody is half-awake, fully awake,
or whatever, he'll sit down with whoever is in the chair. He's definitely not about the dream. He warns the people who come to him
that if they stay their lives are going to change, something is going
to happen. And it does for the people who stick around," Peter
Scarsdale told me. He's been Adya's student for over six years, and
like many of the Open Gate Sangha members, he'd been a spiritual
practitioner long before that.

In Zen the tradition, particularly of late, is *not* to talk about enlightenment experiences unless those experiences are wrapped in
esoteric and mind-boggling language. The reasoning is that people
hearing the tales will get an *idea* of enlightenment stuck in their
heads, and it'll then be harder for them to realize the true experience—too many layers of conceptualization to cut through. It's a
good point, but it has its downside. What is not spoken of almost
always gains mystique and becomes imbued with the notion of a
"secret society." Adya presents awakening in the most transparent
terms. He actively dismantles the mystique surrounding enlightenment while keeping the mystery intact. Actually, the mystery cannot be separated from awakening because they are one and the
same. Awakening is the act of entering the mystery. Adya talks
about, explores, and reveals whatever he can about enlightenment
to demystify what is essentially available to everyone and not just a
select few who have done years of esoteric practices.

Ask Adya's longer-term students about awakening, and they are
very candid about their experiences. "I think it was the second *satsang* and Adya was talking normally to the group and then one moment I was just off somewhere and then back. I don't know what
happened. I knew profoundly that my life would never be the same.

Then Rumi made sense," Hamsa Hilker, a student of Adya's for six years and a long-term seeker, exclaimed. Bonnie had a story, too: "It's like the mind just dropped and there was incredible heart opening and incredible understanding of the source of consciousness and incredible love. I've never felt love like that." These are testimonials, to be sure, and as with any other human enterprise, these stories can stir up jealousies, ego trips, and all kinds of messiness. But the stories, as far as I could tell, were related in the context of both wonder and ordinariness with the conscious sense of normalizing the extraordinary. In fact, in many ways these students were *ending* their spiritual lives, at least that portion of them that was somehow definable in the past. "I've been a spiritual person since I was five years old and it ended when I met Adya," Hamsa told me. "I cannot see that I'm interested in the spiritual life at all, and that baffles me."

Adya is forty-three years old and has been teaching since 1996. He lives with Annie, to whom he has been married for ten years, in a tract home in the suburbs near San Jose, California. When Annie met me at the door of their house for the interview, I joked that it was like coming home because I grew up in the "burbs" not far from there. Adya looks like a cyclist—he has that sinewy, not-an-ounce-of-fat build. He's also an avid backpacker. If you saw him in a diner, perhaps you'd peg him as a bicycle mechanic, which is what he worked at for most of his adult years. He does not have, at first blush, a symphonic personality. "I was underwhelmed, to be honest. He's pulling off his windbreaker and he is just so ordinary I thought, 'I don't know,' " Laura Mackenzie told me, describing the first time she met Adya during a retreat. Laura has been his student for five years. Adya *is* ordinary, but of course he's also not. "When he's not expressing the teaching function, which is how he refers to it, he's a regular guy; he isn't but he is. It's both. He clearly isn't, and if you're sensitive to it it's obvious, but on the other hand he's just regular," Peter told me.

The seeming confusion is understandable. Adya is an extremely powerful teacher in a very plain package. The power and the plainness are not separate, however. The force of his teaching is in his complete lack of rank and pretension—there is simply nothing added to his natural state. "I think the Buddha had it right. I love that the real translation of nirvana is 'cessation.' He got it, that's what it is, cessation of the seeker and the seeking, cessation of illusion. It never was what I got, it's what I lost," Adya explained. For his students, the ones who stay (and there are many; his popularity is exploding), the form of the practice is the clarity of their teacher's presence. In this sense his ordinariness is volatile—it continually morphs from lead into gold and back again.

Laura, soon after being underwhelmed, experienced an elemental shift. "I think I asked the first question [during *satsang*] and it was like water pouring out of my mouth. I said, 'I have this telescoping awareness and the back has fallen out from behind everything so that it is all flat or empty and I can't function,' and it sounded very dramatic. Adya just looked at me and said, 'Oh, this is so common, don't worry about it.' It just floored me. No one had treated my experience that way. No one had recognized it. But what was happening between me and Adya was not in the words at all. He said, 'You're hanging a little too far back. Come forward,' and my whole body jumped and there was a breaking through as if I literally came through the front of my body, like awareness came through. Tears were falling and joy and absolute homecoming."

Hamsa had her eyes closed the first time she met Adya so she could get an impression of his energy. "This person walked by me and I could feel he was super-powerful and super-loving and I didn't want to open my eyes. I did finally open my eyes and I knew on a profound level that I was looking at a young Buddha." These are not pedestrian accounts of a teacher, yet I found, even among the most devotional students, a clear sobriety concerning the student-teacher relationship. They all told me the same thing: Adya is impeccable when it comes to the teacher-student exchange. He does not allow a student's power to be handed over in any form.

A questioner inquired of Adya, "Most students believe that the teacher is more awake or more aware than the students are. Given this belief, how can any student ever have a teacher who he doesn't become attached to or dependent upon?" Adya replied, "The relationship between the teacher and student is precisely for the purpose of removing this very illusion. Most students come to a spiritual teacher with certain dependencies. This is to be expected. However, if the relationship with the teacher is based upon these dependencies, then it is doomed to failure. Like a child who is dependent upon its mother but later grows beyond that dependency, the student should, from the very start, be endeavoring to grow beyond their dependency on the spiritual teacher. This is a very delicate and subtle process that requires a very sincere student and a very clear teacher."[9]

Hamsa tried the worship approach. Soon after she'd met Adya, she fell down on her knees in full prostration before him, and in an instant he was bowing down next to her. "He closed that door. That year was the severance of the dream. Adya often says that he'll hold a student's projection, but not for long. Often someone can't hold the projection of the magnitude of themselves and they will project it onto Adya and he'll hold it for a while, but then that's enough," Hamsa told me.

Bonnie had similar devotional qualities rise up inside and it surprised her. "What happened in my relationship with Adya was this incredible love got projected onto him, all of a sudden I just absolutely loved him. I have a son his age, so it wasn't a romantic kind of love. It made me understand after all these years what the true guru relationship was about because I never quite understood the quality of devotion that people work themselves into, particularly in the Hindu tradition. It's like you're on fire with it, you don't have any choice in the matter. I'm in my late fifties and it's just embarrassing but it's there and I had known for a long time that a resistance to love was my holding point. Adya's so amazing because he just meets it, and this happens a lot with his students. He's just completely available and willing for the love to be there without trying to calm it down or take advantage of it. There's no resistance. I'd tell him, 'This is really embarrassing to have this feeling for you, I'm too old for this.' And he'd say, 'You know it will pass.' And it did," she said.

When Adya first started to teach, he struggled with how to meet a student's devotional energy and he experimented to see what worked, both on a subtle energetic level and on the more overt outward expression of it. "At first I would see what people were doing or trying to do, most of which was unconscious, and with no ill intent, and I would try in some way to see what our relationship was and what they were doing. I found that no strategy worked. It was a losing game from the beginning. I decided to drop any strategy about it. If transference came up, it just wasn't part of the game. I'm not even going to try to play this game. I do my thing, I say what I say to you, I talk, and the rest is up to you."

A student asked Adya, "How does one purely express devotion that is devoid of projection?" Adya responded, "True devotion has no projection. Otherwise it's being devoted to a fantasy, to an image. This is better known as worship. Worshipping is when you put any head above your own. This is simply ignorance and causes further and further separation. Devotion comes out of an intuitive sense of unity or oneness. This oneness can be the source of great devotion and great love. But if your devotion makes you feel separate from the object of your devotion, you have fallen into the ignorance of worship."[10]

Adya also makes it a point to publicly demystify his status as an "enlightened" being as often as possible. He'll mention to retreatants that he went to the Happy Hound for a burger or will appear with a double latte from Starbucks—two things equivalent to Satan worship for many of his politically correct Northern California students. But he's not doing anything outside of his personality. That's who he is. "I tend to tell people that my idea of contemplation is sitting in the backyard with a cheap cup of coffee in a Styrofoam cup and eating Twinkies. And it's true! I like to do that now and then. And I feel great. Some other time I might like sitting in the Himalayas. I don't see any difference, actually, if your mind state is here and now. I often talk about my day-to-day life, which is relatively unimpressive."

He makes it clear, as well, that he has a teacher function, but it is not a permanent identity. He is not the all-suffering gatherer of wayward children to his breast. "I tell people constantly, 'I don't want to be around a bunch of damn students all the time!' It's already surreal enough! The guys who do the monastery thing and are with students all the time, I mean, God bless you! Forget it! It's not my idea of a good time. I love it when I am doing what I do, but I wouldn't want to live in that environment, because there's too much unreality about it. There's just too much living in the world of projection. There's a beauty to it, but there's unreality, too," he told me. When all else fails, Adya will invite a student over to play poker. "Then I take their money and they get a little different view of me."

Adya was born not far from where he lives. He had a very stable and happy childhood and wasn't raised in any particular religion, though there was always talk of spirituality in his family. His aunt Ethyl, an early influence, was a mystic of sorts, and his grandfather

Foster, on his mother's side, was a deacon in the Baptist church. Adya's parents, Larry and Carol, who have been to many of their son's retreats and are a part of his community, occasionally took him to church. Even as a young child he had a strong yearning for truth. When he was put into Sunday school—for a few months only—he thought the whole setup was odd. "Why would I want to be Crayola-coloring pictures of Jesus? I wanted to know something about Jesus."[11]

Adya's early years were infused with what we would call spiritual experiences, but what were for him everyday events. "For a long period I had a nice big white light that hung out at the end of my bed at night and I didn't think anything of it. I had moments when I would sit and stare at my wood dresser and I could disappear into the wood and feel like I *was* the wood."[12] He had a recurring dream in which he was taken underground to a room and taught by an old Asian man. At the time, he'd never heard of Buddhism. During the fifth grade Adya had an experience that he recognized at the time as being different from "normal" life. He didn't feel like a child or an adult, but somehow "outside of time." That event awakened in him an inner guide that he trusted implicitly. "This inner guide taught me that I could know anything I wanted to know; all I had to do was not try to know it. I found that simply by having the question and then not trying to answer it, but just keeping it in my mind, out of nowhere in a few days, sometimes a few weeks, the answer would just pop up."[13]

Adya was a bit of a loner as a child, as he is still, and touched with the usual amount of devilishness—he always had his ear to any closed door and private conversations. But for all intents and purposes Adya had a very normal and healthy childhood that happened to be touched quite frequently by mystical events. "In junior high, three, four, five times a year I would wake up in bed and my perception would be turned on its head from normal. We would call it now being in a very awake condition. I knew as soon as I opened my eyes. I'd just say to myself, 'This is one of those days that I am absolutely one with everything.' I would have to teach myself not to look at people because I would love to do it, because I was them. And if you go to school and start looking at people that way, they get a little weird."[14]

Telling these tales of youth makes Adya a little uneasy. "The reason I almost never talk about these stories is that certain people will put me into some special category. What I found as a teacher is that there is really no such thing as a special category. If you never had any of these odd experiences, it doesn't much matter. But, you know, even though I say this to people, they won't believe it. They'll say, 'Well, of course, you can say that because you had those experiences.' Especially when they hear I had good parents and was cared for really well. But actually there are more awake spiritual people who have had a lot of hardship in their life and childhood than there are not."[15] The point of telling these stories here is that it gives the reader a sense of Adya's motivation as he later searched for a teacher and a spiritual practice. He had little need—with such a rich and textured inner life—for external motivation or discipline or even, for that matter, guidance.

"My relationship with my teacher Arvis was very much like my relationship that I had when I was racing bicycles at a younger age. She was my spiritual coach. It never occurred to me that a teacher can somehow give you something. It was only later that I found out people had that notion in their heads." Arvis, with genuine humility, agreed with her student. "I never set myself up as a teacher. I was more like a hostess and I was sharing my practice with whoever came to my house. If they didn't want anything, I stayed out of it," she told me. Arvis is now eighty years old, retired from being a "hostess," and volunteers one day a week at the Open Gate Sangha office.

The bones of Adya's studentship are what shape the body of his teaching style. There is no notion in his head about giving his students anything. Yet he has tasted a certain spaciousness that arose naturally within him and has experienced as a teacher the ability to help students with their own expansion. "A true teacher is one who opens space within your mind. If you turn your attention away from everything else and merge with that space, you awaken as that consciousness. This space is the true teacher's gift. It is an open door, but you must walk through it."[16]

At eighteen, Adya read a book on Zen and came across the word "enlightenment." It was then that his troubles started. "I had bitten, the hook had been set, and I was on the enlightenment path and then, very quickly, I wasn't just yearning, I was going stark raving bananas. All those little wonderful experiences I had as a child stopped flat, just stopped, and I was on the spiritual path."[17] As is Adya's leaning, he quickly winnowed down his spiritual questions to the essentials: Is life ultimately good and positive, or is it negative, as it is portrayed on television? "I was terrified to find out what was true because I had to equally take the possibility that it could end up being a terrible disaster. I eventually found the strength to entertain that possibility just as much as I entertained the likelihood that it could be good. From about twenty years old on, that was the fuel for my search."[18]

The problem with any deep inquiry is that it's very difficult to know what is true and what is delusion. It's at this point when a clear teacher can help tremendously to guide the student through the minefield of ego blindness and fear, and Adya had the consistent clarity of Arvis and Kwong Roshi to temper his search. But the teacher cannot swim for us; students must rely on their own experience of reality to cut away the blurring fat of ignorance. "The big thing was realizing that any part of the mind or personality or emotions was completely, absolutely untrustworthy as far as the

Truth is concerned. That's the first step. What I found was that when I was able to sustain that, knowing the untrustworthiness of it without collapsing, then that which was trustworthy became obvious."[19]

For twelve years Adya dug deeper and deeper into the question of his own existence. At twenty-five he had a profound awakening that led to the beginning of his liberation. Though Adya's awakening was deep, he still felt there was more, more to cleanse, more to uncover. The seeker was not yet extinguished. These were not necessarily happy years. "Overall, the journey from ages nineteen to thirty-one was, outside of moments of revelation, pretty damn very unpleasant,"[20] he said. When Adya had his "final awakening" the seeker disappeared. When he heard that birdsong, a voice inside him said, "Who hears that sound?" And that was it. Days after the experience he wrote a letter to Kwong Roshi describing what he'd seen. "Instantly the whole world, my perception of it, flipped 180 degrees. Everything dropped away. Everything. I was hearing. I was the bird. I was everything and nothing at all. It's just like waking up from sleep. Nothing special at all. No excitement. No thrills. Nothing like I thought it would be. It's like going home. Finding home."[21] Soon after this experience he began to teach.

Six months after Adya started teaching, he had a sobering insight into the teacher-student relationship. He was driving home from one of his talks and he suddenly realized that he could tell people just about anything and they would believe it. "It really scared me because I'd never seen how vulnerable human beings really are. I'd never totally seen into it until that moment. Even well put-together, smart people—not just dysfunctional people—are reaching out to anything that will help them. When I saw it, it had the effect of someone sucker-punching me. Literally, all the air went out of my lungs as though someone had hit me in the stomach and I was in shock. I immediately sensed the responsibility that goes along with it—if people are that vulnerable, then I've got to be really clear. I've got to really have my head up, really know what I'm doing."

This realization is the reason Adya is so up front about power issues. Teachers don't commonly talk about their own power. When they say it's impossible to really give students anything, it's true—nothing is added to what already exists in a person. But at the same time teachers can be powerful catalysts for the journey inward, and if they do not take responsibility for that power, then the shit can hit the fan. Adya was surprised to find that to some extent what he had realized *could* be transmitted to his students. In Zen it's described as direct transmission, but it is never talked about in much depth. "There is something to the teacher-student relationship that transcends what is said and the teachings themselves and all of it. The most delicate thing in the whole discussion of teachers and students is what I call the 'juice.' It doesn't have to be a teacher. But if someone's got the juice they can be a really powerful catalyst for someone's awakening," he told me.

The need for wisdom in all of this is essential. Power can be applied at inappropriate times; teachers can force the issue and cause their students unwarranted problems. "I realized that if I had an intention behind getting someone to awaken, it didn't always end up well. It's possible to break people open, but they'd usually have an equal and opposite contraction which might leave them in a worse place. Even if a person has an awakening, no teacher can complete the job for them. There's always another element that can't be transmitted," Adya said. It must be noted here that when he speaks of a teacher being a powerful catalyst, he is not speaking of personal power but of the juice of awakening. Whatever skill Adya has as a teacher comes directly from the clarity of the emptiness he realized upon his awakening. On the teacher level it is not Adya meeting either Jack or Jill, it is enlightenment calling forth enlightenment. It is the difference between mind and presence. Teachers get into trouble when they perceive themselves as having some sort of tremendous personal power.

"Adya magnificently represents the mind in its function as opposed to its presence," Peter told me. "The difference became really ripe with me—mind and presence and seeing thoughts as such. It's getting progressively difficult to take any thoughts seriously." This is really the esoteric part of the teaching, the transmission or exchange or dance of subtle energies. This is the mystery. "Early on I found when I talked to people I could kind of guide them," Adya said. "Nowadays I don't do nearly as much guiding. Someone will ask me a question and I'll just start talking. The feeling is that I'm just talking, not with any intention, it just happens, it's like I'm downloading the answer and keeping everything open. I don't really understand; it's not necessary for me to understand. I look at the person and often say, 'You got it?' And they say, 'Yeah.' I didn't really guide them 'there,' I just talked about 'there.' "

"When you have that type of experience of who you really are, the idea of the seeker becomes irrational. You can't imagine why you would want to look for anything. The drive is gone. I could care less if I ever meet another spiritual teacher anywhere," Bonnie told me. Awakening comes and then you must learn to embody it, to find the truth of it in action, in daily life. That is why Adya makes a point of talking continually about the embodiment process.

"Embodiment is usually a gradual process that begins after the event called 'awakening,' so we can't really speak about embodiment in absolute terms. The indications of embodiment are peace, love, wisdom, and enlightened action. What effect we have on others is a good indication of exactly how enlightened we are. If we think we are very enlightened, but have a negative effect on others, we are probably not nearly as enlightened as we'd like to believe. Enlightened action springs from a humility that never makes assumptions about one's own attainment. The more humble you are, the better chance that your behavior will be enlightened."[22]

People can have deep awakenings and unknowingly hide from parts of themselves in transcendence. This is called "spiritual bypass." But it never works. "It's the nature of consciousness, number one, to leave everything, to transcend, and then it's the nature of consciousness to come back for the very stuff it transcended. Quite naturally, consciousness is going to start to move back into the world of form, and so it's going to have to deal with the dark little recesses, the unresolved things, the resentments, the angers, all that stuff is going to have to be seen," Adya explained.

This can be done through psychology, spiritual practice, or a combination of both. Even if you wish and wish that it might be otherwise, it's going to have to be done. Bonnie has made a profession out of helping spiritual seekers along the path and sees psychological work as a good primer for the real gritty spiritual work. "It has always been my observation that people who had done the psychological work had a much easier time navigating the spiritual work. Anything that is left undone, particularly if you've had a traumatic past, is going to come up much more intensely through the spiritual awakening process. And it's harder to deal with objectively if you've never done any psychological work yourself," she told me.

As Adya is always pointing out, awakening is not about gain or accumulation. "Most spirituality is a construction project. We're ascending and ascending—ideas are ascending, kundalini energy is ascending, consciousness is ascending. It just keeps building and a person feels, 'I'm getting better and better.' But enlightenment is a demolition project."

10

ALL THE KING'S HORSES

For greatest scandal waits on greatest state.[1]
—WILLIAM SHAKESPEARE

One of the first bioterrorism attacks in the United States was waged by followers of Bhagwan Shree Rajneesh in 1984. Rajneesh was an Indian guru who moved to America to found a commune. Members of his group, known as Rajneeshees, placed salmonella in the salad bars of ten restaurants in the city of The Dalles in Oregon. They did so in the hope of influencing the county election—sickening people to prevent them from voting, and thus ensuring victory for Rajneeshee candidates. More than 750 people became ill.

By the time Rajneesh (aka Osho, Acharya Rajneesh, or Chandra Mohan Jain) was kicked out of the country (charged with one count of criminal conspiracy and thirty-four counts of making false statements to immigration officials), the list of charges against his followers was as long as a mafia thug's rap sheet. Twenty-five Rajneeshees were charged with electronic eavesdropping conspiracy, thirteen with immigration conspiracy, eight with lying to federal officials, three with harboring a fugitive, three with criminal conspiracy, one with burglary, one with racketeering, one with first-degree arson, two with second-degree assault, three with first-degree assault, and three with attempted murder.[2] This was a "spiritual community."

Six years before the Rajneeshees placed salmonella on alfalfa sprouts and lettuce, 918 Americans died—many of them African

Americans—in a jungle encampment known as Jonestown, in Guyana, South America. Nine hundred of those deaths were from drinking cyanide-laced Flav-R-Aid (a British version of Kool-Aid). This was the largest mass murder–suicide in American history. Just a half-decade before the carnage in Guyana, Jim Jones had opened a Peoples Temple church in the heart of the Fillmore District of San Francisco, an African American ghetto. The interracial church offered free blood pressure and sickle-cell anemia tests and free child care for working parents and was, in the beginning, a respected social advocate for blacks, the elderly, and the poor.

Chögyam Trunga Rinpoche said:

> Whenever we begin to feel any discrepancy or conflict between our actions and the teachings, we immediately interpret the situation in such a way that the conflict is smoothed over. The interpreter is ego in the role of spiritual advisor. The situation is like that of a country where church and state are separate. If the policy of the state is foreign to the teachings of the church, then the automatic reaction of the king is to go to the head of the church, his spiritual advisor, and ask his blessing. The head of the church then works out some justification and gives the policy his blessing under the pretense that the king is the protector of the faith. In an individual's mind, it works out very neatly that way, ego being both king and the head of the church.[3]

Religious scandals and teacher abuses are not unique to any one place on the globe, nor are they confined to a particular religion or spiritual community or time in history. The abuses run the full spectrum of human foolishness, but for the sake of clarity and neatness they are usually lumped into four categories, which, not coincidentally, are the same for politicians, Hollywood stars, and the average Joe. In *The Guru Papers: Masks of Authoritarian Power,* by Joel Kramer and Diana Alstad, the authors break down the categories in this way:

1. Sexual abuse: . . . includes child molestation, rape, promulgating prostitution . . . a pretense of celibacy or monogamy while having clandestine sexual activity.
2. Material abuse: . . . concerns for wealth and luxurious living contradict the stated values of austerity or detachment.
3. Abuse of power: . . . using and abusing others for one's own enhancement and to preserve power.
4. Self abuse: . . . the body is the temple of the spirit and must so be treated: a healthy body is the result of a healthy mind and spirit; tranquility, compassion, and emotional control are signs of arrival. Yet many leaders display the opposite: drunkenness, obesity, vindictiveness, rages. . . .[4]

In real life these "separate" categories are less well delineated. A teacher's sexual and/or material missteps might be the direct result of substance abuse and vice versa. Life *is* messy, but we rightly have expectations that our spiritual leaders have found a toehold a little above the more slippery courses of our earthly wanderings. We are naturally given to outrage in the face of spiritual scandals—if we haven't yet become hopelessly jaded—because religious groups and spiritual practices offer a perennial promise of Truth and by extension justice, compassion, and all the beautiful qualities of what it is to be human.

Karen Armstrong writes, "Like any other human activity, religion can be abused, but it seems to have been something that we have always done. It was not tacked on to a primordially secular nature by manipulative kings and priests but was natural to humanity."[5] I would further clarify that *spirituality* is the natural impulse in humanity and that religion is its necessary twin—the one the bones, the other the flesh. But the point of the matter is that even through all the religious treachery—the "holy" wars, the blatant and outrageous misuses of power, the destructive patriarchal manipulations, and sexual abuses—spirituality has remained a constant flow in our lives. Spiritual leaders throughout history have opened themselves to this flow and have warned against trying to control it or claim it as one's own. Jesus, Muhammad, Buddha—all rejected, in some form or other, the religious status quo, whose spiritual body had long advanced toward rigor mortis.

Spiritual "outsiders" are enticing. The world's religious history is built in large measure upon the actions and words of outlaws. When we witness the horrors of such events as Jonestown or the Branch Davidians,[6] we wonder how a group could have wandered so far from what we take to be the norm. Yet it is that very departure that is central to such a group's appeal. Society is corrupt, the reasoning goes, so therefore a new norm must be established, or in many cases reinvigorated. Saint Benedict, disgusted by the corruption he found in Rome, created a community based on different, more-essential Christian values, and from this Benedictine Catholicism was born. We often hear people in spiritual communities say, "We answer to a higher calling," which in some cases means that they are rejecting, in full or in part, the established secular laws of society. When Gandhi acted against colonial rule and the caste system, he was establishing values based on spiritual truths, not on British colonial law or Hindu societal norms.

What I am getting at here is that when we are on the outside of scandal, looking in, we have a tendency to dismiss the people involved—that is, if they are adults—as too gullible, not educated, foolish, needy, plagued by low self-esteem, or any number of other labels that act to distance "us" from "them." In other words, we want to know that the same thing won't happen to us. But community dynamics and interpersonal relationships are never simple. Being gullible or needy—which we've all experienced at one time or another—do not, on their own, guarantee we'll have problems in a spiritual community. Abuses happen as part of a gestalt that develops over a period of time, usually years. No matter the degree of blindness in a teacher, there is always a measure of complicity within the group. But also, and this is no less important, the community exists within a societal and historic context that has a large impact upon the way it functions. Many of the Hindu and Buddhist scandals in America in the 1970s and 1980s that involved teachers of foreign origin happened in part because of cultural differences—particularly when those teachers arrived in the midst of the West's sexual revolution.

The attraction of "outlaw" spiritual leaders and/or the exoticism of foreign teachers might pull us into a community, yet there is a complex of factors—which change over time—that need to be in place before we find ourselves in dangerous waters. The ingredients for abuse are usually added slowly and are often masked, sometimes quite subtly, by noble-sounding intentions.

In one study of Jonestown, the researchers wrote:

The ideology of Peoples Temple focused on commitment to the community, and to elevating the group above the individual. Members deemed self-sacrifice the highest form of nobility, and selfishness as the lowest of human behavior. Loyalty tests ensured commitment to the cause. No one looked askance at various practices because they made sense within a worldview that anticipated an imminent apocalypse—either through thermonuclear war or genocide against people of color. By fleeing the United States and attempting to create an alternative society, Temple members believed they might survive this harsh inevitability, perhaps even serving as a new model for humanity. But forces arrayed against them, they assumed, conspired to defeat them, and so they were defeated.[7]

When we ask the questions that need asking in response to teacher-student and spiritual community abuses, we are better served by realizing that all of us contain the possibility of health and dysfunction. We all wrestle with the same questions that I am sure plagued the members of Jonestown and the Rajneeshees. Don't we need to trust the teacher implicitly in order to progress along the spiritual path? Can we maintain our personal autonomy and still serve the greater good? Shouldn't we answer to a "higher calling"? There is a measure of blindness in any group toward conflagrations, power struggles, envy, jealousy, and so forth. Luckily, it's rare that these low-level fires erupt into the disasters of Jonestown or the recent sexual scandals in the Catholic Church. But still it is good to remember that there is often a subtle line, as Chögyam Trungpa Rinpoche described, between enlightenment and delusion.

A former follower of Bhagwan Shree Rajneesh writes:

> Rajneesh never lost the ultimate existential truth of being. He only lost the ordinary concept of truth that any normal adult can easily understand. He rationalized his constant lying as "left-handed Tantra," but that too was dishonest. Rajneesh lied to save face, to avoid taking responsibility for his own mistakes, and to gain personal power. Those lies had nothing to do with Tantra or any selfless acts of kindness. Rajneesh knew everything that Buddha knew and he was everything that Buddha was. It was his loss of respect for ordinary truthfulness that destroyed his teaching.[8]

"Awakening is a process marked by profound experiences and periods of integration. However powerful an initial opening is, it inevitably leaves many aspects of our personal life unaffected," writes Jack Kornfield, a psychotherapist and co-founder of the Insight Meditation Center. "A mystical vision or taste of 'enlightenment,' an experience of satori, or awakening, is just the beginning of deep spiritual practice, but these initial experiences can be so powerful that many people begin teaching based on them alone. These unintegrated experiences can easily lead to grandiosity and inflation."[9] Daido Roshi has always said that if you shot up the Buddha with heroin every day for a month, you would have an addict. Enlightenment, even to the degree of the Buddha's attainment, is no absolute guarantee against a teacher dipping into delusion.

Being in the teacher role is a powerful position and, like heroin, such power can be addictive. As students, we often fuel this addiction by giving over our power to the teacher; we become enablers, co-conspirators. Frequently we do so through transference and projection. It is common for students to unconsciously project on or transfer to a teacher characteristics of some significant figure in their past, particularly their parents. Often the unfinished business of family dynamics or past loves leaks into the teacher-student relationship or into the interactions with the spiritual community. These idealizations can be negative (we might have had an overbearing father and see the teacher as a constant bully) or positive (we believe that the teacher will fulfill all our emotional and spiritual needs and see them as the perfect parent).

In these states a student, like a political operative, tends to paint things in simple and shallow terms, glossing over any real human complexities. Depending on the degree and intensity of the transference and, most important, depending on the clarity of the teacher, such episodes can either be part of the natural unfolding of spiritual practice or completely destructive to the individual and the entire spiritual community. "Transference and idealization have a powerful effect on teachers as well as students. They create a climate of unreality, and often feed the teacher's isolation. When the teacher is insecure or lonely, student projections increase these feelings. When students see a teacher as perfect, the teacher may become similarly deluded," writes Kornfield.[10]

Each of us, if we've been in an intimate relationship for any length of time, has experienced some form of projection. In therapy, projection and transference are used consciously (most of the time) as a tool to help the client resolve unfinished family dynamics and unfulfilled desires. Spiritual teachers, though less directive with a student's projection, will also use its presence as a means to illuminate attachments and ego patterns. Teachers are generally aware of the destructive power that transference can wield, but these are subtle exchanges and need continued clarity.

The late 1970s and the entire 1980s were a period of widespread religious scandal. Nearly every spiritual discipline was caught in the tumult: Jonestown and Rajneesh; Jim and Tammy Faye Bakker; the Hare Krishna scandal (brought to an ugly light— sexual misconduct, greed, etc.—by Nori J. Muster's book *Betrayal of the Spirit*); the sexual and financial scandal of Richard Baker and the San Francisco Zen Center (recently described with investigative journalist fervor in the book *Shoes Outside the Door*); Maezumi Roshi at Zen Center of Los Angeles; the Shambhala (Chögyam Trungpa Rinpoche's organization) disaster in which Ösel Tendzin (Thomas Rich), who was Trungpa's successor, had sex with a great many students while knowingly carrying the AIDS virus; the *fatwa* placed on Salman Rushdie for writing *The Satanic Verses.* And there were the first signs and warnings of the Catholic sex-abuse problems that have recently gained media attention; the Rev. Thomas P. Doyle, a Dominican priest, co-authored a report in 1985 that warned of impending pedophile scandals.

Though all of this scandalous behavior might seem bleak and offer little promise for healthy teacher-student relationships in the future, the opposite is true. The abuses, though painful and confusing, have exposed much of the faulty authoritarian structure in the "old-style" guru-disciple relationship. Students are now much more aware of the potential for problems and are willing to take more responsibility for their own spiritual development. We—both teachers and students—are continuing to change our functioning within the established roles. We're learning the landscape of the new paradigm.

Sudha Puri, who is a monastic living within the spiritual community, told me, "The idea of me being the 'mother figure' and that is my title, is a little uncomfortable. This motherly role is the guru role and it's a model of dependence and I don't like that. I think we all need to be very strong and independent. I can have the heart of a mother, but the birds need to be kicked out of the nest so they can all find their own clear voice. That's the teaching of Vedanta. The model of dependence isn't healthy."

Sudha Puri alternates between traditional Indian dress and casual American clothing to upend the static image that some of her students cling to. As a former psychologist, she is very conscious of her students' projections, particularly as they relate to the classic guru model. Many of her students' projections will be wrapped in the guise of devotion. She doesn't deflect their devotion, but neither does she take it personally; there is no willingness on her part to take on that baggage. "Never turn over your sovereignty," Sudha Puri tells me. "If you just turn everything over abjectly, then the mind stops. Don't be a fool. I'm very clear with students and tell them that they can't miss steps; they may be very developed in the spiritual part but undeveloped in the emotional realm. So you've got to work on those things and not be embarrassed by it."

"Most people—in East and West alike—do not realize that putting oneself in the hands of an expert implies no loss of personal importance," writes Idries Shah. "Inconsistently, they will allow a surgeon to remove their appendixes, but will dispute the superior knowledge or experience of a teacher in a field in which they are as ignorant as in surgery."[11] That's the rub. As students we are at a disadvantage, yet this is what we want. We get little value from studying with someone who has less knowledge of the subject than we do. There is no need to throw the baby out with the bathwater because, as students, we still have much to learn, and as teachers we still have much to teach. We don't want to give up the game entirely but simply change a few rules. When we are in need of a doctor's care, it is an acceptable practice nowadays to get second and third opinions and come to the consultation with a good grasp—by way of handy research on the Internet—of the subject at hand.

This doesn't mean (within the new paradigm) that we are asking the teacher to relinquish all responsibility. It is just that we are no longer expecting the teacher to take the entire load. Trust is always going to be central to the spiritual teacher-disciple relationship. We cannot open to the teachings without faith in the teacher's ability to help us along the path. These days trust might take a little longer to develop, but that is not a bad thing. By continuing to question honestly, we can overcome our cynicism and fear. Our faith must now be clear-eyed and unafraid of testing.

Jack Kornfield encourages seekers to take responsibility for their journey, to keep asking the difficult questions. He writes:

> In the spiritual community, are you asked to violate your own sense of ethical conduct or integrity? Is there a dual standard for the community versus the guru and a few people around him? Are there secrets, rumors of difficulty? Do key members misuse sexuality, money, power? Are they mostly asking for your money? Are they asking for your body? Are you not allowed to hang out with your old friends? Do you feel dependent? Addicted? Is the practice humorless? . . . Are you being

asked to believe blindly without being able to see for yourself?...Is there a sense of intolerance? When you look at the
oldest and most senior students, are they happy and mature?
Do they have a place to graduate to, to teach, to express their
own dharma, or are people always kept in the role of students
and children?[12]

The path to trust leads through inquiry, and we should never be
complacent in our discernment. Yet we should also remember that
teachers are human, which means they make mistakes. We also, all
of us, have an honorable capacity for forgiveness. As Arvol Looking Horse writes, "We need a great healing. And we need a great
forgiving. But healing can't begin without forgiveness. We must forgive each other, forgive our loved ones, forgive our friends, forgive
our enemies, forgive ourselves."

The spiritual teacher-disciple relationship is a precious thing. It
can be absolutely life-changing in the most positive way. For every
teacher who goes astray, there are ten who never waver. Each teacher
in this book has helped transform hundreds, sometimes thousands,
of lives, and other teachers are doing the same every day. To open
our hearts and minds is a difficult, often painful thing. But it is a
noble pursuit, as much as we can be noble these days. Simply put,
to take this course, to show willingness to be taught, is to acknowledge that we cannot do it alone and that we realize that we need
each other.

NOTES

1. Returning to the Circle

1 John G. Neihardt, *Black Elk Speaks* (Lincoln, NE: University of Nebraska Press, 1988), p. 194.

2 Red Pine and Mike O'Connor, eds., *The Clouds Should Know Me By Now.* From the poem, "Given to Master Ch'ing-lun of Hsia Mountain," by Chien Chang, translated by Paul Hansen (Boston: Wisdom, 1998), p. 90.

3 William James, *The Varieties of Religious Experience* (New York: Viking Penguin, 1982), p. 485.

4 Martin Buber, *Tales of the Hasidim: Early Masters* (New York: Schocken Books, 1947), p. 151.

5 Thomas Merton, *Thomas Merton: Spiritual Master,* edited by Lawrence S. Cunningham (Mahwah, NJ: Paulist Press, 1992), p. 94.

6 Gary Snyder, *The Practice of the Wild* (San Francisco: North Point Press, 1990), p. 16.

7 Chögyam Trungpa, *The Myth of Freedom and the Way of Meditation,* edited by J. Baker and M. Casper (Boston: Shambhala, 1988), p. 31.

8 James, *The Varieties of Religious Experience,* p. 487.

9 Neihardt, *Black Elk Speaks,* p. 205.

10 Alexander Berzin, *Relating to a Spiritual Teacher: Building a Healthy Relationship* (Ithaca, NY: Snow Lion, 2000), p. 67.

11 Merton, *Thomas Merton: Spiritual Master,* p. 142.

12 Walt Whitman, *Leaves of Grass* (New York: Signet Classic, 1980), p. 51.

2. The Whistleblower: Murat Yagan

1 Sun'ullah Gaïbi, *The Gathering,* translated by Murat Yagan (Vernon, BC: Kebzeh Publications, 1994), p. 86.

2 Idries Shah, *The Sufis* (New York: Doubleday, 1964), p. 396.

3 Murat Yagan, *I Come from Behind Kaf Mountain* (Putney, VT: Threshold Books, 1984), p. ix.

4 Murat Yagan, *The Teachings of Kebzeh* (Vernon, BC: Kebzeh Publications, 1995), p. 4.

5 Ibid, p. 4.

6 Murat Yagan, *Ahmsta Kebzeh: The Science of Universal Awe* (Vernon, BC: Kebzeh Publications, 2003), p. xxvii.

7 Shah, *The Sufis,* p. 395.

8 Yagan, *I Come from Behind Kaf Mountain,* p. 16.

9 Ibid, p. 20.

10 Ibid, p. 18.

11 Ibid, p. 21.

12 Ibid, p. 22.

13 Ibid, p. 24.

14 Ibid, p. 29.

15 Ibid, p. 56.

16 Ibid, p. 56.

17 Ibid, p. 56.

18 Ibid, p. 64.

19 Ibid, p. 67.

Soundings

1 Arvol Looking Horse, *White Buffalo Teachings* (Williamsburg, MA: Dreamkeepers Press, 2001), p. 10.

2 John Daido Loori, *Mountain Record* 28, no. 2 (Mt. Tremper, NY: Dharma Communications, Inc., 1999), p. 10.

3 Murat Yagan, *I Come from Behind Kaf Mountain* (Putney, VT: Threshold Books, 1984), pp. 36, 37.

3. The Keeper: Chief Arvol Looking Horse

1 Dave Chief was a Lakota spiritual leader from the Ogallala Nation, grandson of Red Dog, Crazy Horse's Band. He was a good friend of Arvol's. This quote is from an interview I conducted with him months before he died.

2 Arvol Looking Horse, *White Buffalo Teachings* (Williamsburg, MA: Dreamkeepers Press, 2001), p. 37.

3 The White Buffalo Calf Pipe Bundle was brought to the Nation nineteen generations ago by White Buffalo Calf Woman.

4 Vine Deloria Jr., *For This Land* (New York: Routledge, 1999), p. 134.

5 Frank King, *The Native Voice: Interview with Arvol Looking Horse*, www.homestead.com/arvollookinghorse/articles_on_chief_Arvol_may2002.html.

6 Vine Deloria Jr., *Spirit and Reason* (Golden, CO: Fulcrum Publishing, 1999), p. 48.

7 Vine Deloria Jr., *God Is Red* (Golden, CO: Fulcrum Publishing, 1993), p. 62.

8 Gary Snyder, *The Practice of the Wild* (San Francisco: North Point Press, 1990), p. 64.

9 Ibid, p. 64.

10 Looking Horse, *White Buffalo Teachings*, pp. 42, 43.

11 Ibid, pp. 38, 39.

12 John G. Neihardt, *Black Elk Speaks* (Lincoln, NE: University of Nebraska Press, 1988), p. 270.

13 Snyder, *Practice of the Wild*, p. 63.

14 Vine Deloria Jr., *Custer Died for Your Sins* (New York: Collier Macmillan, 1969), pp. 146, 147.

15 Gathered from website, www.manataka.org/page108.html.

16 www.homestead.com/arvollookinghorse/articles_on_chief_Arvol_may2002.html.

17 "Arvol Tells How He Started on His Path," www.kstrom.net/isk/arvol/arv_path.html.

18 Ibid.

19 Looking Horse, *White Buffalo Teachings,* p. 24.

20 Ibid, p. 25.

21 Ibid, p. 9.

Ego: Good, Bad, and Indifferent

1 Chögyam Trungpa, *Cutting Through Spiritual Materialism* (Boston: Shambhala, 1987), p. 15.

2 Jeremy D. Safran, ed., *Psychoanalysis and Buddhism: An Unfolding Dialogue* (Boston: Wisdom Publications, 2003), p. 36.

3 Vine Deloria Jr., *Spirit and Reason* (Golden, CO: Fulcrum Publishing, 1999), p. 227.

4 Adyashanti, *Emptiness Dancing* (Los Gatos, CA: Open Gate Publishing, 2004), pp. 104, 106.

5 Ibid, p. 107.

6 Jack Kornfield, *A Path with Heart* (New York: Bantam, 1993), p. 198.

4. Untying the Cat: Joan Chittister, OSB

1 Mary Lou Kownacki, *Between Two Souls: Conversations with Ryōkan* (Grand Rapids, MI: Eerdmans, 2004), p. 153.

2 Joan Chittister, *The Way We Were* (Maryknoll, NY: Orbis Books, 2005), p. 17.

3 Annie Dillard, *Living by Fiction* (New York: Harper & Row, 1982), p. 22.

4 "Statement of Sister Christine Vladimiroff," extracted from the Association for the Rights of Catholics in the Church (ARCC) website: www.arcc-catholic-rights.org/prioress.htm.

5 Joan Chittister, *In Search of Belief* (Liguori, MO: Liguori/Triumph, 1999), p. 9.

6 Joan Chittister, *Called to Question* (Lanham, MD: Sheed & Ward, 2004), p. 14.

7 "Statement of Sister Christine Vladimiroff."

8 Joan Chittister, *The Rule of Benedict: Insights for the Ages* (New York: Crossroad, 2003), p. 31.

9 Chittister, *The Way We Were.*

10 Ibid, p. 23.

11 Chittister, *The Rule of Benedict,* p. 36.

12 Ibid, p. 37.

13 Chittister, *The Way We Were,* p. 12.

14 Ibid, pp. 12, 13.

15 Joan Chittister, *Heart of Flesh* (Grand Rapids, MI: Eerdmans, 1998), p. 89.

16 On December 2, 1980, Maryknoll sisters Maura Clarke, Ita Ford, and Dorothy Kazel and lay worker Jean Donovan were raped, mutilated, and murdered because of their work with the poor and destitute in El Salvador.

17 Thomas Merton, *Thomas Merton: Spiritual Master,* edited by Lawrence S. Cunningham (New York: Paulist Press, 1992), p. 233.

18 Joan Chittister, *Wisdom Distilled from the Daily* (San Francisco: HarperSanFrancisco, 1991), p. 62.

5. Tying Shoes: Rabbi Zalman Schachter-Shalomi

1 Martin Buber, *Tales of the Hasidim: Early Masters* (New York: Schocken, 1947), p. 107.

2 Tirzah Firestone, *With Roots in Heaven* (New York: Dutton, 1998), p. 200.

3 Huston Smith, *The World's Religions* (San Francisco: HarperSanFrancisco, 1991), p. 278.

4 Zalman Schachter-Shalomi, *Jewish with Feeling* (New York: Riverhead, 2005), p. 37.

5 Zalman Schachter-Shalomi, *Wrapped in a Holy Flame* (San Francisco: Jossey-Bass, 2003), p. 11.

6 Ibid, p. 13.

7 Ibid, p. 13.

8 Ibid, p. 12.

9 Ibid, p. 12.

10 Ibid, p. 13.

11 Zalman Schachter-Shalomi and Netanel Miles-Yépez, unpublished manuscript.

12 Ibid.

13 Firestone, *With Roots in Heaven,* p. 311.

14 Karl Stern, *The Third Revolution: A Study of Psychiatry and Religion* (Garden City, NY: Image Books, 1961).

15 Schachter-Shalomi and Miles-Yépez, unpublished manuscript.

16 Ibid.

Gratitude

1 Taizan Maezumi Roshi, *Appreciate Your Life* (Boston: Shambhala, 2002), p. 3.

2 Sudha Puri, from talks compiled in manuscript form by Janapriya.

3 Murat Yagan, *The Teachings of Kebzeh* (Vernon, BC: Kebzeh Publications, 1995), p. 46.

4 Gregg Krech, *Naikan* (Berkeley: Stone Bridge Press, 2002), p. 35. Krech is the executive director of the Tōdō Institute, which provides instruction in the Japanese therapies of Naikan and Morita, a psychotherapy developed by Japanese psychiatrist Shoma Morita and based on the principles of Zen.

5 Developed in Japan by Ishin Yoshimoto, Naikan is a deep method of self-examination in which the participant looks at the people and things in their life through the eyes of three questions: "What did I receive from this person or thing?", "What did I give this person or thing?", and "What troubles did I cause this person or thing?"

6 From an interview in *The Sun,* December 2004, p. 10.

6. Master of the Ordinary: Gehlek Rimpoche

1 Allen Ginsberg, "Thoughts on a Breath," *Poems All Over the Place: Mostly Seventies* (Cherry Valley, NY: Cherry Valley Editions, 1978), p. 35.

2 Gehlek Nawang, *Good Life, Good Death* (New York: Riverhead, 2002), p. 12.

3 Ibid, p. xiii.

4 Alexander Berzin, *Relating to a Spiritual Teacher: Building a Healthy Relationship* (Ithaca, NY: Snow Lion, 2000), p. 20.

5 Alexander Berzin, "Making Sense of Tantra: Basic Questions and Doubts," www.berzinarchives.com/e-books/making_sense_tantra/making_sense_tantra_I.html (accessed October 29, 2005).

6 Kalu Rinpoche, *The Dharma: That Illuminates All Beings Impartially Like the Light of the Sun and the Moon* (Albany, NY: State University of New York Press, 1986), p. 109.

7 Huston Smith, *The World's Religions* (San Francisco: HarperSanFrancisco, 1991), p. 142.

8 Gehlek Nawang, *Good Life, Good Death*, pp. 60, 61.

9 Ibid, p. 61.

10 Ibid, p. 68.

11 Ibid, p. 19.

Drawing Boundaries: Community, Cliques, and Clubs

1 Chögyam Trungpa, *Cutting Through Spiritual Materialism* (Boston: Shambhala, 1987), p. 27.

2 Joan Chittister, *Called to Question* (Lanham, MD: Sheed & Ward, 2004), p. 161.

7. A Bridge Home: Reverend Mother Sudha Puri

1 Sara Ann Levinsky, *A Bridge of Dreams* (West Stockbridge, MA: Lindisfarne, 1984), p. 305.

2 Lex Hixon, *Coming Home* (Burdett, NY: Larson Publications, 1995), pp. 26, 27.

3 Ibid, p. 36.

4 Levinsky, *A Bridge of Dreams*, p. 557.

5 Hixon, *Coming Home*, p. 40.

6 Ibid, p. 39.

7 Levinsky, *A Bridge of Dreams*, p. 372.

8 Sudha Ma quote from a manuscript of her talks compiled by Janapriya.

The Healthy Diet of Disillusionment

1 Chögyam Trungpa, *Cutting Through Spiritual Materialism* (Boston: Shambhala, 1987), p. 25.

2 Jack Kornfield, *A Path with Heart* (New York: Bantam, 1993), pp. 268, 269.

3 Adyashanti, *Emptiness Dancing* (Los Gatos, CA: Open Gate, 2004), p. 149.

4 Joel Kramer and Diana Alstad, *The Guru Papers* (Berkeley: Frog Ltd., 1993), p. 155.

5 Joan Chittister, *Called to Question* (Lanham, MD: Sheed & Ward, 2004), p. 55.

8. Undiscovered Genetics: John Daido Loori Roshi

1 Lao-tzu, *Tao Te Ching,* translated by Stephen Mitchell (New York: HarperCollins, 1988), p. 48.

2 Taizan Maezumi Roshi, who died in 1995, was a seminal figure in bringing Zen to America, and was the founder, in 1963, of Zen Center of Los Angeles.

3 David Chadwick, *Crooked Cucumber: The Life and Zen Teaching of Shunryu Suzuki* (New York: Broadway Books, 2000), p. 320.

4 Bernie Tetsugen Glassman is Maezumi Roshi's first dharma heir, founder of Greyston Bakery and the Zen Peacemakers, and author.

5 Huston Smith, *The World's Religions* (San Francisco: HarperSanFrancisco, 1991), p. 133.

6 Koans are stories or dialogues in the Zen (Chan) tradition that confound the intellect and can only be "seen into" by intuition. *Shikantaza,* or "just sitting," is a form of meditation. There is no direction for the mind other than to simply be in the moment.

7 Smith, *The World's Religions,* pp. 136, 137.

8 Eido Tai Shimano Roshi is a Rinzai Zen master who heads the Zen Studies Society and founded the New York Zendo Shobo-Ji and the

Dai Bosatsu Zendo Kongo-Ji in the Catskill Mountains. He received dharma transmission from Soen Nakagawa Roshi in 1972.

9 John Daido Loori, *The Zen of Creativity* (New York: Ballantine, 2004), p. 25.

10 Soen Nakagawa Roshi was a Rinzai Zen master and a seminal figure in bringing Zen to America. He was an extraordinary poet and calligrapher, as well as a gifted yet eccentric teacher.

11 Naropa University (formally Naropa Institute) was founded by the late Trungpa Rinpoche. It is the only major accredited Buddhist university in North America.

12 Kazuaki Tanahashi is an artist and the author of many books, including *Brush Mind*, and is also a well-known translator of Japanese Zen classics.

13 Loori, *The Zen of Creativity*, p. 5.

14 Dogen Zenji was a thirteenth-century Zen master and founder of the Soto School.

15 Joan Chittister, *Called to Question* (Lanham, MD: Sheed & Ward, 2004), p. 14.

16 John Daido Loori, *The Eight Gates of Zen* (Mt. Tremper, NY: Dharma Communications, 1992), p. 24.

9. *Traveling Without a Passport: Adyashanti*

1 Nisargadatta Maharaj, *I Am That* (Durham, NC: Acorn Press, 1973), p. 443.

2 Adyashanti, *Emptiness Dancing* (Los Gatos, CA: Open Gate, 2004), p. 3.

3 Ibid, p. 5.

4 Adyashanti, *The Impact of Awakening* (Los Gatos, CA: Open Gate, 2005), p. 103.

5 Yasutani Hakuun Roshi was one of the most influential Zen teachers in the West and a teacher to, among others, Taizan Maezumi Roshi, who was also a seminal figure in Western Zen and founded the Zen Center of Los Angeles. Eido Shimano Roshi received dharma

transmission from Soen Nakagawa Roshi and is the founder and abbot of Dai Bosatsu and Zendo Shobo-Ji.

6 Shunryu Suzuki Roshi was the founder of the San Francisco Zen Center, Green Gulch Farm, and Tassajara Zen Mountain Center— the first Zen training monastery in the West.

7 Adyashanti, *Emptiness Dancing*, p. 2.

8 Dogen Zenji, thirteenth-century master and founder of the Soto School, is a forceful influence on modern Zen.

9 Adyashanti, *The Impact of Awakening*, pp. 110, 111.

10 Ibid, pp. 105, 106.

11 Adyashanti, from a private interview, March 7, 1999, www.wheniawoke .com/sages/adyashanti.html.

12 Ibid.

13 Ibid.

14 Ibid.

15 Ibid.

16 Adyashanti, *The Impact of Awakening*, p. 107.

17 Adyashanti, from a private interview, March 7, 1999.

18 Ibid.

19 Ibid.

20 Ibid.

21 Ibid.

22 Adyashanti, *The Impact of Awakening*, pp. 64, 65.

10. All the King's Horses

1 William Shakespeare, *The Rape of Lucrece* (The Riverside Shakespeare: Boston: Houghton Mifflin, 1974), p. 1733.

2 Sven Davisson, *The Rise and Fall of Rajneeshpuram*, www.ashe-prem.org/ two/davisson.shtml (accessed December 15, 2005).

3 Chögyam Trungpa, *Cutting Through Spiritual Materialism* (Boston: Shambhala, 1987), pp. 13, 14.

4 Joel Kramer and Diana Alstad, *The Guru Papers: Masks of Authoritarian Power* (Berkeley, CA: Frog Ltd., 1993), pp. 50, 51.

5 Karen Armstrong, *A History of God* (New York: Alfred A. Knopf, 1993), p. xix.

6 The Branch Davidians came from within the structure of Seventh-Day Adventist Christianity. In the early 1980s, Vernon Howell, who would soon change his name to David Koresh, took over the leadership role. In the spring of 1993, Koresh and seventy-nine other Branch Davidians perished in a shootout and fire during an FBI raid on their compound in Waco, Texas.

7 Peoples Temple (Jonestown) article from the University of Virginia's *The Religious Movements Homepage Project* website, http://religiousmovements .lib.virginia.edu/nrms/Jonestwn.html (accessed December 16, 2005).

8 Christopher Calder, *Osho, Bhagwan Rajneesh, and the Lost Truth*, http:// rajneesh.info/ (accessed December 17, 2005).

9 Jack Kornfield, *A Path with Heart* (New York: Bantam, 1993), p. 258.

10 Ibid, p. 261.

11 Idries Shah, *The Sufis* (New York: Anchor Books, 1990), pp. 389, 390.

12 Kornfield, *A Path with Heart*, p. 262.

FURTHER READING

ADYASHANTI

Books by Adyashanti

Emptiness Dancing. Los Gatos, CA: Open Gate, 2004.

The Impact of Awakening: Excerpts from the Teachings of Adyashanti. Los Gatos, CA: Open Gate, 2000.

My Secret Is Silence: Poetry and Sayings of Adyashanti. Los Gatos, CA: Open Gate, 2003.

Related Books

Deutsch, Eliot. *Advaita Vedanta: A Philosophical Reconstruction.* Honolulu: University of Hawaii Press, 1969.

Hixon, Lex. *Mother of the Buddhas.* Wheaton, IL: Quest, 1993.

King, Richard. *Early Advaita Vedanta and Buddhism: The Mahayana Context of the Gaudapadiya-Karika.* Albany: State University of New York Press, 1995.

Maharshi, Sri Ramana. *Be as You Are: The Teachings of Sri Ramana Maharshi.* Edited by David Goodman. New York: Penguin, 1985.

Nisargadatta Maharaj. *I Am That: Talks with Sri Nisargadatta.* Translated by Maurice Frydman. Kala Ghoda, Mumbai, India: Chetana Private Ltd., 1999.

Poonja, H. W. L. *The Truth Is.* Compiled by Prashanti De Jager. York Beach, ME: Samuel Weiser, 2000.

Sheng-yen. *Faith in Mind: A Guide to Chan Practice.* Berkeley, CA: Dharma Publications, 1987.

Teresa of Avila. *The Collected Works of Saint Teresa of Avila.* Translated by Otilio Rodriguez. Washington, DC: ICS Publications, 1976.

JOAN CHITTISTER, OSB

BOOKS BY JOAN CHITTISTER (A SELECTION)

Becoming Fully Human: The Greatest Glory of God. Lanham, MD: Sheed & Ward, 2005.

Called to Question: A Spiritual Memoir. Lanham, MD: Sheed & Ward, 2004.

Heart of Flesh: A Feminist Spirituality for Women and Men. Grand Rapids, MI: Wm. B. Eerdmans, 1998.

In Search of Belief. Liguori, MO: Liguori Publications, 1999.

In the Heart of the Temple: My Spiritual Vision for Today's World. New York: Blue-Bridge, 2004.

Listen with the Heart: Sacred Moments in Everyday Life. Lanham, MD: Sheed & Ward, 2003.

A Passion for Life: Fragments of the Face of God. Maryknoll, NY: Orbis, 2001.

The Rule of Benedict: Insights for the Ages. New York: Crossroad, 2003.

Scarred by Struggle, Transformed by Hope. Grand Rapids, MI: Wm. B. Eerdmans, 2003.

Seeing with Our Souls: Monastic Wisdom for Every Day. Lanham, MD: Sheed & Ward, 2002.

The Story of Ruth: Twelve Moments in Every Woman's Life. Lanham, MD: Sheed & Ward, 2000.

The Way We Were: A Story of Conversion and Renewal. Maryknoll, NY: Orbis, 2001.

Wisdom Distilled from the Daily: Living the Rule of St. Benedict Today. San Francisco: HarperSanFrancisco, 1991.

RELATED BOOKS

Armstrong, Karen. *The Spiral Staircase: My Climb Out of Darkness.* New York: Alfred A. Knopf, 2004.

Fischer, Norman, et al. *Benedict's Dharma: Buddhists Reflect on the Rule of Saint Benedict.* New York: Riverhead, 2001.

Kownacki, Mary Lou. *Between Two Souls: Conversations with Ryōkan.* Grand Rapids, MI: Wm. B. Eerdmans, 2004.

Merton, Thomas. *The Ascent to Truth.* New York: Harcourt Brace, 1951.

———. *The Seven Storey Mountain.* New York: Harcourt Brace, 1948.

GEHLEK RIMPOCHE

BOOKS BY GEHLEK NAWANG RIMPOCHE

Good Life, Good Death. New York: Riverhead, 2002.

with Brenda Rosen. *The Tara Box: Rituals for Protection and Healing from the Female Buddha.* Novato, CA: New World Library, 2004.

RELATED BOOKS

Berzin, Alexander. *Relating to a Spiritual Teacher: Building a Healthy Relationship.* Ithaca, NY: Snow Lion, 2000.

Dalai Lama. *My Land and My People: The Original Autobiography of His Holiness the Dalai Lama of Tibet.* New York: McGraw-Hill, 1962.

——— et al. *MindScience: An East-West Dialogue.* Somerville, MA: Wisdom Publications, 1993.

Glaser, Aura. *A Call to Compassion: Bringing Buddhist Practices of the Heart into the Soul of Psychology.* Berwick, ME: Nicolas-Hays, 2005.

Khyentse, Dilgo. *Enlightened Courage: A Commentary on the Seven Point Mind Training.* Ithaca, NY: Snow Lion, 1993.

Lati Rimpoche and Jeffrey Hopkins. *Death, Intermediate State and Rebirth in Tibetan Buddhism.* Ithaca, NY: Snow Lion, 1981.

Shantideva. *A Guide to the Bodhisattva Way of Life.* Translated by Vesna A. Wallace and B. Alan Wallace. Ithaca, NY: Snow Lion, 1997.

Thurman, Robert A. F. *Life and Teachings of Tsong Khapa.* New Delhi: Paljor Publications, 1993.

Trungpa, Chögyam. *Cutting Through Spiritual Materialism.* Boston: Shambhala, 1987.

———. *The Myth of Freedom and the Way of Meditation.* Boston: Shambhala, 1988.

ARVOL LOOKING HORSE

Books by Arvol Looking Horse

White Buffalo Teachings. Williamsburg, MA: Dreamkeepers Press, 2001.

Related Books

Black Elk (with John G. Neihardt). *Black Elk Speaks: Being the Life Story of a Holy Man of the Oglala Sioux.* Lincoln: University of Nebraska Press, 2000.

Brown, Dee. *Bury My Heart at Wounded Knee: An Indian History of the American West.* New York: Henry Holt, 2001.

Brown, Joseph Epes. *Animals of the Soul: Sacred Animals of the Oglala Sioux.* Dorset, England: Element, 1993.

———. *The Sacred Pipe: Black Elk's Account of the Seven Rites of the Oglala Sioux.* New York: MJF Books, 1996.

Crow Dog, Mary. *Lakota Woman.* New York: HarperPerennial, 1991.

Curtis, Edward (with Joseph Epes Brown). *The North American Indians.* New York: Aperture, 2002.

Deloria, Vine Jr. *Custer Died for Your Sins: An Indian Manifesto.* Norman: University of Oklahoma Press, 1988.

———. *God Is Red: A Native View of Religion.* Golden, CO: Fulcrum, 2003.

———. *Red Earth, White Lies: Native Americans and the Myth of Scientific Fact.* New York: Scribner, 1995.

Matthiessen, Peter. *In the Spirit of Crazy Horse.* New York: Viking, 1991.

Welch, James. *Fools Crow.* New York: Viking, 1986.

——— with Stekler, Paul. *Killing Custer: The Battle of the Little Bighorn and the Fate of the Plains Indians.* New York: W. W. Norton, 1994.

JOHN DAIDO LOORI

Books by John Daido Loori (a selection)

Cave of Tigers: Modern Zen Encounters. Boston: Weatherhill, 2000.

Hearing with the Eye: Photographs from Point Lobos. Mt. Tremper, NY: Dharma Communications, 2004.

The Heart of Being: Moral and Ethical Teachings of Zen Buddhism. North Clarendon, VT: Tuttle, 1996.

Making Love with Light. Mt. Tremper, NY: Dharma Communications, 2004.

Mountain Record of Zen Talks. Boston: Shambhala, 1988.

Teachings of the Insentient. Mt. Tremper, NY: Dharma Communications, 1999.

The True Dharma Eye: Zen Master Dogen's Three Hundred Koans. Boston: Shambhala, 2005.

Two Arrows Meeting in Mid-Air: The Zen Koan. North Clarendon, VT: Tuttle, 1994.

The Zen of Creativity: Cultivating Your Artistic Life. New York: Ballantine, 2004.

Related Books

Cleary, Thomas, trans. *The Flower Ornament Scripture: The Avatamsaka Sutra—Volumes 1–4.* Boston: Shambhala, 1993.

Dogen, Eihei. *How to Raise an Ox: Zen Practice as Taught in Zen Master Dogen's Shobogenzo.* Translated by Francis Harold Cook. Los Angeles: Center Publications, 1990.

———. *Moon in a Dewdrop: Writings of Zen Master Dogen.* Translated and edited by Kazuaki Tanahashi. New York: Farrar, Straus & Giroux, 1995.

Maezumi, Taizan. *Appreciate Your Life.* Edited by Wendy Egyoku Nakao and Eve Myonen Marko. Boston: Shambhala, 2002.

Matthiessen, Peter. *Nine-Headed Dragon River: Zen Journals 1969–1982.* Boston: Shambhala, 1986.

Snyder, Gary. *The Practice of the Wild.* New York: North Point Press, 1990.

Underhill, Evelyn. *Mysticism: The Nature and Development of Spiritual Consciousness.* Chatham, NY: Oneworld Publications, 1993.

SUDHA PURI

Related Books

Devi, Srimata Gayatri. *One Life's Pilgrimage.* Cohasset, MA: Vedanta Centre Publishing, 1977.

Hixon, Lex. *Great Swan: Meetings with Ramakrishna.* Boston: Shambhala, 1992.

Levinsky, Sarah Ann. *A Bridge of Dreams: The Story of Paramananda.* West Stockbridge, MA: Lindisfarne, 1984.

Paramananda, Swami. *The Essential Writings of Swami Paramananda.* Whitefish, MT: Kessinger Publishing, 2005.

———. *Srimad-Bhagavad-Gita.* Cohasset, MA: Vedanta Centre Publishing, 1981.

———, trans. *The Upanishads.* Cohasset, MA: Vedanta Centre Publishing, 1981.

Ramakrishna, Sri. *The Gospel of Sri Ramakrishna.* Translated by Swami Nikhilananda. New York: Ramakrishna-Vivekananda Center, 1985.

Tripurari, Swami B. V., et al. *Aesthetic Vedanta: The Sacred Path of Passionate Love.* San Rafael, CA: Mandala, 1998.

Vivekananda, Swami. *Complete Works of Swami Vivekananda.* Kolkata, India: Advaita Ashrama, 1947.

———. *Vedanta: Voice of Freedom.* St. Louis, MO: Vedanta Society of St. Louis, 1990.

RABBI ZALMAN SCHACHTER-SHALOMI

Books by Rabbi Zalman Schachter-Shalomi (a selection)

First Steps to a New Jewish Spirit. New York: Bantam, 1983.

Fragments of a Future Scroll: Hassidism for the Here and Now. Germantown, PA: Leaves of Grass Press, 1975.

From Age-ing to Sage-ing (with Ronald S. Miller). New York: Warner, 1995.

Jewish with Feeling: A Guide to Meaningful Jewish Practice (with Joel Segel). New York: Riverhead, 2005.

Sparks of Light (with Edward Hoffman). Boston: Shambhala, 2001.

Spiritual Intimacy: A Study of Counseling in Hasidism. Northvale, NJ: Jason Aronson, 1996.

Wrapped in a Holy Flame: Teachings and Tales of the Hasidic Masters. Edited by Nataniel M. Miles-Yepez. San Francisco: Jossey-Bass, 2003.

RELATED BOOKS

Carlebach, Shlomo. *Shlomo's Stories: Selected Tales.* Northvale, NJ: Jason Aronson, 1994.

Firestone, Rabbi Tirzah. *With Roots in Heaven: One Woman's Passionate Journey into the Heart of Her Faith.* New York: E. P. Dutton, 1998.

Heschel, Abraham Joshua. *A Passion for Truth.* New York: Farrar, Straus and Giroux, 1973.

———. *The Sabbath.* New York: Farrar, Straus and Giroux, 1951.

Kamenetz, Rodger. *The Jew in the Lotus: A Poet's Re-Discovery of Jewish Identity in Buddhist India.* San Francisco: HarperSanFrancisco, 1994.

———. *Stalking Elijah: Adventures with Today's Jewish Mystical Masters.* San Francisco: HarperSanFrancisco, 1997.

Schneersohn, Yosef Yitzchak. *The Principles of Education and Guidance.* Brooklyn, NY: Kehot Publication Society, 2004.

Schwartz, Howard. *The Dream Assembly: Tales of Rabbi Zalman Schachter-Shalomi.* Warwick, NY: Amity House, 1988.

Shapiro, Rami. *Minyan: Ten Principles for Living a Life of Integrity.* New York: Bell Tower, 1997.

———. *Wisdom of the Jewish Sages: A Modern Reading of* Pirke Avot. New York: Bell Tower, 1995.

MURAT YAGAN

BOOKS BY MURAT YAGAN

The Abkhazian Book of Longevity and Well-Being. Vernon, BC: Kebzeh Publications, 1999.

Ahmsta Kebzeh: The Science of Universal Awe, vol. I. Vernon, BC: Kebzeh Publications, 2003.

I Come from Behind Kaf Mountain: The Spiritual Autobiography of Murat Yagan. Putney, VT: Threshold, 1984.

The Teachings of Kebzeh: Essentials of Sufism from the Caucasus Mountains. Vernon, BC: Kebzeh Publications, 1995.

TRANSLATIONS BY MURAT YAGAN

Gaïbi: The Gathering: The Mystical Poetry of a Sufi Master of Melâmet. Vernon, BC: Kebzeh Publications, 1994.

I Wrapped Myself in Flesh and Bones and Appeared as Yunus: Translations of Yunus Emre. Vernon, BC: Kebzeh Publications, 1998.

RELATED BOOKS

Colarusso, John. *Nart Sagas from the Caucasus: Myths and Legends from the Circassians, Abazas, Abkhaz, and Ubykhs.* Princeton, NJ: Princeton University Press, 2002.

Fadiman, James and Robert Frager, eds. *Essential Sufism.* San Francisco: HarperSanFrancisco, 1999.

Griffin, Nicholas. *Caucasus: A Journey to the Land between Christianity and Islam.* Chicago: University of Chicago Press, 2004.

Gurdjieff, G. I. *Life Is Real Only Then, When I Am.* New York: Viking, 1991.

Rumi, Jalal al-Din. *The Essential Rumi.* Translated by Coleman Barks with John Moyne. San Francisco: HarperSanFrancisco, 1997.

Shah, Idries. *The Sufis.* New York: Anchor, 1971.

———. *The Way of the Sufis.* New York: Penguin, 1991.

ACKNOWLEDGMENTS

This book would not have been possible without the gracious support of the many teachers and students who lent their patience, voices, and wisdom to the weave of these pages. I was continually humbled by their warm hospitality and insights, and deeply touched by their dedication to the path; a deep bow for their practice. Also, my sincere gratitude to my editor (and publisher), Toinette Lippe, for guiding this project from its infancy—when it was a mere wisp of an idea—to the solid shape it now holds. Her skill and expertise have sweetened the struggle of this work considerably.

To my parents, James and Dorothy, my love and admiration for such an example of graceful aging and a marriage that continues to blossom even in its fifty-fifth year. And for the rest of my family: Douglas, Susan and Dena, Scott and Linda and Rena and Jesse, Kathy and Gordon and Benjamin. To my good friends and writing companions all these years, James Taylor III and Eric Shaffer, I couldn't have done this without you—all the poems, all the miles and adventure, the river days and late-night dialogues, have formed a magnificent geology in my life. And thanks to the other Fire Gigglers—those wayward poets, musicians, painters, actors, and malcontents—for the songs and the blazes, particularly Padma Thornlyer, for believing in my poems, and Michael and Claire, for the dexterous words and the camping spot.

Much gratitude as well to John Montaña, for giving me work when I needed it, advice when I asked, and putting up with two days of vehicular insanity. Also thanks to a long list of friends, work companions, and acquaintances: Bruce and Wendy Barry; Don Boucher, a splendid neighbor; Mark Bruak; Dr. Carla Cesario, always an inspiration; Karen DeTomasi; George Dukas (the Count); Carol Dysinger, for impeccable risotto and lasting friendship; Kathryn Haber; Martha Helliesen; Lynn Hoberg; John Isaacs; Richard Johnstone and Pam Tristram; Hettie Jones; John Killebrew and Kristin Rainer; Gregg Krech and Linda Anderson Krech; Jenny Langsam; Vicki Lindner, for getting the ball rolling; Alex McMullan, for much support and inspiration; Sean Murphy, for sound advice; Alfonse Palumbo; Enid Sanford; Eliza Schwarz, for warmth and boundless creative energy; James Shaheen at *Tricycle* and Melvin McLeod at *Shambhala Sun,* for publishing my work; Mary Talbot and Todd Pitman; Bonnie Myotai Treace, for her wonderful writing ear and eye; Helen Tworkov. Also thanks to the Mount Tremper gang: Amy and Julie, Bear and Danica, Bethany and Thayer, Kathy Nolan, Matt and Ansley, Michelle and Bernie, Nita Freidman, Troy and Scola, and too many others to mention.

Finally, thanks to the monks and dedicated practitioners of Zen Mountain Monastery who helped start this fire, particularly John Daido Loori Roshi for his consistent vision, Shugen Sensei for his strength and strong heart, Yukon for his deep friendship, and Jimon, Ryushin, Hojin, Kaijun, and Hogen for continuing to hold the flame, and to Vanessa Suizei Goddard, who entered the monastery when I did and stayed to do the hard work. And much gratefulness to the Ashland gang for putting up with my hibernation—Diana Hartel, Lenore Shisler, Stuart Gray, Sarah Biles, and the rest. For those I've forgotten, and I'm sure there are many, sincere apologies; my faulty memory is a poor advocate for my genuine appreciation.

PERMISSIONS ACKNOWLEDGMENTS

Grateful acknowledgment is made to the following for permission to use their photographs:
Lima Wright: Murat Yagan (p. 11); Sarah Penman: Chief Arvol Looking
Horse (p. 41); Joan Chittister, OSB: Joan Chittister, OSB (photo by
Rick Klein, p. 71); James Royce Young: Rabbi Zalman Schachter-
Shalomi (p. 97); Jennifer Girard Photography: Gehlek Rimpoche (p.
125); Walker Bob: Reverend Mother Sudha Puri (p. 157); Zen Moun-
tain Monastery Archive: John Daido Loori Roshi (p. 185); Annie
Gray: Adyashanti (p. 215).

*Grateful acknowledgment is made to the following for permission to reprint from these
previously published works:*
Wisdom Publications, Somerville, MA, for an excerpt from "Given to
Master Ch'ing-Lun of Hsia Mountain" by Chien Chang, translated
by Paul Hansen, in *The Clouds Should Know Me By Now*, edited by Red
Pine and Mike O'Connor. Copyright © Paul Hansen, 1998.
Murat Yagan for excerpts from *I Come from Behind Kaf Mountain* by Murat
Yagan. Copyright © Murat Yagan 1984. *Gaïbi: The Gathering* translated
by Murat Yagan. Copyright © Kebzeh Publications 1994. *The Teachings
of Kebzeh* by Murat Yagan. Copyright © Kebzeh Publications 1995.
Ahmsta Kebzeh by Murat Yagan. Copyright © Murat Yagan 2003. All
published by Kebzeh Publications.
Arvol Looking Horse for excerpts from *White Buffalo Teachings* by Arvol
Looking Horse, published by Dreamkeepers Press. Copyright ©
2002 by Arvol Looking Horse.
Mary Lou Kownacki for an excerpt from *Between Two Souls: Conversations*

ABOUT THE AUTHOR

John Kain has been a practicing Buddhist for ten years and has studied with Zen master John Daido Loori for seven years. He is a poet and writer who has worked as a landscaper, carpenter, house painter, truck driver, cattle hand, magazine publisher, advertising copy editor, and legal researcher. He has published numerous articles and poems in magazines and journals including *Tricycle: The Buddhist Review, Stick, Yoga Journal, Terra Nova, Grand Tour, Shambhala Sun,* Beliefnet, and *EarthFirst! Journal.* He lives in Ashland, Oregon.